15.9

The Royal Air Force
A Personal Experience

SIR PETER LE CHEMINANT
GBE, KCB, DFC*, FRUSI (RAF retd)

Ian Allan
PUBLISHING

Dedication

To Sylvia, who played her part to
perfection, shifting camp every $2^1/_2$ years
without complaint, and never in need of
counselling.

First published 2001

ISBN 0 7110 2786 2

© Sir Peter Le Cheminant 2001

Published by Ian Allan Publishing

an imprint of Ian Allan Publishing Ltd, Hersham,
Surrey KT12 4RG.

Printed by Ian Allan Printing Ltd, Hersham,
Surrey KT12 4RG.

Code: 0104/B

Title page:
The Vampire — a change from the Sunderland.

Contents

Acknowledgements

My thanks are due to Sir Michael Beetham for his generous foreword; Squadron Leader Peter Singleton for his unstinting help in searching out relevant Crown Copyright photographs, and for waiving that said copyright thereafter; Nick Grant for his perceptive and sympathetic editing; and finally to Norma Gardiner, MVO, for typing the MS with unrivalled speed, accuracy and grace.

Previous Books by the Author

(Writing as Desmond Walker) *Bedlam in the Bailiwicks*, 1987, Alan Sutton Publishing
   (printed by the Guernsey Press Co Ltd, Guernsey, Channel Islands)
(Writing as Desmond Walker) *Task Force Channel Islands*, 1989, Alan Sutton Publishing
   (printed by the Guernsey Press Co Ltd, Guernsey, Channel Islands)

Foreword

There can be few, if any, officers in the Royal Air Force who have had a more varied, interesting or challenging career than Peter Le Cheminant.

Starting as a Cranwell cadet just before the outbreak of World War II, he was quickly thrust, with minimal training, into operational service on squadrons, first in France during the so-called 'Phoney War', then in North Africa, Malta, Sicily and Italy with the Desert Air Force. Experience came quickly in the hard school of war with early responsibility given to those who could handle it. Peter certainly could, rising rapidly to the rank of Wing Commander at the age of 22. It was all very exciting for a young man in those days but the cost was high, 17 of Peter's entry of 25 at Cranwell losing their lives during the conflict.

Rested after completing 83 operations with Desert Air Force, he returned home in 1944 to do Staff College — important for a career officer. Postwar, and for the rest of his career, his postings mainly alternated between flying, much of it in the Far East Air Force, and the staff, mainly in Whitehall.

The Far East Air Force seemed to have been a particular magnet for him as he served three tours there in ranks from Squadron Leader to Air Vice-Marshal, which covered the Korean War, confrontation with Indonesia and the defeat of Communist insurgency culminating in the independence of Malaya.

Whitehall did not perhaps have the same attraction for him personally but his staff ability was such that he was selected to fill key policy and planning appointments in every rank from Wing Commander upwards until finally he became Vice Chief of Defence Staff.

To round off his 41 years in the Royal Air Force he filled two influential international appointments, firstly in CENTO and finally in NATO as D/CinCent where his diplomatic skills were well tested and his military experience of great value to the Alliance.

The story he tells brings vividly to life what it was like to serve on operational squadrons and stations in the Royal Air Force and on the staff in an eventful period covering the spectrum of full-scale war, limited war and cold war. It is told with a light touch and in an easy flowing style.

To those who were in the Royal Air Force over this period, there were ample opportunities to serve in different parts of the world and to show one's metal in testing circumstances. Perforce there were times where rules were often treated more for guidance rather than to be strictly obeyed. This was seldom abused. I often wish the same applied today.

Sir Michael Beetham
Marshal of the Royal Air Force

1. Pre-Blitzkrieg: January 1939–May 1940

This book is not an autobiography in the normal sense. It is more a collection of jottings on those incidents which, for varying reasons, remain clear in my memory of 41 years' service in the Royal Air Force. I have sought to eliminate the boring bits, mostly excised from my memory anyway, and concentrate on that which may entertain, inform or amuse. Apart from my log books, which ensure accuracy as to dates and places, a diary which I kept for three months following Operation Torch, the invasion of Northwest Africa, and my engagement diaries for the later years, I have no written record of events. There is therefore little verbatim detail and remembered dialogue as I do not have the total recall apparently enjoyed by some who seek to set out their reminiscences.

I made up my mind that I wanted to be a pilot in the Royal Air Force in 1937, having previously flirted with the idea of the Royal Navy or the Indian Army. My motivation was unashamedly shallow; nothing in my imagination could compare with the thrill of flying the Spitfire, then just about to come into service, and nothing at that time, if one was keen on young females, matched the pulling power of RAF wings. Added to that, I had had a wild and wicked uncle in the Royal Flying Corps in the 1914-18 war and had been an avid reader of Biggles, whose inventor Captain W. E. Johns has been the best recruiting sergeant the Royal Air Force has ever had.

My father was not encouraging. The Royal Air Force was expanding rapidly at that time and a short service commission, if you were fit, was not hard to come by. Those were the days when the service was dubbed 'The Brylcreem Boys' and the saying, 'Don't tell my mother I've joined the RAF, she still thinks I'm playing the piano in a brothel', was considered the height of wit. Whilst many would-be pilots were rich young men with long scarves and Bentleys, and many more were fine keen specimens from the dominions and colonies, there is no doubt that there was a sprinkling of acting pilot officers on probation who would not have been granted a commission in either of the other two services. My father was aware of all this and also of the fact that, if an officer was not granted a permanent commission at the end of one's short service one, he would be out on his ear after five years with no readily marketable skill. He therefore dismissed any idea of my taking a short service commission and ruled that, if I really was hell-bent on the Air Force, I would have to pass the entrance exam for the Royal Air Force College Cranwell, something which he predicted I had not a cat in hell's chance of doing. In the event he was very nearly right as in the November 1938 exam I just squeaked into Cranwell in 16th out of 20 competitive places (another five being reserved for ex-Halton apprentices), with marks which would have got me into Sandhurst, my second choice, in fifth place out of 200.

My mother had elected to leave my father in 1928 and so, on my leaving school, the headmaster's wife felt it incumbent on her to stand in my mother's place and offer some worldly-wise advice. She came up with — and here I think that unusually I can quote from memory — 'Don't be taken in by all those nude women in nightclubs; they're not nude really, they're all wearing body stockings.' Buttressed by this faulty intelligence, presumably vouchsafed her by her husband, I felt ready to face the full rigours of adult life.

For me Cranwell, in January 1939, was exciting, even at times slightly daunting. I was 18 and had spent my whole life in Guernsey. True, I had been to London occasionally, had worked on a farm in Wiltshire for two summers and been to OTC camp three times. I had also been on two cruises, then just becoming popular, and had been to Canada in 1937 to shoot for the Public Schools VIII against the Canadian Cadets. But none the less I was a country cousin, unfamiliar with many places and rituals that my more sophisticated mainland contemporaries took for granted.

There were two others on my term who felt slightly out of place from time to time: Andrew Humphrey whose parents were, I think, in India and who had largely been brought up by his grandmother, and Peter Balean who had passed into Cranwell offering Latin and Greek as his main subjects and whose hobby at the age of 18 was collecting antique furniture. Andrew gave an early demonstration of his determination by conquering the air sickness which made his first 50 flying hours a major trial. He went on to become a highly skilled pilot and was only the second Old Cranwellian to become Chief of the Air Staff, the first being Sir Dermot Boyle, at that time Squadron Leader Boyle and the Chief Flying Instructor at Cranwell. Andrew sadly died at the early age of 56 soon after becoming Chief of Defence Staff and the Air Force was thereby denied what would have been an influential voice in the House of Lords. Peter elected to retire soon after the war, finding the service, in that immediate aftermath, not entirely to his taste. He delighted in teasing people, particularly by arousing their suspicion that he might have homosexual tendencies, and sadly died last year, as witty and debonair as ever. I count both him and Andrew amongst my handful of life-long friends.

I had other friends who were somewhat wilder and I used on occasion to spend the night in London in their carefree company, returning by milk train in time for the 08.00 hours parade. One of this number who, perhaps in some ways fortuitously, died in the Battle of Britain claimed to be a bigamist at the age of 19. Of the 25 on my term 17 were to die in the war, but we had no inkling of this likely outcome, although war was clearly coming, as we settled down in January 1939 to absorb the training which was supposed to fit us to hold permanent commissions and thus to be the future backbone of our service.

This training lacked firm direction, although I suppose one did not think so at the time, and had not accommodated to changed circumstances. I cannot

Right: The author as a cadet at Cranwell in 1939.

Below: The November 1938 entry at the RAF College, Cranwell. The author is first from the right, front row; Peter Balean is third from the right, front row; Freddie Ball, later Air Marshal Sir Alfred, is extreme left, front row. Andrew Humphrey away sick.

The author in a Hart.

now remember whether the prewar Cranwell course was 2½ or 3 years, but it was apparent that my course would be considerably shortened. In the event we were commissioned after one year.

For the first eight months of 1939 we followed the old syllabus which gave some prominence to the academic side. Although new subjects such as Theory of Flight and Navigation bulked large we still spent many hours on History and Military Geography relearning the lessons of our Imperial past with which we were already familiar from our schooldays. We were reminded of how we had constantly vanquished presumptuous foreigners, notably the French and the Spanish, to say nothing of the Dutch and the Portuguese, but no suggestion was offered as to how we might defeat the menace of Nazi Germany. Not that we worried unduly. We were shielded by our insularity, confident that our aircraft, our tactics and our crews were the best, that Hitler was an ex-corporal who was reliably reported to be deficient of one ball, that the Maginot Line was impregnable and that the Royal Navy still had the whip hand at sea. With the possible exception of Hitler's physiognomy, all our comfortable assumptions were to prove false.

This training for peace rather than for war lasted right up until 3 September when we all gathered in the main hall to hear Chamberlain's sombre words. On the following day we ceased to be flight cadets and were sworn in as aircraftsmen second class and promoted to leading aircraftsmen on 5 September. This was thought necessary because as flight cadets we were not subject to Air Force law; our parents were paying, and paying heavily — £300 a year in 1939 money — for the privilege of us being cadets, and we could have walked out at any time. On 5 September we could no longer walk out, but since we were now paid 12s 6d (62.5p) a day as LACs rather than 5s (25p) a day as flight cadets and our parents no longer had to pay fees, everyone was happy.

With the declaration of war things changed, but it was not a sea change. There was less emphasis on drill, on which we had the presumption to rank ourselves on a par with Sandhurst, the Guards and the Royal Marines, and general academic studies no longer featured. There were still such anachronisms as learning to splice wire rope, but the biggest and most welcome change was the new emphasis given to flying.

Cranwell cadets, prewar, reached wings' standard after some two years, whilst their short service contemporaries gained their wings and were commissioned, admittedly 'on probation', in about half that time. We now set about catching up. By the end of March 1939 we had all done some 50 hours on the Avro Tutor, a delightful little aircraft, sturdy and forgiving and easier to fly than the DH Tiger Moth with which the Flying Training Schools were equipped. At that stage, we split into Singles and Twins, Singles going on to the biplane Hawker Hart and its variants, the Audax, the Hind and the Fury, and Twins going on to the Airspeed Oxford, a monoplane of more modern construction. By the beginning of September 1939 I had only some 30 hours on the Hart and even with the new priority given to flying had raised that to only some 70-odd hours by December. I was commissioned on the 23rd of that month with 133 hours 45 minutes flying time. That day was when we all learnt what our immediate future was to be, and those of us in the Singles stream were all hoping for fighters and had visions of ourselves in either Spitfires or Hurricanes. It was not to be; with, I think, only two exceptions we were posted to No 1 School of Army Co-operation at Old Sarum, there to fly Lysanders.

I have often idly speculated as to why Army Co-operation Squadrons were originally so-named and have been tempted to the conclusion that it was in order to differentiate those squadrons that were prepared to co-operate with the Army from those which were not. Similarly I have sometimes wondered whether there was something more than mere chance, or expediency, amongst the postings staff that sent so many ex-flight cadets onto Lysanders at that time. It could, most improbably, have been a desire to put permanent commissioned officers into a perceived low risk role, in which case seldom has a greater misjudgement been made; it could, perhaps slightly less improbably, have been a desire to present a polite and well scrubbed face to the Army; almost certainly it was neither of these but no more than a need to fill vacancies in the squadrons in France, which spelt death to many and disappointment to all.

The Lysander was a curious beast. It met its specification perfectly, the only trouble being that that specification had been drawn up by the Army to meet the needs of static warfare on the 1918 model. It would have been fine on the Northwest Frontier, or anywhere where there was no serious opposition, but it was, like the Fairey Battle, totally unable to live in the France of 1940. For a single-engined aircraft it was quite massive with its heavy fixed undercarriage and strong struts supporting its high wing, fitted with slots and flaps, which gave it its remarkable short field performance. It was slow and extremely stable so that one could easily fly it with one's knees, which was just as well as a Lysander pilot was busy indeed. He sat high up in a large perspex canopy and had an excellent field of vision except to the rear which was covered more in hope than in expectation by an air gunner with a single .303 calibre Vickers K gun. He had a message pad strapped to his right knee on which he wrote the details of what he saw if doing a Tac/R or tactical reconnaissance, or plotted the fall of shot if spotting for the guns in what was known as an Arty/R or artillery reconnaissance. There was a Morse buzzer on the starboard side of the cockpit for the pilot to transmit this information by W/T, as the only effective R/T sets were all needed for fighters. Left-handed pilots must have managed with considerable difficulty and it was not all that easy for right-handed pilots either as one was supposed to be able to send and receive at 15 words a minute, a feat I was unable to achieve, even on the ground, unless the message had an inordinate number of two-, three- or four-letter words. The pilot had also to be proficient in aerial photography as the Lysander could be fitted with cameras for either oblique or vertical photography. All of this was fine in peacetime conditions but, predictably, was not viable in the face of fighters and anti-aircraft fire.

After 17 hours on Lysanders and 11 hours on Hectors, another Hart variant with a potent Napier Dagger engine, I was posted to 4 Squadron at Monchy Lagache near Peronne. I had a total of 163 flying hours of which all but 17 were on totally outmoded biplanes. None of my contemporaries were any better placed; we were all effectively untrained, the 1940 equivalents of the RFC pilots who were posted to the Western Front with as little as eight hours total flying. We were mercifully unaware of this at the time, filled as we were with totally unjustified pride and self-confidence.

I remember little of that time in France when the so-called Phoney War was about to come to an abrupt end. It was a somewhat unreal atmosphere, living as we did surrounded by the battlefields and graves of the 1914–18 war whilst waiting for our war to start in earnest. We trained as we would have done in England, religiously rehearsing our outmoded procedures as we became familiar with that rather featureless part of northeast France. Everything seemed in the grip of lethargy, almost paralysis. We were close to the coal-mining heart of the country but there was no coal to be had; *pas de charbon* was accepted with a shrug as part of life, after all it was only the English who were mad enough to want hot baths. Distribution seemed to be the main problem. Seen from the air the roads were largely empty; the great railway terminus of Lille was not far away but a train was a rare sight. I was billeted on an elderly couple in the little village of Estrées. Their house had been occupied by the Germans in the Great War and they were apprehensive that history might repeat itself, as indeed it was about to. I did my best to reassure them, foolishly believing my own words. After all, we had beaten them in 1918 and Hitler was only a jumped-up Marx Brothers-type corporal. Their attitude and their doubts were typical of the older generation; they had seen it all before, and they were fearful.

There were few young men about but no shortage of young women, mostly of a certain type. Our airmen loved it and could not believe their luck. They were amazed at the abandon and expertise of these girls and recounted their experiences in great detail in letters home to their male friends, letters which had to be censored by an officer in case they gave away any military information which, in my experience, they never did. Censoring was by and large a dull and intrusive chore but it did have occasional moments of entertainment and wonder. There were what purported to be officers' brothels with higher class or better looking girls, but the received wisdom was that they were the same brothels, with the same girls but with two separate entrances, one for officers and one for other ranks. There was of course strict segregation and inevitably the better, and more expensive, restaurants and bars were reserved for officers. I remember that one of these, in Amiens, was particularly popular because one of the barmaids could pick up francs, placed on the table edge, by suction alone. As 19 year olds we were enthralled by this Gallic *tour de force* and contributed generously to what no doubt became her dowry.

On 3 May, a few days before the German offensive began, the CO of 4 Squadron, Squadron Leader Guy Charles, received a signal ordering him to return two pilots to England to take part in an operation that was about to be mounted. By the old trade union rule of 'last in, first out' the two most recently arrived pilots on the squadron, of whom I was one, were selected. What the operation was to be was unclear but we were told that it would involve flying off an aircraft carrier to operate in either Finland or Norway. I was sad to be leaving my friends on the squadron but excited by what promised to be a fascinating assignment. I was also thrilled at the prospect of seeing my fiancée — I had become engaged in December 1939 — much sooner than I had expected. I reported to my new squadron, No 613, at RAF Odiham in Hampshire a few days later to find things in a state of uncertainty to say the least. It has since transpired that the German invasion of Norway on 9 April had put an end to the plan to support Finland, already virtually abandoned in mid-March, and for which an air component headquarters, two bomber squadrons, three fighter squadrons and one and a half Army co-operation squadrons had been earmarked. No one knew what we were to do other than to train for carrier landings, but even that was overtaken by the German Blitzkrieg. In the event we did nothing and my sense of anti-climax was heightened by the information that I had been posted to 613 Squadron in error and that I was now to be posted to 614 Squadron, also at Odiham.

No 614 was a Welsh Auxiliary Squadron, County of Glamorgan, and very proud of its roots. The airmen were Taffys to a man and remained together throughout the entire war. I joined the squadron on 4 May and was to stay with it, apart from a two-month break in 1942, until 16 February 1943. Most of those 2½ years plus, though not entirely incident free, as I shall recount, were by and large exceedingly frustrating and constituted what I increasingly came to look upon as my own 'phoney war'.

2. War Part Time: May 1940–November 1942
Army Co-operation Command

On the 7 June 1940, just over a month after I joined the squadron, 'B' Flight was detached to Inverness to fly anti-invasion patrols. We were billeted in the Caledonian Hotel in great style and flew from a short grass strip near the gasometer, which was what then passed for Inverness Airport and was used by the DH Rapide biplanes of the local airline. Although the risk of invasion by German troops based in Norway must have been judged low, it was none the less a virtually undefended coastline and we patrolled at dawn and at dusk, one aircraft flying east to cover as far as Kinnairds Head and the other north past Wick to Duncansby Head. We were armed with 20lb anti-personnel bombs on wing racks and, after a while, with ungainly Hispano Suiza cannon attached to our undercarriage. What effect this armament would have had on any invasion barges was problematic.

On 21 June I set off by train for London in order to get married, having been granted six days leave, three of which were spent travelling. The date of the marriage was advanced, and indeed virtually dictated, by the imminence of the German occupation of the Channel Islands. My father, then an instructor at the Aldershot OCTU, arranged for the banns to be called and Sylvia managed to slip out, with one suitcase, on one of the last boats. The wedding was to have been at 11.00 on the 22nd in a registry office in Aldershot. My train to London was 3½ hours late because of an air raid on Newcastle and I eventually arrived at 14.30 to the relief of those present. A friend of mine at Odiham, one of the many Johnny Johnsons, had an old car but no petrol coupons. I on the other hand had petrol coupons, granted for disembarkation leave, but no car. He very generously insisted that Sylvia and I should take the car, drive it as far as it would go and then abandon it in the nearest barn. This we did, getting as far as Andover on the 22nd and finding a barn for it on the 23rd near Bath, where we spent the last two nights of our rather basic honeymoon before setting off back to Inverness by rail. I regret to say that I lost touch with Johnny and don't know whether he survived the war and, if he did, whether he succeeded in retrieving that stately carriage which served Sylvia and I so well.

I arrived back on the 27th and flew two sorties on the 28th and three on the 29th. Patrolling continued on a daily basis, the weather was glorious and nothing in my service life had changed except that I had to move out of the Caledonian to a less grand establishment.

A fairly indulgent view was taken towards accidents in 1940, the philosophy seeming to be that accidents, if not inevitable, were certainly very likely and that, if you survived, you would have learnt something and thereby become a better pilot. So far I had had a fairly clean bill of health, my only stupidity being to attempt a take-off in a short field in coarse, as opposed to fine, pitch whilst at Old Sarum. As a result I dragged my tailplane through the hedge, causing little more than cosmetic damage, but earning me a very mild rocket from the Commandant in whose house I was to live some 28 years later. But now I was to have two accidents in a fairly short space of time. On 11 July I had been airborne for just over 10 minutes on a local W/T test when a haar suddenly came up, reducing visibility to a few hundred yards almost instantaneously. I had no chance of getting back to the airfield and knew that it was imperative to land immediately whilst I could still see something. This would have been simple enough except that the available fields of any size had all been dutifully planted with upright poles to prevent German airborne troops landing by glider. The only field not so covered was minute, but the Lysander was capable of a very short landing run indeed and I thought that I might just make it; I was also acutely aware that I had no other hole to go to. In the event I was very nearly right. I dropped it in very slow, just over the hedge and started to brake as soon as I dared. The Lysander brake lever was in the spade-grip control column and I am sure that, had I not been wearing gloves, my knuckles would have shown white. We had slowed to walking pace and I was beginning to think that I'd pulled off a splendid piece of airmanship when, a few feet from the boundary hedge, it all proved too much for the old beast and she reared up very slowly and gently and stood on her nose. I had cut the engine so that the propeller was no more than badly bent, but it had been a very alarming few moments.

The second accident, which was to be a different matter altogether, happened on 10 August. I had been detached to Montrose, south of Aberdeen, to fly anti-invasion patrols north to Kinnairds Head and south to Berwick upon Tweed. I had flown the southerly dawn patrol that morning and was detailed to practise evasive tactics with another aircraft in the afternoon. The other aircraft was piloted by Flying Officer Merrett. Evasive tactics could easily degenerate into a dogfight, and that is what happened on this occasion. Something went disastrously wrong and we were suddenly on a head-on collision course only yards apart. We collided starboard wing to starboard wing, with Merrett's wing being slightly lower and hitting my struts. His wing came off either on that initial impact or on a secondary impact with my tailplane which jammed my elevators and rudder. Although we were at 3,000ft and one or more of them bailed out, their parachutes did not deploy in time and Merrett, his air gunner and a medical officer passenger were all killed. I was, of course, unaware of this at the time and was anxious as to whether my own starboard wing would stay in place. Although the struts were very severely damaged they were of solid construction and looked as though they would hold. Despite having no elevator or rudder control my ailerons were undamaged and I gradually turned the aircraft until it was pointing at the airfield and managed to juggle the airspeed and rate of descent on the throttle sufficiently to land in one piece. As was customary in those days I was sent up again immediately to make sure that my nerve had not gone. After searching for and locating the crashed aircraft I was flown back to Grangemouth and tasked to fly a Tiger Moth to Prestwick and return.

During my detachment to Montrose, 'B' Flight moved from Inverness to Grangemouth on the Firth of Forth, to join up with 'A' and 'C' Flights. Until the middle of October 1940 we patrolled from Berwick to Kinnairds Head whenever conditions were favourable for invasion. For some reason, which we now know to be ill-founded, fear or expectation of invasion seemed to be heightened. There was the night when, by mistake, the church bells — the signal that the invasion had started — rang all over the country. Our readiness was heightened and for 21 nights running 'B' Flight pilots slept in the dispersal hut and stood-to at dawn. It was a relief when winter came. For the first three weeks of November I was at Tangmere on air-sea rescue standby. It was frustrating in the extreme to be with the Hurricane pilots but not one of them. I remember in particular envying the pilots of 43 Squadron, 'The Fighting Cocks', whose CO at that time was Max Aitken. Their morale and exuberance were at a high level and their expectation of daily action gave their lives an edge which was altogether missing in a Lysander squadron. I was scrambled on a number of occasions, mostly to search for downed Hurricane pilots and once for the crew of a Hampden. The information given to guide the searches was very vague and could cover a large area — south of Selsey Bill, southeast of St Caths, south of Hayling Isle were typical. Sadly, but not surprisingly, I made no sightings.

One small and somewhat unlikely incident coincided with my leaving Grangemouth. Sylvia and I were accosted by the Corporal of the Guard who turned out to be a schoolfriend called Charles Frossard. Charles was soon thereafter commissioned into the Dogras and subsequently served with the Tochi Scouts and the Chitral Scouts. Many years later as Sir Charles Frossard KBE he was to be Bailiff of Guernsey during the last $2\frac{1}{2}$ years of my time as Lieutenant-Governor. We play golf together regularly.

The squadron moved to Tranent, a small grass field east of Edinburgh, in March 1941 and from then until we converted to Blenheims in the following July we trained incessantly, though to what end was not entirely clear to us at the time. In fact what was happening was simply that all the Lysander squadrons of Army Co-operation Command were destined to receive more battle-worthy aircraft and were kept in being during this waiting period achieving little more than building up the individual pilots' flying experience. I now had about 500 hours on Lysanders, and this would have been fairly typical throughout the command. In parentheses it has always struck me as odd that this large reservoir of Lysander

The Lysander.

experience was not tapped to supply the pilots who flew agents in and out of occupied France. So far as I am aware, that small handful of pilots, and certainly the ones I came to know later, notably Hugh Verity and Bob Hodges, later ACM Sir Lewis Hodges, had never flown Lysanders before.

During this dull period I started a process, which I kept up throughout my service life, of flying any and every new type I could lay my hands on. I had already managed to fly a few small and unexciting aircraft, notably the Tiger Moth, the Magister, the Mentor, the Moth Minor and the Proctor. Now, by dint of having a friend in 213 Squadron at Turnhouse, I had the huge thrill of getting my hands on a Hurricane and flying a total of 11 sorties with that squadron before my friend was posted and my back door and amateur attempt to become a DIY fighter pilot came to an end. In the same month that I first flew a Hurricane I managed to get my hands on a Gladiator at Arbroath and my own squadron took delivery of a DH Rapide, my first twin-engined aircraft. The Rapide was on our strength for the purpose of ferrying senior Army officers around. No one else was particularly keen so I did the bulk of this work and had some interesting flights, notably carrying the GOC Scotland, General Thorne, to the Orkneys and back, and, when Hitler invaded Russia, flying a certain Colonel Firebrace, who was an expert on the Russian Army, down to London so that he could brief the War Cabinet.

Domestically our time at Tranent was marked by two major events: the birth of our first child and the purchase of our first car. The first was a girl and the second was a 1928 Austin Seven tourer. A baby daughter necessitated the purchase of a pretty plush pram which cost £8. I remember this in particular as I bought the car on the same day for £5. Almost inevitably it was christened 'The Pram' and went like the clappers when, on occasion, a little 100 octane was added to its normal fuel. I eventually sold it, still in good working order, for £3.

On 27 July 1941 Flight Lieutenant 'Ace' Newman arrived to convert us on to Blenheims. This process consisted of two hours dual on a Mk I 'Shortnose' with three hours solo before moving on to the Mk IV 'Longnose' which had no dual controls. From then on the bulk of our flying was on Blenheims although we kept the DH Rapide and at least one Lysander on strength until the following June.

'The Pram' — with Sylvia aboard.

Flying a Blenheim in and out of Tranent, or Macmerry as it was increasingly coming to be called, was no sinecure; there was room, but only just. Nothing much other than accidents and near misses happened to give variety to our days. I had two of these. On 23 November my starboard tyre burst on take-off and my airscrew hit the ground towards the end of the take-off run. I was forced to collapse my undercarriage and slide ignominiously along the ground on a full bomb load, hoping against hope that all pins were securely in place, and would remain so.

A 'Longnose' — Blenheim Mk IV — at Macmerry.

Some two months later on 10 January 1942 I lost control in a snowstorm and very nearly killed myself and my crew. Out of Benson, near Henley, bound for Macmerry I ran into heavy snowfall near York and, with the cloud base down to 300ft, resolved to turn back. I made the mistake of taking my eyes off the instruments and sticking my head in the bubble canopy to make sure that all was clear as I turned to port. When I looked back at my instruments my gyro-horizon had toppled, my altitude was about 1,000ft and my airspeed was down to 100mph. As I had gone into the turn at 250ft and 150mph it was quite evident that I had established a gentle climbing turn and gone onto my back in the process. Whether I was still on my back or had rolled through into the upright, or was betwixt and between, I had no immediate means of knowing.

There have been a number of times in my flying life when I knew I had little chance of surviving, but on this occasion I thought I had none whatsoever. I remember a stillness as the aircraft hung there and a feeling of calm and resignation. I thought I was about to die and had no feeling of panic or even fear. I suppose that, although my reason told me that we had no chance of survival, my subconscious was determined to fight on. I just centralised the controls and waited to see what would happen. The airspeed started to build up, slowly at first and then quite rapidly as the altimeter unwound. It was evident that we were in a dive so I cut the throttles and started to pull back on the control column. We broke cloud at 300ft heading straight for the top of a haystack. It looked huge and vertically below us but I think our angle must have been less, possibly somewhere between 60° and 45°, otherwise I could never have pulled her through. Heaven knows what G she withstood but my navigator's metal seat in the nose just buckled under him.

On landing I put it to my crew that they would never wish to fly with me again but they, in their ignorance, maintained that I had done such a marvellous job that they would never wish to fly with any other pilot. I had landed in a small field, so small that the aircraft had to be dismantled and recovered by road. Instead of a well-deserved reprimand from Command Headquarters I was awarded what was known as a 'Green Endorsement' and my Log Book was endorsed with the words 'a difficult precautionary landing carried out skilfully and successfully'. Seldom was any laudatory endorsement less well deserved.

I took command of 'B' Flight in September 1941 and was promoted to flight lieutenant in December and although I was happy to be a flight commander I still had this feeling that we were never going to get into action. Whenever a request for volunteers had been received — for fighters in 1940 and for PRU Spitfires in 1941 — I had put my name forward but had either never been accepted or never been allowed to go. I think all the pilots felt the same and we had become rather slack, not really believing in what we were being required to do. This at all events appears to have been the perception at Command Headquarters as, in 1941, we were sent a new CO, Wing Commander Dick Skelton, who had evidently been briefed to smarten us up.

He was a seconded Army officer, formerly a major in the Royal Tank Corps I believe, and he set about his task with apparent enthusiasm, instituting early morning parades initially in full webbing with water bottle, pistols and gas masks, the men with rifles. It was, I think, intended as a short sharp shock and achieved its purpose to a degree, though at some cost. The squadron had been diversified somewhat by the addition of four seconded Army officers and a few VRs (Volunteer Reserves) but the old prewar hands, the senior flight lieutenants, were Auxiliaries to a man, all having joined the squadron in Cardiff on commissioning, and found this new broom not at all to their taste. They were wealthy young men who had joined the service with the intention of fighting the Germans, should war come, and had certainly not bargained for, as they saw it, being buggered about by some Army type. They hastened slowly to conform to some of the new CO's requirements and he, for his part, recognised quite quickly that there were limits beyond which it would not be sensible for him to push. The hallmark of the new regime was the early morning parade, and the tensions which this new institution had aroused were dissolved in farce when, owing to some clock changing confusion, we paraded in full darkness. Good humour was restored, both sides recognised the need to modify their stance, and, without anything being said, the parades were reduced in frequency and subsequently dropped, and the senior Auxiliary pilots fell into line.

May 1942 was a more exciting month than usual. It had been realised in France in 1940 that tactical reconnaissance, whether by eyeball or camera, was going to be possible only in fast single-seat fighter-type aircraft operating at low level. The Tac/R squadrons had had a long wait but in early 1942 they began to be re-equipped with P-40 Tomahawks. Later they were to get P-51 Mustangs, one of the best aircraft of the war. In mid-May I was in York for a low-level bombing display and on the 13th managed to get my hands on a Tomahawk. It was only the second modern fighter I had flown at that time and I had nothing to compare it with but the Hurricane. It did not compare all that favourably, the Allison engine being no match for the Rolls-Royce Merlin and, with its huge nose, it was awkward on take-off and landing. Nevertheless it was a quantum leap in the right direction and the pilots of the squadron based at York — No 4 I think — were delighted to be discarding their Lysanders in its favour.

However, the really big thing about May was that the first thousand-bomber raid took place on the 30th against Cologne, and we had some small part to play in it. We now know that just about every aircraft capable of dropping a bomb was pressed into service in order to make up the magic number, including Bomber Command OCU aircraft, flown by instructors, Coastal Command aircraft and the two Blenheim squadrons of Army Co-operation Command. We operated from West Raynham and our task was to help suppress the German night fighters. My target on 30 May and again on 1 June, when the main force went against Essen, was the fighter base at Twente. It was a beautiful full moon period and I remember in particular the excitement on the 30th of crossing the enemy coast for the first time.

I believe 614 flew intruder operations, again from West Raynham, during the next moon period but I was not with them as I had been posted to No 2 School of Army Co-operation, or 42 OTU at Andover as the reconnaissance instructor on 14 June. I was not a happy officer in that role and I am glad to say my stay there was short, the only plus side being that I got some more Hurricane flying and added four new types, the Whitley, the Anson, the Whitney Straight and the Messerschmitt 108, a delightful little communications aircraft.

It had taken me nearly two months to find somewhere to live close to Andover and Sylvia had just joined me in early August when, on the 10th, I was posted back to 614 Squadron this time as an acting squadron leader, again in command of 'B' Flight. We had already lived in seven different places, one of them being in one room of a farm cottage that had only two rooms plus a kitchen and bathroom. We were soon to move to our ninth location which was to be the George at Odiham, a lovely old coaching inn which has hardly changed to this day. This came about because, following my posting to Andover, the squadron had been brought south to Odiham. I rejoined them at Thruxton which had long runways and where preparations were being made for some major operation which turned out in the event to be the celebrated raid on Dieppe. I, of course, had no crew but happily one of the pilots went sick and I inherited his crew the day before the operation. By strange coincidence the navigator was a Guernseyman, a Pilot Officer Leonard Quevâtre. We had been in the same form at school but had not seen one another since 1938. We only flew together on those two sorties at Dieppe as I was able to pick up a new crew some three days later. The air gunner with Quevâtre was a French Canadian, Sergeant Limoges, who was to visit Guernsey some 40 years later.

It is hard to think of any incident or action in the war, with the exception of Arnhem, that caused more excitement at the time. Some 6,000 troops were landed, 5,000 of them being Canadian, the remainder being British Commandos and a small force of American Rangers. The Canadians in particular suffered very severe casualties but lessons were learned, albeit costly ones, that proved invaluable in the mounting of subsequent invasions and in particular the D-Day landings. Perhaps the most important of these, amongst many, was that it would not be possible to capture a French port without a degree of destruction which would render it useless to the Allies. From this realisation the Mulberry Harbours were conceived. But the real excitement was engendered by the size of the air battle. On the Allied side, 73 squadrons were employed, made up of 47 Spitfire squadrons, 8 Hurricane, 3 Typhoon, 4 Boston, 2 Blenheim, 1 Beaufighter, 4 Mustang and 4 B-17. Losses were high on both sides, the RAF losing 70 aircraft. Overall it was felt to be a success and was hailed by the press as a glorious victory.

The air involvement in this combined operation and the great air battle that ensued is covered in detail in a book by Norman Franks titled *The Greatest Air Battle*. The timings are given to the minute — aircraft numbering, pilots' surnames and initials or Christian names are all recorded — and the overall impression is that this is the definitive work covering all aspects of air operations on 19 August. By and large this is probably so as representatives of most squadrons have clearly been consulted by the author. Unfortunately he can have made no contact with any member of 614 Squadron as his account of the squadron's participation is shot through with error. My name is mentioned twice, once as Squadron Leader P. de Le Cheminent and once as Squadron Leader P. D. Le Cheminent; in the index I am run together as LeCheminent. My aircraft is given as V6002 but was in fact Z6002. The CO is named as Wing Commander H. C. Sutton whereas he was H. T. Sutton; two pilots' names are incorrectly spelt, Robarts given as Roberts and Baelz as Baely.

On the first sortie Pilot Officer Hanbury did not hit a car on the runway. He taxied into a ditch. On the second sortie we were not recalled 25 miles south of Selsey Bill after 15 minutes flying. My Log Book reads 'recalled when off the French Coast' and the sortie lasted 1 hour 20 minutes. Neither were we 'recalled by radio' but by Spitfires from our escort diving across our bows.

The third sortie, in which we laid a smoke-screen over the beach, is accurately reported but Appendix F does not record the categories of damage inflicted on the five participating aircraft. I cannot recall precise categories but they were all taken off squadron strength. My memory of that operation is quite sharp. We came over the beach low in close line astern and received intense light AA fire from the cliff top. I was directly behind Harry Sutton and could see his aircraft being hit repeatedly in and just forward of the tail section. I in turn took most of my five major hits in that same area, as did the following aircraft. I think we were saved from taking our major damage in the cockpit area by the fact that we had been preceded over the target area by Bostons of 225 Squadron dropping at 300mph whilst we dropped at 180mph. This would almost certainly have caused the Germans to allow too much deflection, with the result that we were probably being hit by fire intended for the aircraft immediately astern of us. Either way it was a brisk and energising few moments. We split up and came home individually at low level, initially in +9 override boost which just about gave us 200mph.

By August 1942 the Blenheim IV was coming to the end of its service life and was only marginally fit for its role. Considering that fact, the two Blenheim squadrons employed, Nos 13 and 614, could be thought to have got off lightly. Each squadron lost one aircraft destroyed, 13 had three aircrew killed whilst 614 had two killed and one severely wounded. True, their aircraft had suffered severe damage — I don't believe that any of the 614 aircraft ever flew again — but as the Blenheim IV was about to be phased out of the front line, that was of little consequence.

3. War Full Time (Part 1): November 1942–May 1943 Flight Commander Nos 614 and 114 Squadrons

For the last few days of August it was strongly rumoured that we were going to be re-equipped with Bostons or A-20s, to give them their US designation, the light bomber that could outrun a Spitfire or an Me109 at low level, that had such beautiful lines and which, with its modern tricycle undercarriage, was so easy to take off and land. Then, suddenly, the blow fell and we took delivery of our first Bisley. It is difficult at this distance in time to envisage how the production of that aircraft was ever authorised. Not to put too fine a point on it, it was an abortion, a cobbled-up disgrace to Bristols, not fit to operate in the air environment of late 1942 and inferior in almost every way to the Blenheim IV that it was replacing. Its history as a light bomber was predictably short and inglorious as I shall relate.

The Bisley, to the lasting shame of its perpetrators, was the Blenheim V and was not fit to be the last of that honourable line. I felt so strongly about it that, although I flew the aircraft for more than 100 hours, the name Bisley does not appear in my Log Book. The entry for 2 September, the first time I flew the Bisley, reads 'Blenheim BA743 — Experience on type'. We set about doing what we could to remedy the worst fault of the aircraft which was its excessive weight. This was caused by three changes from the Mk IV, the power-operated mid-upper turret, a great deal of additional armour plating and a large and heavy Heath Robinson device whereby through a system of mirrors the navigator could fire two .303s rearward from the nose. We judged that this contraption would be largely impractical and its removal enabled us to get rid of a lot of counter-balancing armour plate. We could not remove the power-operated turret, nor did we wish to as this was the one particular in which the Mk V was an improvement on the Mk IV.

With the delivery of 18 Bisleys came the news that the squadron was earmarked for overseas although the destination was not disclosed. No 13 Squadron, to whom Odiham had been home since prewar days, also took delivery of 18 Bisleys and we learnt that we were to form a wing of 72 aircraft along with two 2 Group squadrons of Bomber Command, No 18 and No 114. The rest of September and the first three weeks of October, so far as the aircrew were concerned, were spent in getting familiar with the aircraft and carrying out consumption tests and D/F loop calibration, necessary precursors to any long distance flight. The squadron was organised in two flights, each of nine aircraft. Charles Bonner, who commanded 'A' Flight, was a seconded Territorial Army officer and went on to command 614. I believe he now lives in Wales and is the popular doyen of 614 reunions. The new squadron commander who succeeded Dick Skelton was Harry Sutton, a multi-talented man who fired the enthusiasm and quickly attracted the loyalty of the whole squadron.

During this work-up and preparation period we were visited from time to time by the commander designate of No 323 Wing, Group Captain Laurence Sinclair GC. Sinclair, known as Laurie to his contemporaries, and about to become Sinc to us, was a charming man. Very Public School, a keen rider to hounds, tall and saturnine, he was old school and had terrific charisma, enhanced by his being awarded the George Cross for pulling someone clear of a burning aircraft at great risk to his own life. He enthused us with the prospect of the adventure which lay ahead — and indeed the knowledge that we would be going to war, 72 aircraft strong, somewhere overseas was exciting — but he was too experienced a pilot to try and sell us the Bisley; he knew a dud when he saw one. He retired as Air Vice-Marshal Sir Laurence Sinclair having been knighted for his successful prosecution of the Radfan campaign, whilst Air Officer Commanding (AOC) Aden. In an earlier AVM appointment he had preceded me by several removes at Old Sarum and he came to visit me there in 1968 when I myself had become an air vice-marshal in turn.

But for the moment all effort was directed towards getting the heavy equipment ready for despatch, and the men themselves kitted out, inoculated and readied for bloc embarkation

Gibraltar 1942.

leave. We were issued with tropical kit of venerable design, complete with very long shorts and solar topees and had our camp kits brought up to scale. These, as I recall, included a canvas chair, a washstand, a canvas bucket and a very solid camp bed, all contained in a great canvas roll, no doubt designed to be portable by a native bearer but beyond the compass of an average officer.

Apart from a 20-minute air test on 7 November, I did not fly from 21 October until 16 November, the day fixed for departure. Once the Torch landings began on 8 November it was pretty clear where we were going and excitement rose. There was a last minute panic on the 16th getting everything set. Briefing was at 11.00 and take-offs were to start at 12.30. I said goodbye to Sylvia at 12.00 and remember the group of wives waving us off as, one by one, we lined up and opened the throttles. I took-off one from last with the CO the last to leave. I can remember that it all felt slightly unreal. Our final departure airfield was Portreath and we got there without incident although the weather was rather dirty.

There was a lot of dithering and indecision as to route and take-off times. Our destination was Blida, just west of Algiers, and the original intention had been to fly there direct via Cape Finisterre, along the line of the Pyrenees to the Mediterranean and then south. It was absolutely on our limits for fuel, even with long range tanks installed, and with no aids and possibly dirty weather it did not seem sensible to me. The 2 Group squadrons had preceded us and word had got back that, of four 18 Squadron aircraft despatched by that route, only one had reached Blida. Two had crash-landed out of fuel, one on the coast and one in the sea, and the fourth aircraft just disappeared. The alternative route was via Gibraltar, and this seemed to have everything to recommend it, apart from the prevalence of Ju88s over the Bay of Biscay, which were in any event common to both routes.

I personally had no problem with all this uncertainty. I was determined to go by day as I had less than full confidence in my artificial horizon. On a flight in October in good weather when I was fully visual and had no need of my artificial horizon it suddenly started rotating. It was an unnerving sight as, had it happened in cloud or at night, I would have had no reason to disbelieve it, would have followed it and almost certainly have been killed. The instrument repairer was confident that it was now fully serviceable, but I was still haunted by the memory of it going round and round and half expected it to happen again.

Eventually it was agreed that we should all go via Gibraltar and take-off times were settled, most going that night to have less risk of being intercepted by Ju88s. I played poker until 01.00 and won £20, a large sum in those days, from a chap in another squadron whose name I forget. He was going to pay me in Gibraltar but unfortunately for me, and even more unfortunately for him, he never made it and was seen to fly into the sea just short of the Straits. I was up at 04.00 and saw the last of the night take-offs at 04.30. All had got off safely except Peter Robarts, a particular friend of ours and godfather to our baby daughter, who had taxied into a wire fence. He was a seconded Yeomanry Officer and was always good fun. An Old Etonian, whose elder brother ran Robarts Bank, he survived the war but was killed as a test pilot a few years later.

After a Met briefing I took-off at 08.10 and climbed on course to 7,000ft. Visibility was good and I could see both Land's End and the Scillies as we coasted out. It was an uneventful flight although at the same time exciting. The longest flight I had made at that time, the knowledge that it was the start of what could prove to be a great adventure and the total lack of knowledge of what to expect combined to give a sense of exhilaration. We landed at Gib after exactly seven hours in the air having seen only one aircraft, a Portuguese fighter which intercepted us near Lisbon. The airfield was jam-packed with aeroplanes, and taxying was a somewhat hazardous business. I recorded in my diary that 'Gib seems pretty shambolic — very little organisation'. This was probably a harsh judgement considering the numbers of transients the permanent staff were having to handle.

Once we had established the arrangements for the next morning my crew and I went into town and had a celebration dinner against the backdrop of a brilliantly lighted Rock. The contrast with the blacked-out Britain we had just left could hardly have been more stark. My crew, who had been with me since September, were now a fixture. Both were pilot officers and, curiously enough, both were redheads. Bill Service, the navigator, was pale ginger with freckles and was a very steady, solid Canadian from British Columbia who could be relied on

Below: The Northwest African campaign.

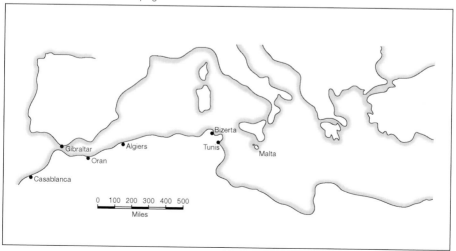

Above: Refuelling at Blida.

Left: The author (centre) with Ginger (left) and Bill (right).

at all times. Ginger Ryder, the wireless operator/air gunner had very red hair and a high complexion, with a temperament to match. He was excitable, always in high spirits, and wanted to be a pilot, an ambition he realised after the war when he went into civil aviation. Sadly, he was killed but Bill Service was going strong until just recently.

After shaving in salt water, a pretty horrific operation with the razor blades of those days, we took-off at 10.30 and reached Blida 3 hours 35 minutes later to be greeted whilst clambering down the wing by a cheerful aircraftsman saying, 'Lost 5 out of 12 yesterday, sir.' My first impressions were 'Blida populated with fairly friendly Vichy — the usual ropey l'Armée de l'Air types and their still ropier aircraft. Aerodrome set in a basin surrounded on three sides by hills with mountains rising sheer to the south. The town lies at the foot of these, 2 kilometres away. The atmosphere simply reeks of the Foreign Legion, very colourful with the Tricolour still flying — sanitation of course nil.'

That last remark would have been recorded after I had seen our quarters which were in a barrack block just vacated by a regiment of 'Goums', French colonial troops whose favourite weapon was a very large knife, not unlike our Gurkhas' kukri, and with which later in Italy they used to cut the throats of German sentries. But, fighters though they were, they could never be held up as a model of hygiene. The latrine in our block was a large rectangular room with perhaps 12 square holes cut in the stone floor on the side of the room furthest from the door. When I say that you could not open the door without pushing faeces with it, it gives you some idea of the sight. At some stage the holes had been missed and a gradual retreat towards the door had begun and appeared to have been completed to coincide with our arrival. Whether this was coincidence or whether the French officers had spurred their troops on to give a Gallic Harvey Smith to the *perfides Anglais* who can say. Either way our inheritance was a horror in that department, as were the bed bugs and lice in our iron bedsteads until we burned them out with blow lamps.

My diary records that we played poker that first night and that, as we had no money with which to play, the CO authorised the opening of our escape wallets which contained French francs, US dollars and a small number of gold Maria Theresa coins of, I think, 20 franc denomination but worth a considerable amount of money. We were on our honour to return any lost francs and reseal the wallets as soon as an accounts officer should arrive to pay us. The exchange rate was 300 francs to the £ and I lost 500 francs on that first evening, not very satisfactory but not disastrous.

The following day there was a good deal of scurrying around removing our long range tanks, checking the aircraft over and getting bombed up. All this took a long time as none of our equipment or transport had arrived and we were dependent on makeshift arrangements. Indeed none of our own ground crews had yet arrived either and we had to rely on a handful of very keen young airmen called servicing commandos who had come ashore by landing craft. Most of us got into Blida for a very late lunch, all carrying arms, as the natives were reported as occasionally hostile. There was no sign of any hostility, in fact the reverse, with the local population very friendly. We had an excellent five course lunch, including a magnificent omelette, which must have seemed amazing after UK rationing. I bought a bottle of Chanel No 5 for 250 francs and we returned to camp in a flea-ridden Arab *gharri* for what I recorded as 'an exorbitant sum'. We were just going to bed when all crews were ordered to the ops room in flying kit. The target was Bizerta docks, which I was to bomb later but not on that night, as the group captain had laid down that when the CO was flying, one of the two squadron leaders had to stay behind and that night it fell to me to be grounded. All aircraft got back but one was badly flak damaged and crash-landed. That was our second aircraft lost as we had received confirmation of a non-arrival at Gibraltar.

I took-off for Bizerta at 02.00 the following night and flew straight over a convoy near Algiers at 800ft and 140mph. Suddenly the sky was full of LAA tracer and I was down at 50ft and 200mph. Both Bill and Ginger said that they could smell burning so I landed back at Blida only to find that there was negligible damage. Most frustrating. The following night we did bomb the docks. It was a long way to go in an aircraft that would only cruise at 140mph in order to drop 1,000lb of bombs. That sortie in fact took 6 hours 25 minutes.

This sortie, and others like it, was typical of the tactical disarray which was obvious to the pilots and was no doubt being grappled with by the staffs. Initially, that is to say from 17 November, the 323 Wing squadrons had been deployed and expected to fly by daylight against targets in support of First Army. In practice this didn't happen. The targets were more strategic than tactical: Bizerta docks, Tunis harbour, El Aouina airfield, Sidi Ahmed airfield. First Army had advanced more rapidly than expected, Blida was too far to the rear and all attacks for the rest of November were carried out individually, either by night or by day using cloud cover. Because there was not a lot of cloud by day the balance lay in favour of night operations and by 3 December I had flown four sorties by night and two by day, all of about six hours duration.

Below: The Tunisian campaign.

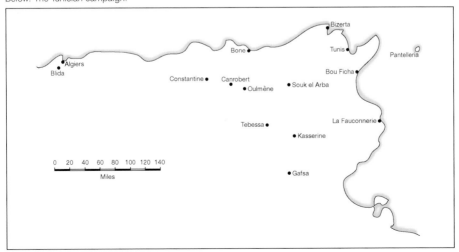

I use 3 December as a marker for a number of reasons. On the personal side it was the last raid I carried out from Blida, and very nearly my last raid of any sort. I had bombed Bizerta docks and had been briefed to follow this up by strafing Sidi Ahmed airfield from low level. It was a beautiful moonlit night and I naively steamed straight up the runway at 300ft, no doubt presenting a good silhouette to the German LAA batteries sited to either side. All might possibly have been well except that Ginger had neglected to change to night tracer so that when I ordered him to open fire we presumably became a dream target with our day tracer illuminating our exact position most effectively. At all events, no sooner had he opened fire than both batteries opened up simultaneously and we were suddenly caught in a cone of 40mm fire, most of it passing just above the canopy, although the guns on the port side scored at least one hit in my engine and managed to make great holes in my wing and to shoot away most of my aileron on that side. Until that moment I would not have contemplated a near vertical dive at night from 300ft, but it seemed preferable to the alternative of being shot out of the sky. I recovered very low indeed and, having got clear, faced some 2½ hours back to Blida with a barely controllable aircraft. I soon realised that I would not have the strength to keep up the necessary downforce to starboard with my arms alone and passed most of that seemingly endless flight back to base with my right knee crooked over the control column.

The watershed on the day versus night controversy came on 3 December. Still hankering to employ the Bisley by daylight, the operations staff had ordered 18 Squadron forward to Canrobert and thence to Souk El Arba. On the afternoon of the 4th the squadron was given the landing ground of Chouigui as its target. The attack, with a Spitfire escort, was to be carried out by 11 aircraft, led by the CO, Wing Commander Hugh Malcolm. Just before take-off Malcolm was told that there had been a change and that in place of an escort there would be a fighter sweep across the area. Precisely what happened then is still not clear. The official version of events is that the decision as to whether or not to go without a fighter escort was left up to Malcolm and that he volunteered to go. Our understanding at the time was that the decision was taken by the senior operations officer, a fighter boy who did not fully appreciate the vulnerability of the Bisley and that Malcolm acquiesced rather than appear to be questioning an order. Either way Hugh Malcolm was undoubtedly brave, and the 11 Bisleys lined up. One burst a tyre and crashed on take-off and one crash-landed soon after becoming airborne so that in the event it was a formation of nine aircraft that set course for the target at 15.15.

Approaching the target they were jumped by some 50 to 60 Me109s and Fw190s. At first they tried to press on but, realising the odds were hopeless, they jettisoned their bombs and tried to fight their way back to Souk El Arba. Still maintaining formation they were shot down one by one. The last aircraft crashed close to our troops' forward positions and the crew, of which Leonard Quevâtre was the navigator, survived the impact and managed to walk to safety. This disastrous action, which was marked by the posthumous award of the VC to Hugh Malcolm, finally put an end to even the occasional use of the Bisley by day, except for the action which took place on 7 December.

Sinc, perhaps worried that wing morale might suffer as a result of 18 Squadron's plight (the squadron had had losses on the flight out and other losses before the disaster and was now non-operational, with something like two serviceable aircraft remaining) and perhaps partly motivated by a desire to stick two fingers up at the Germans, decided that he would lead a small select force of 614 Squadron by daylight against a target in the same area. The formation was six aircraft strong, flying as two vics of 3 rather than as one box of 6. Sinc led the first vic with me as his number 2 and Charles Bonner as number 3. The second vic was led by the CO with Peter Robarts at 2 and Philip Hanbury at 3. We had an escort of 24 Spitfires and were supposed to have had a top cover of US Lightnings, but they never showed up. Two Hurricanes of 225 Squadron took advantage of our escort to carry out Tac/R at the same time. Our escort looked after us, shooting down one Me109 in the process, and we successfully bombed our target, the road/rail junction at Tebourba. Admittedly we bombed from 6,000ft as opposed to 18 Squadron's planned 1,000ft, but to a degree it was felt that honour had been satisfied. Sinclair had taken quite a chance, and for this demonstration of defiance and for his leadership of the wing in very adverse circumstances he was awarded a bar to his DSO.

No 18 Squadron had already been called forward and on the afternoon of the 4th the whole wing was ordered to move to Canrobert, a grass strip to the east of Constantine, on the following day. There was a glorious sunrise and all looked set fair. The road detail had moved during the night except for one lorry carrying the officers' camp kits and suitcases. Owing to some muddle, this vehicle and its high priority load had been left driverless and, as my aircraft was a write-off, I resolved to make sure that 'the mail got through'. We accordingly set off at 14.00 with Derek Wallace as navigator. I had never driven a 3 tonner before, but found it a delightful vehicle, which was just as well as I was to drive it for 18 hours, arriving the following day having taken the route Algiers, Palestro, Sétif, Constantine, Canrobert. My diary records that it was glorious scenery between Algiers and Palestro, reminiscent of the Balearic Islands and that at some stage we negotiated a zigzag track through precipitous mountains. We noticed also an interesting change in type of Arab, from city dwellers to fine-looking Berbers.

And so it had been a final and abrupt farewell to Blida — I had been in the middle of a game of chess with Derek Wallace when the order to move to Canrobert came through — and I do not think any of us had regrets. We had come out as daylight low-level bombers and had been employed at night at long range, a role with which we were totally unfamiliar. As the Official History puts it 'in the absence of navigational facilities, night operations conducted at long range over mountainous country might well have daunted the stoutest hearts.' Whilst that is true to a degree it misses the main point — the total inadequacy of the Bisley. The two Wellington squadrons that now took over the night role, Nos 142 and 150, operated against the same targets with very much lighter casualties.

It had been an incident-packed 19 days that seemed very much longer in retrospect. From our disorganised shambolic arrival, without our ground crew and without transport, without even the sacred Form 700 — the True Cross of an aircraft's fitness for flight and of the pilot's acceptance of any stated minor deficiencies — everything had to be improvised. We had to do things we had never done before, like taking-off without a flare path on one occasion because of Ju88s above. More importantly in relation to our losses, because of the weights at which we were operating we had as a matter of routine to take off in +9 emergency boost. If a tyre burst occurred in that configuration, as it not infrequently did, because of all the large flints in the soil, it was virtually impossible to hold the swing and the airscrew would hit the ground, the undercarriage collapse on that side and, with or without fire, the aircraft would be a write-off.

At Canrobert — Bill is on the far left and Ginger immediately to the right of the author (third from the right).

The wing had sustained a lot of losses during the Blida period, including non-arrivals on the flight out. What the precise figure was I do not know but I would put it at about 30 aircraft. The loss in crews was nothing like proportionate as a good number of the losses were crashes, whether or not caused by enemy action, from which the crews walked away. Every instance of major damage on the other hand was an aircraft lost as at that time we had no facilities or organisation capable of major repair.

The move to Canrobert brought us to within 180 miles of Tunis and Bizerta, our likely target area. This was still too far away to get an appreciable increase in sortie rate but it did enable us to increase our bomb load by carrying a 250lb bomb under each wing on bomb racks quickly improvised by the 614 armament and engineer staff. Flying in December was somewhat restricted by weather — I had flown some 35 hours in the last two weeks of November but logged only 21 hours in the whole of December. The trouble was mud caused by heavy rain. This affected all our forward airfields and the fighter squadrons at Souk El Arba were similarly bogged down. To quote the Official History again, 'On this airfield [Souk el Arba] as elsewhere, efforts were being made to lay steel matting; but some 2,000 tons of this — or two days' carrying capacity of the entire railway system in the forward area — were required for a single runway. And when laid, it tended simply to disappear into the mud. Like everything else on our side, the provision of hard runways suffered from the long, thin line of communication and the appalling weather.'

Although I did little flying in December some of it was more stimulating than I would have wished. On the 17th I was briefed to attack Tunis harbour. My own aircraft, 'R', was unserviceable and I took 'K', the CO's. In +9 boost, opposite No 3 flare my starboard tyre burst. The aircraft swung violently but I thought I was going slowly enough to stop. However, almost immediately, the port tyre also burst, accentuating my correction to port.

The port undercarriage collapsed, the port engine was wrenched from the wing and a fire started. It was clearly no place to be and the three of us ran like hell for the ops room. Strangely enough 'K' didn't blow up for some minutes, by which time we had been given a swig of whisky and were being congratulated on our escape.

Weather prevented any flying for the next seven days but cleared slightly on the 25th when I did a 30-minute air test in my own aircraft 'R'. It was a strange Christmas Day starting with a visit from a reconnaissance Ju88 which photographed the airfield to its heart's content, our own sparse heavy AA being pathetically inaccurate. We served the airmen a traditional Christmas dinner in the local church which my diary records as a great success; also that I had

No 614 Squadron mess at Canrobert.

delicious cakes for tea with a certain Madame Casanova. Scheduled ops were cancelled at 17.00 because of the weather and we had an enjoyable dinner in the squadron mess with Sinc as our guest of honour. He rose to the occasion with great panache and gave us a very funny song about shooting bear in India.

The following night the weather was fine and I prepared for an armed recce of the road from Tunis to Pont du Fahs. Take-off was at 02.15 and when I was given the Form 700 to sign it was apparent that my outer tanks had not been filled, owing to some strange error. I therefore had the choice of taking off late with full tanks or taking off on time with inner tanks only. As it was a beautiful night I foolishly elected to go on time. There was no convoy on the road so we bombed Pont du Fahs railway station, the alternative target, before turning for home. The beautiful night had been deceptive; by the time we had cleared the high mountain range and let down towards Canrobert a dense ground fog had suddenly come up. Ginger could get nothing out of the D/F loop and in any event I calculated I had less than an hour's fuel remaining so a diversion, even if we had known where we were, was not really an option.

It was two hours to dawn so it seemed to me that we were faced with either baling out or attempting a crash-landing in the dark if there was any break in the fog within the hour. I looked on baling out as very much a last resort, to be postponed as long as possible, and started to fly for endurance, remaining over terrain which, though high, we knew to be relatively flat. After a while I spotted a small hole in the fog through which in the moonlight I could get occasional glimpses of the ground, and I determined to stay with that hole come what may.

The hour passed and I was still registering a flicker of fuel and I began to wonder if there was any hope of remaining airborne, if not until dawn, perhaps until the pre-dawn lightening of the sky might show me something of the ground through my providential hole. We were flying at about 200ft just above the fog and I had in mind all the time the critical balance between staying up as long as possible on the one hand and on the other keeping sufficient fuel to climb up to a safe height for baling out. As time went on and the sky showed the first signs of lightening I discarded the baling out option and decided that I would land through the hole in the fog either when my engines cut out or, I was beginning to hope, under power when there was enough light to see by. After I had hung on my props for one and three quarter hours and I knew that my fuel must be virtually exhausted I was committed to land. I could vaguely see the ground as I came below the fog and decided to attempt a wheels-down precautionary landing. I came in very slowly with full flap and dropped it in.

The undercarriage stood up to it and I was a pretty relieved captain of aircraft when after no more than 400yd we stopped without having hit any of the extremely large boulders that lay to either side. My crew were no doubt even more relieved — I had tried to keep them informed of the situation as we went along but they cannot have been greatly reassured by my evident uncertainty. When eventually the ground crew checked the aircraft, there was not enough fuel in the tanks to register on a dip-stick. I had stayed airborne for 5 hours on inner tanks alone, which must, I believe, be a record, albeit not one I would wish to relive. The two aircraft which took-off at about the same time as I did also came to grief; a 114 aircraft crashed, killing the crew, and Charles Bonner crash-landed on a beach along the line of the surf, writing off his aircraft but saving his crew.

To revert to our situation, we had only the vaguest idea of where we were but it turned out that we were near a small town called Auguste Comte, about 20 minutes flying time from Canrobert. At the time of course we didn't know this, but we could see that there was a railway line a few hundred yards away and it seemed that our best course of action was to stop the next train and hitch to the nearest bit of civilisation. We didn't know whether the train would be along that day or the next, but we were so pleased to be alive that we did not greatly care. Soon after we had landed and whilst we were still taking stock of our position we found ourselves effectively surrounded by a large body of Bedouin horsemen. I don't know how many there were but they looked to be more numerous than the Household Cavalry on the Queen's Birthday. We had a moment's anxiety when suddenly confronted by this wild-looking and colourful band, but they immediately turned out to be extremely friendly.

The leader — some Sheikh, I imagine, by his bearing and accoutrements — made it clear that he would like to have a close look at 'R'. That done, he went on to indicate that he would be happy to afford me the honour of riding his horse, a terrifying-looking animal. Luckily I had done a bit or riding, albeit of more docile creatures, whilst at Canrobert and was accustomed to the high pommel, so much more accommodating and forgiving than the English saddle. No sooner was I mounted than he dealt his steed a fearful thwack and I was off from standstill to instant full gallop, like an equine Formula One. His followers, like the crowd at a Roman circus, were in good voice, clearly thirsting for a kill in the form of my being thrown by this fearsome stallion. Sadly for them he gradually tired of his mad gallop and returned, in auto and with no guidance from the pilot, to his master's side and I was accorded an enthusiastic, though exceedingly ill-earned, welcome. Shortly after that we heard a train coming and, having stopped it, Ginger and I set off for Auguste Comte leaving Bill to look after 'R'. Arrived at Auguste Comte, I arranged for a guard of Spahis to relieve Bill and then rejoined the waiting train for Khenchela where we were warmly welcomed in the French cavalry mess prior to being driven back to Canrobert in a classic prewar Citroën with those beautiful simple lines and a dashboard gear change.

(Left to right:) the author, A. N. Other, Harry Sutton, Ian MacDougal, Derek Wallace, Peter Robarts and Charles Bonner at Canrobert, December 1942.

The next three days the weather was atrocious and gave no hope of recovering 'R'. However, on the 30th it was cold and hard, like Scotland in March, and I set off with Ginger, Sergeant Belt and Corporal Beall in the 15cwt to see what we could do. The longest run was 550yd with a 30° bend halfway, much of it over plough and stubble. I thought it would be just possible with minimum fuel and at minimum weight, so we transferred anything movable to the 15cwt. and I decided even to leave poor Ginger behind. I had a terrific audience of excited Arabs and rather anxious guards and managed just to get her off the ground in +9 boost with 30° of flap.

I got her bombed up and on the battle order as soon as we got back, the target being road convoys near Tunis. Take-off was to be at 04.00 but operations were cancelled at 00.15 because of an expected front. The day of New Year's Eve was spent dispersing aircraft and lashing everything down ahead of this monster front which was expected to bring snow and make the airfield unusable for a fortnight or so. Certainly the sky was unusual to say the least. I described it in my diary in words which now bring faint embarrassment: 'Most glorious and frightening sunset that I've ever seen. To the west, lowering clouds made purple by the last rays of sunlight, just caressing the stark silhouette of the distant range, with the valleys, in striking contrast, the deepest orange.'

During the afternoon came news that there were 18 bags of mail awaiting collection at Constantine and this was terrific news indeed. There were many deficiencies during the Northwest African campaign and the irregularity and uncertainty of the mail was one of the worst. Weeks might pass without a letter and then one would get six or seven together, very similar to the London bus system. To the person in the field it caused no more than unhappiness; to the wife or sweetheart waiting at home without word it must on occasion have been agonising. The evening went well. We had done our best to get hold of as much drink as we could and my diary says that the 'B' Flight party went with a terrific swing.

If my estimate of 30 aircraft lost by the beginning of December was roughly correct then we must have lost another 25 or so during December because by 31 December we had 16 aircraft remaining out of the original 72. On 1 January six new aircraft arrived, bringing the wing up to 22 and on the 2nd a further six, but on 6 January Sinclair reported to headquarters that he had only 12 serviceable aircraft. On the 13th I did an analysis of the fate of the 18 aircraft with which 614 had left England and found that only 4 of the originals remained on squadron strength; 10 had been written off and 4 given away to plug gaps elsewhere in the wing.

We were not alone in scattering our aircraft over the Algerian and Tunisian countryside. On the 2nd I flew to Bône to calibrate the HF/DF and arrived to find them a bit shaken. Two ships were burning in the harbour, one of which blew up at 13.30. A large force of Ju87s, put at 40 plus, had attacked at dawn escorted by Me109s and Fw190s. The 190s also carried bombs and the attack was followed up by a force of Me110s. The airfield was littered with broken aircraft, and others lay in surrounding fields. They had lost 10 Spitfires and had 12 remaining. Whilst I was ringing up operations from the duty pilot's tent I heard an American reporting the result of a dogfight to the controller — six Huns down out to sea for the loss of two Spits. On the same line I heard the controller giving instructions to call for two squadrons from Souk El Arba — he apparently had something on the plot and was expecting further action. Soon after that I took-off on my calibration flight and at 5,000ft straight and level-heading east in a clear blue sky felt somewhat exposed.

The first half of January was marked by filthy weather, rumour, order and counter-order and by the loss of yet more aircraft. On the 2nd we were told that 614 was to be made up to 12 aircraft and was to practise flying in two boxes of six for escorted daylight operations. On the 3rd we were ordered to be prepared to move to Souk El Arba and were ready by 11.00. I personally welcomed the idea because, although we would meet a lot of flak, provided our escort did its job I felt it would be less hazardous and certainly more exciting than the night operations that were remorselessly eating away at our numbers. On the 4th, typical of the times, the whole idea was abandoned as there were insufficient fighters left to escort us.

The CO felt we needed some sort of break and he set off for Batna and Biskra on the 5th. He arrived back on the 7th full of enthusiasm and kindly offered me his Humber staff car to do the same run. It must have been a bit of a squash because in addition to Bill and Ginger I took Peter, David Smyth and Philip Hanbury. We reached Batna that night and stayed at the Hôtel des Orients where the food was magnificent.

Shopping the next day I bought two rings, one purporting to be a *vrai rubie* which the patriotic French jeweller had resolutely refused to sell to the *sales Boches* (none of whom so far as I know had been within 350 miles of Batna) and had been saving until the day that he could sell it — at a loss naturally, but what was that to compare to the pleasure it gave him to advance the *Entente Cordiale*? — to a gallant *pilote de l'Armée de l'Air Britannique* such as myself. I should have seen him coming a mile away — in fact I think I did — but he was such a likeable rogue that I succumbed. The other thing I remember about that morning is that a young French girl, perhaps about 18, remarked to her friend with seeming astonishment and enthusiasm that I had blue eyes. Whilst not unflattered by her attention I was none the less amazed that blue eyes should be such a rarity.

We drove on to Biskra through simply lovely scenery, stopping en route for a picnic lunch by the side of a stream in a very picturesque gorge; the weather was perfect, like a really hot English summer's day. We took rooms at the Hôtel de l'Oasis overlooking the barracks of the 9th Spahis, whose adjutant, a most accommodating officer, laid on some dancing girls, the famed 'Ouiled Nials', to perform for us that night. It was a most exotic and uninhibited show and Bill and Ginger — both red haired and beloved of the Prophet — were particularly at risk. We spent the next night at Batna and arrived back at Canrobert to find that a move forward to Oulmène, a much larger grass field some 20 minutes flying time further east, was imminent.

There was no flying until the 17th when a limited effort of four aircraft was ordered from an advanced landing ground in the desert. We taxied out at 14.30, bombed up, and the CO took-off without incident followed by Peter. Philip got off the ground but his starboard engine cut and he crash-landed straight ahead. Halfway through my take-off run my port tyre burst. The violence of the swing wiped off my entire undercarriage and 'R' ended up in small pieces. This time thankfully there was no fire. Neither Philip's crew nor mine were hurt but two aircraft destroyed reduced the squadron to the ridiculous figure of four. On the next night but one we had three aircraft serviceable and managed to fly three sorties per aircraft. I took-off at 18.15 slightly worried as the weather seemed to be building up. However, it stayed relatively fine and we located and bombed a convoy on the Cheylus–Pont du Fahs road. Word was received that Wing Commander Tucker, the CO of 18, was missing believed killed from a similar attack on the Sousse–Sfax road.

We kept up these harassing attacks every night that the weather allowed and I personally flew two more sorties in January, on the first one bombing a vehicle concentration and on the second a road/rail junction north of Pont du Fahs. Both these sorties had minor excitements. On the first my starboard engine cut immediately after take-off but picked up again and, on the second, I had a hair-raising practically blind take-off because the windows were frosted and iced up.

We continued to lose aircraft at a ridiculous rate, most of them in no way due to enemy action. Weather took quite a toll, but the prime cause was having to operate a heavy under-powered aircraft at altitude and at night off grass airfields covered in sharp flints. At the weights at which we were operating there was no chance of remaining airborne if you lost an engine. Although complete engine failure was a rarity, partial loss of power from which the engine recovered was commonplace. I wrote in my diary at the time, 'most people getting rather jittery about flying these bloody aircraft — engine cuts getting more and more frequent.' There were the odd signs of the beginning of a morale problem, which was hardly surprisingly considering our loss rate. The new replacement pilots must have wondered what on earth they had come to. We had two flamers on take-off, both fatal, during the last half of January. The morning after the second one a crew of 18 Squadron came to me as controller and especially asked to be left off the battle order as they didn't feel like flying after the previous night's fatality. The pilot had been a friend of theirs and they were very shaken. They said that they didn't even want to fly by day. How the new CO of 18 — the third since leaving England — coped with this I don't know as I didn't follow it up, but I found it disturbing. In today's changed environment they might even have been given counselling but I expect that Sandeman booted them back into the air to take their chance with the other crews.

There was little flying in the first half of February and rumour and counter-rumour held sway. The whole wing was going to be re-equipped with Mitchells, 18 and 114 were going to get Bostons while 13 and 614 would carry on the night role with Wellingtons; each day brought its new solution, the least attractive of which was that 13, 18 and 114 would re-equip with Bostons leaving 614 with the surviving Bisleys. Our appetites were sharpened by being able to look over two Mitchells which had landed to refuel. I wrote in my diary, 'it was practically agony looking over the B-25s — they really are the last word in what an aircraft should be.' I wrote that before I had seen a Boston, the A-20, which was to become my favourite aircraft — certainly of the war, if not of all time. The Mitchell crews were typically American and shot the most terrific line for 30 minutes non-stop. Their group had apparently flown 32 operational sorties since 7 December, mostly in formations of 16, and had lost only one aircraft. After telling us how dangerous it was over Tunis and Bizerta they asked us how many aircraft we had at Canrobert. Playing the laid-back ultra-cool Brit of American imagination I said, '14 now. We started with 72.' One of them, impressed, said, 'Gee, did you lose many pilots?' allowing me the malicious knockout of, 'Oh no, only about 30.' They were a harmless bunch but we enjoyed their discomfiture greatly.

On the night of the 15th we managed to get 16 aircraft off, 11 from Oulmène and five from Ain Tukka, the desert satellite. I was controller at Oulmène. After all 11 had taken off without incident a new pilot, Ross-Gower, took-off to do some circuits. He burst a tyre on his first landing, caught fire and burnt out. The flare path had to be shifted and whilst this was being done the aircraft started coming back. By the time the new flare path was ready I had 11 aircraft on the circuit, one of them not showing IFF. There wasn't much to be done about it and I decided to take the risk of it being a German and to bring them in. The first four aircraft landed safely but the fifth stalled straight into the ground and burnt up. It had all become too difficult so I diverted the remainder to Canrobert. Eventually I got to bed in my tent only to be rung by the CO from Canrobert to order three aircraft loaded with supply containers to be ready for take-off in an hour's time. No further details. After an hour and a quarter the projected operation was cancelled. My diary entry records that it was the most shattering night on the ground that I remembered.

On the following day the CO told me that he had agreed my posting to 114 as a flight commander which would allow a charming Scot, Ian MacDougal, to be promoted to squadron leader and to take over 'B' Flight of 614 from me. The CO said that Thomson would soon be going home, he thought on compassionate grounds, and that I would be taking over the squadron. It all sounded great in theory, provided the Bostons really did materialise. At that date 114 had only received one, and that was unserviceable. Five days later it became serviceable and I flew it for the first time. A dream aircraft, easy to take off and land because of its tricycle undercarriage — very much a novelty in those days — capable of over 300mph at sea level and able, low down, to outrun any fighter. I could find no fault with it — the contrast with the dreaded Bisley was absolute.

Before I got to fly the Boston the military picture had suddenly changed as the Germans thrust westwards for the Kasserine Pass. On the 17th 10th Panzer Division was reported to be advancing rapidly and to be only 40 miles from Tebessa, three hours by road from Canrobert. On the 18th we learnt that the thrust against Tebessa was not 10th but 15th Panzer Division and was a major effort. Feriana and Thelepte had been occupied and US II Corps had been badly mauled. If the Germans could get through the pass to Tebessa then there would be nothing to stop a rapid further advance as the area to the north was held by the very ill-equipped French XIX Corps and there was nothing to the south.

It seemed to us that, from the German point of view, the attack was very risky as the Eighth Army was only about 150 miles from Gafsa and going strong. It was decided that in this emergency 18 and 114 were to become operational again on Bisleys and on the 19th there was much scurrying around in preparation for attacks on German formations in or around the Kasserine Pass. On the 19th the possibility of the Germans breaking through and reaching Canrobert was beginning to be taken seriously. There was a lot of rumour flying about such as that the Huns were only six miles from Tebessa and consequently a certain amount of panic in the camp. Sinc, true to form, responded in swashbuckling terms and announced that, if there was a breakthrough, the aircrew would take to the local mountain that overlooked the village and operate as guerrillas. My diary entry reads 'not my cup of tea at all!'

On the 21st we were briefed to attack concentrations of armour in the Kasserine Pass. The weather was foul and I had a tyre burst whilst taxying out. Those who did get off saw nothing because of low cloud.

Right & below:
The Beast at Oulmène.
Crown Copyright

On the 22nd a repeat attack was ordered. It was the same story with the weather and we had a lousy trip dicing in and out of low cloud. We saw nothing because of the cloud and poor visibility and bombed Feriana as the alternative.

The next day the news from the front was much better. Although 15th Panzer had broken through the pass they were being held by 16th Armoured Brigade, and First Army were confident that the Germans would have to withdraw as they, and 10th Panzer at Pont du Fahs, were the only armoured formations available to oppose Eighth Army once it was ready to attack the Mareth Line. A breakthrough there was expected to come soon as Rommel had left its defence to four Italian divisions and was reported to have withdrawn all their transport so that they would be unable to retreat.

Aircraft from 18 and 114 were out that night but attacks were largely ineffective because of the weather. The cost was high: three aircraft written off and one WOp/AG killed trying to bale out. On the night of the 24th I was briefed to bomb Gafsa with incendiaries and left it burning satisfactorily. I had no compunction as, in the face of the German advance, the local population had turned on the French civilians, raping, killing and mutilating. The landing back was hazardous because of the mist covering the airfield. Most of us got in all right but there was one fatal crash, which burnt out, and a number of aircraft diverted.

Although I had not known it at the time, that was to be my last Bisley sortie. I had flown 17 operational sorties for a total of 109 hours and had written off two of them. The wing had been reinforced by a further 25 aircraft on top of the first reinforcement of 12 and now had 30 aircraft on strength. Our losses had therefore amounted to 79 aircraft in not much over three months. Admittedly the loss in life was a lot less, though still considerable, but even taking the most favourable view, the operations of the Bisley wing can only be seen as a minor disaster. Now, after 57 years, I'm prepared to concede that it may well have been necessary to have a British light bomber in production to tide some squadrons over until enough Bostons and Mitchells became available. What I do not concede is that it should have been the Bisley; we would all have been far happier with an extended run of the Blenheim Mk IV, the old 'Longnose'. If you can show me a pilot who liked the Bisley, you show me an unusual person. Looking back I suppose I must accept that the decision to put the Bisley into production — misguided and near criminal though it was — was taken with the best of intentions. Writing in February 1942 at the age of 22 I was not prepared to accept any excuse that those behind the Bisley might have offered. I wrote, on the same day that I last flew a Bisley, 'I wish we'd get rid of these bastard aircraft. God rot the sods who are sitting back and making money out of them.' Intemperate yes, but deeply felt and, I would wager, an accurate reflection of the private thoughts of every pilot in the wing.

At 12.30 on the 25th Thomson, the CO, called Bob Molesworth the other flight commander and myself into his office and told us that selected pilots were to go back to England to collect our Bostons, that we would leave Canrobert by Dakota and that we were to be on standby to do so from midday the next day. I need hardly say how magical those words sounded. In the event, 22 aircrew left for Maison Blanche, at Algiers, on 2 March. This represented 11 aircraft as each pilot could take only one member of crew. I don't remember how it was resolved but Bill stayed behind, perhaps because his family was in Canada, and Ginger came with me. We all had an exceedingly educational night in the Casbah and flew on to Marrakesh, again by Dakota on the 3rd. I am surprised to see from my Log Book that the flight took 5 hours and 30 minutes — a long time in a paratrooper's metal seat — but we were all too excited even to feel tired. We stayed in the La Mamounia for three nights and sadly I can remember little of it except that it was perfect weather and that, for the first time, I was given lime in my gin and tonic rather than lemon. On the night of the 6th we set off in a Skymaster — the last word in passenger longhaul — for a 9 hour 10 minute flight to Prestwick. From there we were flown by Harrow to Hendon, granted 10 days' leave and told to report to West Raynham on the 16th.

I air-tested my new 'R' on the 16th for an hour and after two consumption tests with a certain Flying Officer Langdon as navigator and a Sergeant Russell, who was to stay with me throughout my time on 114, as air gunner we set off for Portreath on the 23rd. Bad weather forced a stay but we eventually took-off for Gibraltar on the morning of the 28th. I had a

The beautiful Boston.

grand total on type of 6 hours 50 minutes and was nearly to double that with 5 hours 10 minutes to Gibraltar. We dropped off Langdon there and I flew on to Blida the next day and thence to Canrobert on the 30th without a navigator as the weather was fair. For the next three weeks we flew every day but two; short sorties, a lot of them in formation, getting really to know this beautiful aircraft.

During this period it was thought it would be a good idea if the lead pilots, of whom I would be one, could see how the Americans flew the sort of mission that we would soon be flying. Accordingly, on 4 April, I flew as a passenger in a Mitchell captained by a Lieutenant Sheffield. Strangely, with a relatively junior officer as captain, we were lead aircraft of three boxes of six. We had a Spitfire escort and the target was St Marie du Zit airfield. Everything went much as I would have expected, except that they seemed a bit more tense and excitable than a British crew would have been, until we started to run up on the target. At that juncture, on Sheffield's order, they all produced steel helmets; of the five crew most put them on their heads but some, I think two, elected to sit on them. It was a weird performance, and whether it was unique to that crew or was a standard operating procedure for all bomber crews, I never discovered. The heavy flak was fairly accurate but only moderate in intensity so their procedure seemed very over-dramatic to British eyes and not one that I could see being adopted by Royal Air Force squadrons.

The squadron moved forward to Souk El Khemis on the 18th and began operating on the 21st. This airfield was only 30 minutes flying from the German positions so we were able to fly two sorties a day and on occasion three. It also had a runway of pierced steel planking or PSP so the days of burst tyres were over. Three of our first four sorties were against strongpoints on Longstop Hill, that commanding height that had changed hands so many times, and was now finally to fall to the Guards. I visited it a few days later as part of an initiative whereby RAF aircrew could go and see how the Army worked and Army officers could get a taste of flying. It seemed like a good idea, but didn't really work as each was uneasy, if not terrified, in the other's environment — I certainly found coming under shellfire on the ground more animating than seeing 88mm shells bursting close to my aircraft. We operated flat out to the end of April for the loss of two aircraft, one spinning in after a collision in formation and one, flying number 6 in a box, being neatly picked off by an Me109 en passant. On 2 May, with no warning or even an inkling of what was afoot, I was promoted to acting wing commander and posted to command No 223 Squadron of the famed Desert Air Force. The squadron at that time was at La Fauconnerie in southern Tunisia and was equipped with Martin Baltimores. I bade a hasty farewell to 114, a squadron I had been with for only two and a half months but which, because of the Boston, I remember with great pleasure. (Although I did not know it at the time Lieutenant-Colonel Michael Carver, with whom I was to have a good deal to do later on, had taken command of 1st Royal Tanks in 22nd Armoured Brigade some two weeks previously on 14 April, not far from La Fauconnerie, and had been switched to First Army near Medjez el Bab on 2 May for the final advance on Tunis.)

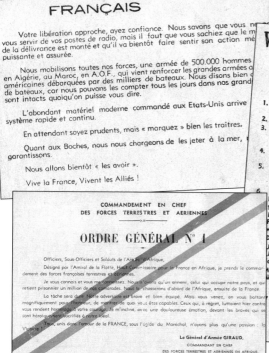

World War 2 leaflets — North African campaign.

FRANÇAIS

Votre libération approche, ayez confiance. Nous savons que vous ne
vous servir de vos postes de radio, mais il faut que vous sachiez que le m
de la délivrance est monté et qu'il va bientôt faire sentir son action m
puissante et assurée.

Nous mobilisons toutes nos forces, une armée de 500.000 hommes
en Algérie, au Maroc, en A.O.F., qui vient renforcer les grandes armées
américaines débarquées par des milliers de bateaux. Nous disons bien
de bateaux, car nous pouvons les compter tous les jours dans nos grand
sont intacts quoiqu'on puisse vous dire.

L'abondant matériel moderne commandé aux Etats-Unis arrive
système rapide et continu.

En attendant soyez prudents, mais « marquez » bien les traîtres.

Quant aux Boches, nous nous chargeons de les jeter à la mer,
garantissons.

Nous allons bientôt « les avoir ».

Vive la France, Vivent les Alliés !

WILLST DU NACH HAUSE KOMMEN,
DEUTSCHER SOLDAT ?

DENK DANN ÜBER FOLGENDEM NACH :—

1. Wenn wir losschlagen, wird es nur zweierlei deutsche Soldaten in
Afrika bleiben : die Gefangenen und die Toten.
2. Die Toten kommen nicht nach Hause.
3. Alle in Tunisien gemachten Kriegsgefangenen werden nach Amerika
gebracht. Nach Ende des Krieges, kehren sie nach Deutschland wieder
zurück, und werden mit ihren Geliebten wieder vereinigt.
4. Hitler kann den Krieg nicht mehr gewinnen : er kann ihn nur
verlangern. DU aber kannst ihn verkürzen.
5. Du glaubst nicht mehr an Sieg, aber Du willst Frieden haben.
Du kannst deinen eigenen Frieden erkämpfen, und dadurch den
allgemeinen Frieden naher bringen !
6. Du bist von Hitler in eine Falle geschickt worden. Niemand weiss
besser als er, dass die deutschen Truppen in Afrika nur als Gefan-
gene, wenn überhaupt, nach Hause kommen können.
Dir hilft es nicht, dass immer noch andere deutsche Soldaten in die
Falle geflogen kommen. Aber uns kann das nur recht sein. Wir
warten ab.
DU aber brauchst nicht zu warten, bis sich die Falle zuschliesst.
Umseitig stehender Schein erlaubt Dich, unversehrt durch die alliierte
linie zu gehen. Dieser Schein stellt ja Deine beste Hoffnung dar,
dass Du doch nach Hause kommst.
Mach von diesem Schein Gebrauch ! Er ist überall und zu jeder Zeit
gültig. Du wirst bei weitem nicht der Erste sein !

KANNST ES,
WENN DU WILLST !

COMMANDEMENT EN CHEF
DES FORCES TERRESTRES ET AÉRIENNES

ORDRE GÉNÉRAL Nº 1

Officiers, Sous-Officiers et Soldats de l'Armée d'Afrique,

Désigné par l'Amiral de la Flotte, Haut-Commissaire pour la France en Afrique, je prends le commandement des forces françaises terrestres et aériennes.

Je vous connais et vous me connaissez. Nous n'avons qu'un ennemi, celui qui occupe notre pays, et qui
retient prisonnier un million de nos camarades. Nous le chasserons d'abord de l'Afrique, ensuite de la France.

La tâche sera dure. Notre adversaire est brave et bien équipé. Mais vous venez, en vous battant
magnifiquement pour l'honneur, de montrer de quoi vous êtes capables. Ceux qui, de regret, luttaient hier contre
vous rendent hommage à votre courage. Je m'incline, avec une douloureuse émotion, devant les braves qui se
sont héroïquement sacrifiés à notre idéal.

Tous, unis dans l'amour de la FRANCE, sous l'égide du Maréchal, n'ayons plus qu'une passion : la
Victoire.

Le Général d'Armée GIRAUD,
COMMANDANT EN CHEF
DES FORCES TERRESTRES ET AÉRIENNES EN AFRIQUE.

Officers of No 223 Squadron.

4. War Full Time (Part 2): May 1943–March 1944 Squadron Commander No 223 Squadron

I flew down to La Fauconnerie on 3 May with Bill and Ginger and Sergeant Russell, also posted to 223, flying a Boston for the last time. My predecessor, a near legendary figure called Tommy Horgan who left the service immediately after the war, had already gone, on promotion to acting group captain at the age of 25, possibly a record. Looking back I suppose my acting wing commander at 22 might also possibly have been a record, although at the time it seemed perfectly natural and something that followed inevitably from my experience. No 223 Squadron was one of the two squadrons in No 232 Wing, the other being No 55, commanded at that time by Jack Roulston, a tough and likeable Rhodesian who had been with the squadron since the Abyssinian campaign and was a comparatively old man of perhaps 28. Jack was short service during the war but Larry Stokes, or Stokey, who commanded the wing, was a regular and very much an old man, in his late thirties if not early forties.

Both squadrons, hardened and honed by experience, were superbly efficient and were an eye-opener to me, coming from what was by comparison a fairly ramshackle and inexperienced, albeit keen, command. Each consisted of 18 Baltimores, 18 crews, 500 men, 80 prime movers and 80 trailers, were totally under canvas and could be packed up and on the move in two hours. They were truly mobile squadrons — the product of years of experience — which have never been bettered nor, since the war, even equalled.

When I had called on Stokey, I and my crew were whisked off by the squadron adjutant and the squadron warrant officer to the squadron tailor, all three of whom were horrified at our First Army lack of sartorial elegance. Away went the long shorts and dark khaki UK-issue stockings and in no time we were dressed as paid-up members of the Desert Air Force in short shorts and stockings bordering on yellow. Only then was I allowed to meet my flight commanders, a South African and an Australian, both nearing the end of their tours.

Above: Flying No 4, 8 May 1943.

Left:
Briefing for the last raid of
the North African campaign.
(The scene was posed after
the event, 12 May 1943.)

On the 4th I think I must have been busy with the formalities of taking over and of meeting key people because I did not fly the Baltimore until the 5th. Most of the pilots turned out for this event, rather as aficionados might watch an unknown bullfighter take on a particularly savage bull. The Baltimore had, I think, a rather undeserved reputation as a difficult aircraft to handle because of its tendency to swing quite savagely to starboard on take-off. But if one was prepared for the swing it was quite easy to control and otherwise the aircraft handled nicely. In spite of the fact that the United States Army Air Force never accepted it for squadron service, it was a very good fighting aircraft. Powered, like the Boston, with two Wright Cyclones, it was not quite as fast at low level but carried a good bomb load, could take a lot of flak damage and was well armed, with two .5-inch machine guns in the turret in addition to the four .303s firing downwards through the rear hatch.

I made a respectable first solo on type, probably to the disappointment of my audience, and took my crew up for the first time on the 7th. On the 8th, 9th and 10th we bombed Pantelleria aerodrome, each time as part of a large 'Balbo' of 90 aircraft including 55 Squadron, 3 SAAF Wing and 12th Bombardment Group flying Mitchells. On the first two raids I flew as number 4 in our first box and saw little except the underside of the lead aircraft's tailplane. We had a Warhawk escort who on the 8th had to deal with Macchi 303s, one of whom was shot down by a 223 gunner. I was alarmed at one point by what appeared to be strikes on my port wing but which turned out to be spent cartridge cases from the aircraft on which I was formating. On the third raid I was flying the lead aircraft of 223 for the first time and was able to get a good view of the phenomenon I had only got glimpses of on the first two occasions. This amazing sight, as the leading aircraft approached the island, was a sky nearly black with anti-aircraft bursts, which ceased whilst one bombed and the Italians took to their shelters, and became black again once the last formation had bombed and turned away. Not surprisingly we lost no aircraft but bombed so effectively that fires could be seen from 90 miles away on our return flight.

On 12 May I led a box of 18 aircraft on what was to be the last bombing raid of the North African campaign. We had a Warhawk escort and bombed the remnants of the 90th Light Division near Bou Ficha to such good effect that they surrendered. The squadron received a congratulatory signal from the Army saying that the bombing was so demoralising that 'white flags sprang up like mushrooms'.

For the rest of May the squadron was effectively stood down. No operations were ordered and I made day visits to Souk el Khemis and to Oulmène to see old friends. This was my first experience of command — as a flight commander you are still accepted and to a degree remain one of the boys — and the subtle isolation of being the commanding officer took a little getting used to, especially as, perhaps ironically, I was the youngest officer on the squadron.

During this period I got clearance to move the aircrew for five days to the sea, if I could find a suitable site. There was a wonderful site on the Gulf of Hammamet that I had spotted from the air, custom built for our requirements but, and this could have been a big but, it was on ground allocated to the Free French and would need their agreement. I set off to seek their permission and expected to see perhaps a commandant or at most a colonel but was wheeled up in front of the legendary General de Lattre de Tassigny. He was resplendent in impeccably tailored uniform complete with collar and tie, everything crisp and freshly ironed and, to my added discomfiture, was several inches taller than me. I was dressed in an open-necked shirt, with sleeves rolled up, and shorts and have seldom if ever felt at a greater disadvantage. He no doubt spoke perfect English but, like all French generals, would never admit to that weakness and it was only the fact that I could speak reasonable French that carried the day. With a solemnity that would have befitted the surrender of a fortress, or of his sword, he granted leave for us to use a portion of that wonderful beach. We did so for five days and it was just perfect.

Soon after that my life was changed quite dramatically. The end of the Tunisian Campaign saw the surrender of 250,000 Germans and at least two Alsatian dogs. These two, who had been mine-detecting dogs, were offered to 232 Wing, and the group captain, who by this time was Jack Roulston, said he would have the dog. I said I would have the bitch, named Gretil. I thought no more of it until a few days later, on landing from some flight, I was told that Gretil had been delivered and was waiting for me in the mess. The mess was a large marquee with several upright poles. Chained to one of these was a distressed and seemingly fierce Gretil who had defied anyone's attempt to approach her. She was my problem, and I could sense the feeling amongst my officers that how I handled the next few minutes was going to be crucial to my standing in their eyes. Gretil certainly looked fierce, snarling and pulling on her chain, but I'd had quite a lot to do with dogs as providentially my aunt ran a kennels, so I just walked up to her and called her bluff, patted her and talked to her, and she was instantly my dog. She never left my side from then on, unless I was flying. She terrorised my adjutant, she slept beside me and she was exceedingly menacing to anyone whom she sensed had not my full trust and friendship. She was a quite wonderful animal and I mourn her to this day.

Gretil.

We started operating again on 6 June and on that day, and on the 8th I led a box of 12 and on the 11th a box of 18 against Pantelleria's coastal batteries, each time with Warhawk escort. The flak, so impressive and dense in early May, had thinned out almost pathetically and the island surrendered to bombardment on the 11th to units of 3rd Infantry Brigade Group, landings being in progress during our last raid.

The last two weeks of June were taken up with a move northwards to Bou Ficha, with practice bombing and with fighter affiliation and we did not operate again until early July when we started day and night attacks on Sicilian airfields. My only excitement was on 4 July when I was severely flak damaged and landed without brakes or flaps. In the middle of July we switched for a few days, to night operations, and my Log Book records that on the 10th I bombed Trapani Milo airfield and was held by approximately 15 searchlights. How I can have assessed the number I don't know, but I can still remember the feeling that we were a sitting duck for any night fighter that happened to be around. I flew my last night sortie on the 15th and on the 20th we moved to Luqa in Malta leaving the bulk of the ground element behind. We ran an 18 dog sortie to Luqa, including Gretil, but they had to be returned to Bou Ficha because Malta's quarantine regulations were still in operation. They all subsequently followed on by sea once we had moved to Sicily.

We continued pounding Sicily from Malta until the landings were secure, when we moved forward on 10 August to Gela/Monte Lunga on the south coast of Sicily. From Malta a lot of our targets had been German positions on the foothills of Mount Etna as they retreated to the north and east and our first target after our move seemed to confirm this pattern of a slow retreat. Then things moved with startling rapidity. In the four days leading up to 15 August the Germans fell back on the beaches north of Messina, moving mostly at night, and prepared to withdraw across the Straits to the mainland of Italy. On the 15th we mounted a massive attack whilst the evacuation was in progress. I led 12 aircraft of 223 as part of a force of 89 light bombers and 60 fighter-bombers. As was to be expected, the heavy flak was very intense and accurate.

The next week was spent in moving to Gerbini/Sigonella and bringing in the rear element from North Africa. By 22 August the squadron was once again complete and in one place. Gerbini/Sigonella was one of six satellite airfields surrounding Gerbini Main on the large plain to the west of Catania. Sigonella was a very large field littered with well over a hundred Me109s and Fw190s in varying states of disrepair. Most were wrecks but the Luftwaffe had pulled out in a hurry and my flight sergeant thought he could make at least one serviceable Me109 out of what was lying around. He asked me if I would like him to do that and I said yes, thinking, if I thought at all, that it would give the men a challenge and that we would probably have moved again before they were finished anyway.

I was therefore very surprised and somewhat disconcerted when two days later he beamingly informed me that the squadron now had a serviceable Me109G which he had had sprayed red all over for recognition purposes. It was his clear expectation, and that of his team, that I would now fly the thing. To this day I don't know whether they thought they were giving me a lovely present or whether they were secretly hoping that I would break my neck, but either way I was committed.

Rather as my officers had gathered in the expectation of seeing me savaged by a dog, they gathered again, expecting I know not what. Dual controls were very uncommon during the war, and were of course non-existent in single-seaters, so one was accustomed to taking on a new aircraft without tuition, but one normally had words of advice from someone experienced on type and, crucially, one had Pilots' Notes. In this instance I had nothing, not even an ability to read German. The ground crew had managed to install an airspeed indicator calibrated in mph so at least I was spared having to cope with km/h. On running

Below: A box of six Baltimores over Sicily. *Crown Copyright*

Above: No 223 Squadron at Luqa, August 1943.

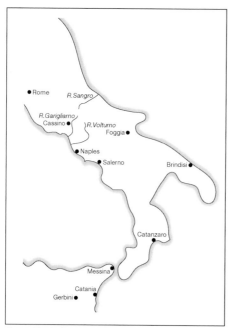

Above: The Italian campaign.

through the cockpit with the aid of my flight sergeant most things were self-explanatory. The controls were pretty standard, the only difference that I can remember was that there was no flap selector but instead a large wheel on the port side with which one wound on flap as required. I found it preferable to our normal system as there was no sudden change in trim.

At that time I had not flown a Spitfire and had only the Hurricane and Tomahawk to guide me, which was not really a lot of use. I scared myself to death on start-up because I had the throttle a bit too far advanced and the Daimler Benz 605 engine started with a huge roar so that the aircraft was straining on the chocks for the split second before I throttled back. After that it was relatively plain sailing, the only snags being the lack of vision when taxying and the very narrow undercarriage. I flew it on that occasion for 30 minutes and to my great relief managed to pull off a very respectable landing. Although more powerful, it was not as nice to fly as the Hurricane and the ailerons were distinctly heavy. I flew it again the next day and regularly until mid-September, often with Freddie Rothwell, a new flight commander, for whom the ground staff had put together a second Me109G, this time primrose yellow. We flew in the early morning and NOTAMS (Notices to Airmen) were issued warning that two friendly 109s painted red and yellow would be flying in the area. This didn't stop us being beaten up on one occasion by 12 US Lightning P-38s in line astern. We were not sure they had seen the NOTAMS so, to be on the safe side, as they started to dive on us we cut our speed right back, lowered our undercarriage and waggled our wings.

On the 13th I flew to the main US transport base to see if I could swap a 109 for a Dakota as I knew their CO had powers of write-off and I felt that a Dakota would be a great asset to the squadron. The colonel was most enthusiastic and the deal was nearly agreed until at the last moment he realised that the 109 was what he called 'a one place ship'. He apparently thought I had been offering a two-seat 109 which, so far as I know, never existed, and wanted no part of a single-seater.

Two days later I flew my 109 for the last time. In the afternoon Sinclair, promoted air commodore and commanding the Tactical Bomber Force, came to call. Seeing my 109, nothing would do but he had to fly it, so I briefed him on the cockpit, paying particular attention to the operation of the undercarriage, which was slightly complicated until you got used to it. He seemed to take it all in and took-off in fine form. He was an exceptional pilot and after some 30 minutes getting used to the aircraft he treated us to a smooth display of the most elegant low, indeed very low, aerobatics. He then came in for a tight turn on to finals, rolled out and landed, the only snag being that his undercarriage was still up and he ended up in a somewhat dramatic cloud of dust. I went out in a Jeep to bring him back, expecting him to be full of apologies for breaking my splendid aeroplane. To my total astonishment, so far from being contrite, he tore me off a tremendous strip for not having briefed him properly. How he had the barefaced gall to do it I don't know, but perversely I have always admired him for it — *l' audace, toujours l'audace!*

All this while we had been operating steadily, initially in support of the Eighth Army landings across the Straits of Messina on 3 and 4 September. Most of these raids were short affairs of under two hours with two and sometimes three boxes of 12 with either a Spitfire or

No 223 Squadron at work.

Warhawk escort. An exception to this was a longer sortie on 27 August against Catanzaro, which was to be on the line of advance of 1st Canadian Division. It was quite a large effort with six boxes of 12, Baltimores, Bostons, Mitchells and Marauders, and we met intense heavy flak over the target and extending westwards right across the toe of Italy, there at about its narrowest. We bombed from 9,000ft and possibly hit a large ammunition dump as we could feel the explosion even at that height.

From 10–25 September we flew rather longer sorties against targets in the Naples area in support of the Fifth Army landings at Salerno These operations lent a welcome variety in that they involved a relatively long sea crossing and we could see the invasion fleet in the Gulf. Navigation could if necessary have been by volcano: leave Etna to port, overfly Stromboli and Vesuvius is dead ahead.

The 25th marked our last operation from Sicily and on the 27th the squadron moved to the Italian Air Force base at Campo Casale in Brindisi. I say the squadron, but initially it was just the aircrew and the aircraft and it was fairly shambolic for a few days. Some trucks were supplied, and quarters of a sort on the airfield. I commandeered a little Fiat 500 for myself which, though driven by an Italian, turned out to belong to the British Control Commission who promptly demanded its return. I ignored the demand and got away with it until our own transport arrived.

Although I had only joined them in Tunisia, the squadron had been under canvas continuously, apart from a very short period in Malta, since leaving Egypt. It seemed therefore that the civilised surroundings of Brindisi held out hope of a welcome change. With the aid of my Fiat 500 I found a charming villa, just large enough for a mess and, having got a taste for the procedure, duly commandeered it, complete with its cellar which included 500 bottles of champagne. This, sadly, was my only personal experience of looting. We stayed in that house with its lovely garden for almost exactly a month and, quite remarkably, it was not really a great success. People had got so used to being permanently outdoors and under canvas that any building, however grand, seemed restrictive.

Our rear party arrived in Brindisi within a matter of days and we flew our first sortie on 6 October. For the remainder of the month our targets were exclusively in support of Fifth Army, including attacks on Monte Cassino, and we met intense and accurate heavy flak. Although we lost only two aircraft during that period, we took an awful lot of minor damage. Our respect for the German 88mm anti-aircraft crews, already considerable, was heightened still further; I remember, always flying as formation leader, that whatever decision you made on changes of altitude or direction, as often as not they had anticipated your move, and the black puffs, if not the sharp crack of an especially close burst, were all around you yet again.

The mess at Brindisi,
September/October 1943.

On 28 October the squadron moved to Foggia/Celone, one of the five airfields on Foggia plain. We were switched to support of Eighth Army and from the middle of November were unescorted, as air superiority was near total. We also met far less flak but had a new enemy in the weather. I do not know whether records would back me up but I would think the winter of 1943/44 on the Foggia plain was unique. We had winds that flattened canvas, we had snow and rain and, above all, we had mud, mud on a par with that in Flanders in 1914–18. The weather was atrocious throughout central and southern Italy and the Allied advance slowed right down. Throughout November and December we repeatedly attacked German positions along the line of the rivers Sangro and Garigliano where the defence was tenacious. The attacks were relatively small scale, mostly with 12 aircraft though sometimes 24, and became somewhat monotonous. There were only two occasions that lent variety to this pattern: on 3 December we flew in support of Fifth Army and bombed Monte Cassino once more, and on 9 December I led a larger attack of 48 aircraft against enemy gun positions near Miglianico. In that raid we met very intense and very accurate heavy flak and most aircraft needed a lot of patching up.

Throughout the early winter period the squadron did well; casualties were relatively light and we received our fair share of DFCs and DFMs. The same was true of 55 Squadron, now commanded by Lloyd Joel, a New Zealander who was to become a great family friend after the war. The fact that the wing had acquitted itself well was recognised by the award of the DSO to Jack Roulston.

My number of operational sorties had been steadily mounting and it was looking increasingly unlikely that I would complete a year in command before being put on rest. Jack asked me what I would like to do and agreed with my suggestion that, as a regular officer, the short wartime Staff College course might be a good idea. As Haifa Staff College was still operating under prewar rules and did not accept students under 30 this would automatically mean my returning to the UK as I was still only 23. Jack was very helpful in pushing for this as he knew that Sylvia was very much on her own, with her parents under German occupation in Guernsey, her brother and elder sister prisoners of the Japanese, and her two younger sisters evacuated to the north of England and dependent on her in holiday time.

By the end of December I had flown 83 operations and, although it was not official, it had become pretty clear that I would soon be repatriated, tour-expired. This brought up the immediate prospect of saying goodbye not only to the squadron but, more personally, to my crew who would become tour-expired with me and, by far the most difficult, to Gretil. On taking over 223 I had kept Bill and Ginger and taken on Flight Sergeant King DFM, a cheerful and experienced NCO as straight air gunner. He remained with me throughout, becoming a warrant officer at the end of September. The irrepressible Ginger, who had first joined my crew in April 1942 as Sergeant Ryder, had remained with me throughout and was now Flying Officer Ryder DFC. Sadly Bill, though remaining on the squadron, ceased to be my navigator in mid-June. Looking back on it I'm not at all sure I was fair to him but I allowed Jack to talk me into accepting a navigator more experienced in the role of lead bombardier. As in a box of 6 or 12 all aircraft bombed on the leader, the role of lead bombardier was critical to the success of any mission, and there was no gainsaying the fact that Flight Sergeant Hutchinson was an experienced man. Quiet and determined, he was a most likeable and reliable operator and deservedly won a commission and a DFC.

This left poor Gretil. By force of circumstances of being left behind to move with the rear party by sea she had become more tractable and had been further changed, at least temporarily, by having six puppies, the result of mating with Jack Roulston's dog. This great event was not universally applauded by my officers as she elected to have them behind the bar and allowed no one to approach, not even me, for three days. That incident over and the pups growing up, she reverted to one-man-dog status though never quite so fiercely as before. In December she developed some form of goitre and was operated on by Doc Arthur, our mad Irish MO, who had little to do in contrast to Toothy Harvey whose dental caravan was always busy. The operation was temporarily successful but had to be repeated. She died three months after I left.

The winter of 1943-4, at Foggia. *Crown Copyright*

On 14 January I flew my last operation with the squadron and on the 24th said goodbye and left by Dakota from Bari. We flew to Catania then on to Luqa and stopped that night in the Tunis transit camp after 5 hours 10 minutes passenger time. The following day we flew on to Maison Blanche at Algiers and, I think, embarked immediately. That voyage, which lasted nine days and took us very far west sailing independently and at high speed, is only a blur in my memory. I cannot even remember the name of the ship, nor of the officers who were briefly my companions. I must have gone by train from Liverpool to London as I did not fly again until 10 May.

5. Anticlimax: March 1944–October 1948
Staff and Staff College

The Staff College course was not due to start until 20 June and I was posted in the meantime, after a month's disembarkation leave, to Combined Operations Headquarters in Richmond Terrace, Whitehall. I had dropped my acting rank on relinquishing command of 223 and so started at COHQ on 1 March as a squadron leader. I was assigned to the plans division and so immediately became privy to the plans for the D-Day invasion, then only some three months away. It was my first experience of access to 'Top Secret' papers and thus to knowledge which was often of great sensitivity and almost always vital to national security. It was a heady experience for a young man — although I certainly did not feel young at the time — but also one which induced a great sense of strangely personal responsibility. I remember walking from Whitehall across the West End to the American Embassy with the up-to-the-minute air plans for the invasion in my pocket and keeping my hand on them all the way in case some unspecified but probably imminent disaster would strike before I could deliver them.

My 3½ months at COHQ passed quickly, D-Day came and went and I duly reported to Bulstrode Park, between Gerrards Cross and Beaconsfield, on 20 June, a few days after my 24th birthday. We had been given a pretty daunting list of pre-course reading, some of which, such as Fowler's *English Usage* and A. P. Herbert's *What a Word*, I greatly enjoyed. It was a bruising course trying to cram the essentials of a year's study into less than three months and it was necessary to work on Saturdays and Sundays as well in order to complete the demanding syllabus. No one in particular amongst the students stands out in my memory but my syndicate DS (Directing Staff — Staff College instructor) was Group Captain Georgie Ward who was subsequently to become an MP and then Secretary of State for Air. The Commandant was Air Vice-Marshal Charles Medhurst, an odd choice as public speaking was clearly a torture to him. He had been Assistant Chief of Air Staff (Intelligence) and in that capacity had successfully negotiated with the Portuguese for the use of the Azores. He went on postwar to be AOC-in-C Middle East Command but never overcame his nervousness in public.

Surprisingly, so soon after D-Day, a number of senior commanders found time to come and talk to us. Amongst them was Trafford Leigh-Mallory, who made a distinctly unfavourable impression, appearing to be full of self-importance. Those of us who knew of his differences with Keith Park — and that was most if not all of us — knew whom we would prefer to serve under. The course was due to finish in early September and sometime in July those of us who wished for a flying as opposed to a staff appointment were allowed to go to the appropriate headquarters to try and arrange a posting. I was quite clear, and had been even before leaving Italy, that I wanted to command either a Boston or a Mosquito squadron in 2 Group. I was already amply qualified on the Boston and, in May, had flown a Tiger Moth from Hendon to Bicester and had soloed on the Mosquito after 30 minutes dual. That under my belt, and my Blenheim, Boston and Baltimore background, a DFC and nearly a year's experience of command made me, or so I thought, an ideal candidate for a command in 2 Group. I had reckoned without Embry and without the stresses and personality clashes of which at that time I knew nothing.

Air Vice-Marshal Basil Embry was one of the most, if not the most, courageous RAF officers to rise to high operational command during the war. Shot down on 27 May 1940 as a wing commander in command of No 107 Blenheim Squadron he eventually reached England 10 weeks later via Gibraltar. Having been made a POW after baling out, he escaped from a marching column of prisoners, discarded his uniform and dressed himself in clothes taken from a scarecrow. Captured again, and under threat of being shot, he escaped again, injuring two and, so the story has it, killing a third guard in the process. As a result he was a wanted man by the Gestapo and had been forbidden, by Bert Harris, to operate over Europe again. Typically he ignored the order and operated as a squadron leader under an assumed name.

Essential training at Allied Staff College.

I waited in his outer office for an hour or so during which time he returned from some sortie wearing squadron leader badges of rank and with his navigator, Air Commodore David Atcherley similarly dressed. Eventually I was called in to be confronted by this frightening little man — he was quite short — who advanced on you as he spoke, forcing you to retreat step by step. He had obviously been told what I was hoping for because he demanded to know why I felt I was in any way fitted to take command of one of his squadrons.

When I told him why, giving emphasis to the fact that I had commanded a Desert Air Force light bomber squadron, he was totally dismissive saying that not only would he not give me a squadron but he would not even give me a flight. He did say, however, that he might consider taking me on as a supernumerary squadron leader, in other words as a squadron leader pilot with no other responsibilities. I was totally shattered by his attitude. Hurt, mortification and a sense of total injustice churned together to produce anger. Why, I thought, was this fierce little man apparently going out of his way to snub and demean someone he did not know, someone who after all was seeking to serve under him in action rather than to take a staff posting which was the normal follow-on to Staff College? The reason, which I was to learn later, was petty but in some way consistent with the man. He and Harry Broadhurst, who had been my AOC in Desert Air Force, had no love for one another and were arch-rivals. It followed, inexorably, that no one who had commanded a squadron under Broadhurst could expect to be acceptable to Embry. So, by foible, was my immediate future decided. Looking back, I could have swallowed my pride and agreed to join 2 Group as a spare pilot, but I was so outraged and insulted by his attitude in the face of my eagerness to get back to flying that anger prevailed and I refused his contemptuous offer with such composure as I could muster.

The result of that interview with Embry was that I was to embark on a number of staff posts that would keep me off flying for the next four years. My first appointment was the result of someone realising that the war might soon end and that, with the exception of the Assistant Chief of Air Staff, there was not a single regular officer in the whole of the Royal Air Force Intelligence staff. They set about rectifying this by attaching six of us off the course, all regulars, to ACAS(I)'s department for six months. It was a good idea and a staggering education for six young officers but, as with so many good ideas, I do not think it was followed up as, so far as I know, none of us took up senior Intelligence posts after the war.

But the six-month indoctrination was quite fascinating. We spent time with literally every branch and sub-branch of Intelligence and were immediately signed on for Ultra, the product of Enigma, and were reading decoded German signals in plain language every day. An immediate result of this was that we had to sign to the effect that we would never disclose anything to do with Enigma or Ultra, and the more practical result was that we were barred from flying over enemy territory for the rest of the war. It was all fascinating and gave one the very highest sense of regard for one's country's brilliance of achievement and depth of talent.

Two memories that stand out are of time spent in the political section with James Pope-Hennessey, afterwards to run the Victoria and Albert Museum and, in the Joint Intelligence Staff with Noel Annan, later to become Lord Annan, Vice-Chancellor of the University of London. I had not until that time met anyone of real intellectual stature and watching and listening to them was an education in itself. One other member of the JIS was a certain Wing Commander Thompson, chairman of an advertising company, who subsequently made me the only offer of a civilian job I have ever had. One minor rub-off of this time is, I believe, that my name shows as Duty Officer in the Cabinet Office historical display of a typical night in 1944/5. One thing that I remember clearly from that fascinating period is that we had notification on Ultra of the Luftwaffe plans to attack Allied airfields on 1 January 1945 and an equally clear memory that those attacks were extremely successful. Either our knowledge was not passed on or, if it was, it was ignored with disastrous results.

At the end of this educational six months I was posted as Intelligence Officer to Tiger Force, then just a planning headquarters at Richmond Park. Tiger Force, under command of Air Marshal Sir Hugh Pughe Lloyd, had been formed to control an RAF bomber force of Lincolns to be operated against Japan from Okinawa. At the end of May 1945 I was sent to Washington to arrange for the supply of various items such as maps and escape aids and for the flow of top level intelligence that Tiger Force would need if it was to operate successfully in theatre.

The journey stands out in my memory as the first of many visits. It was by flying boat from Poole, pioneering what was to become a British Overseas Airways Corporation route. We were taken by train from Victoria Station to Poole in carriages of Queen Victoria's Royal Train. There we embarked in a BOAC Boeing 'Clipper' and took-off for our first leg to Foynes in Ireland, arriving there after 2 hours 35 minutes. From there we made the main crossing to Botwood, in Newfoundland, in 12 hours 45 minutes and felt that the flight had been somehow special. From there, to Baltimore, the nearest alighting area to Washington, took a further 9 hours and 30 minutes thus making a total of 24 hours and 50 minutes flying time since leaving England. It was a preview of things to come and of how the 'Empire' Flying Boats would be run within a few years. Travelling by 'Clipper' in 1945, with your private cabin and bunk, was a new dimension in passenger travel and one which, for comfort, cannot be equalled today.

I stayed in Washington for three weeks and the visit remains clear in my mind for a number of reasons. First was how beautiful the city of Washington was and how co-operative the Americans were. As a squadron leader my allowances were far from generous and I ate largely in drug-stores and in Chinese restaurants and acquired a taste for iced milk. Before leaving England I had enquired of DAFL, the Department of Air Force Liaison, what uniform was appropriate in Washington in June to be told that their spring was the same as ours and that I should wear blue. June of 1944 was, I believe, particularly hot and humid and I have never been more uncomfortable as a result of this ludicrous bit of misinformation. Air-conditioning was far from universal and only the best hotels had it in 1944. Mine was not amongst them, and I accordingly spent many more hours in the Pentagon, which was beautifully air-conditioned, than I would otherwise have done. On the plus side I had an interesting weekend in New York and was introduced to the delights of whiskey sours and mint juleps. I managed eventually to get agreement to virtually everything we asked for and on the 17th left for Montreal by train, well pleased. On the 18th I flew by BOAC Liberator to Goose Bay in 3 hours 45 minutes and from there to Prestwick in a further 9 hours 45. The following day I flew on to Hendon by DH Rapide.

August saw the Japanese surrender and the end of Tiger Force. It was quite a relief no longer to be faced by an overseas staff tour of indefinite length and a move to some other Intelligence post seemed probable, as indeed turned out to be the case. On 28 August I was posted as an acting wing commander to be the Command Intelligence Officer of Transport Command and told to set about tailoring the Intelligence staff to peacetime needs. Transport Command, under Air Marshal the Hon Sir Ralph Cochrane, was at that time a worldwide command and retained operational command of all transport aircraft. The transport groups overseas had operational control and operated their aircraft to the requirements of the appropriate theatre commander, though they were not directly answerable to him. Not surprisingly this arrangement was far from popular with theatre commanders who resented their lack of direct control and looked on Cochrane as an empire builder.

At that time there were 112 Intelligence officers in the Command, mostly overseas in the group headquarters in Delhi and in Rangoon. Now that the war had ended there was little for them to do and I set off at the beginning of November to assess what the peacetime establishment should be. On 3 November I flew by York of 511 Squadron to Luqa in Malta where we night-stopped after a flight of 6 hours 15 minutes. On the day of the 4th and the night of the 4th/5th we flew on to Shaibah, on the Persian Gulf, refuelling at El Maza and arriving at Shaibah in bitter cold just before dawn after a total of 10 hours 35 minutes in the air. At Shaibah we had breakfast and then flew on to Karachi arriving 6 hours 45 minutes later, some three days after leaving Lyneham.

At the transit camp in Mauripur, where I spent two nights, I had to deal with a bumptious power-crazed wing commander who as SPSO (Senior Personnel Staff Officer) claimed that any officer under the rank of group captain arriving on the sub-continent, whatever their previous standing, once they set foot in the command were subject to him for posting purposes. After I had informed him that if he dared even to try and interfere with my arrangements he would catch an extremely severe cold he ceased to block my onward flight to Delhi which took place on the 7th. That flight was especially memorable because of the antiquity of the aircraft, a prewar Imperial Airways Ensign being operated by BOAC. We refuelled at Jodhpur and I was fascinated to see the palace and the polo ground with its association of *chukkas* and *chota pegs*.

I spent longer in Delhi than I had expected as I went down with dengue fever. I remember jumping out of the back of a 15cwt and suddenly realising from the jarring of my spine and the pain in my head that something was seriously wrong. I remember little more as I became delirious and came round three days later feeling weak but otherwise fine, much to the surprise of the MO who had apparently not expected me to survive. I enjoyed Delhi greatly as, unlike Karachi, which was dirty and dusty, it still had the feel of the Raj about it and an undimmed splendour. It was my first real taste of the East. The splendid and exclusive Gymkhana Club, the world of bearers, of *dhobi wallahs*, of *tonga wallahs* and of the huge Sikh *jagas* appealed to me instantly and I revelled in the feeling of exoticism and romance that it engendered.

On the 15th I set out for Rangoon by a very roundabout route that was to involve nearly 16 hours flying. That day we flew to Bombay, getting a good view of the city, and then on to Ratmalana in Ceylon where we night-stopped. The next day was a long haul, again by Liberator, to Pegu and then a short hop by Dakota to Rangoon's Mingaladon airfield. I spent four days in Rangoon, which was quite long enough. It was very hot and humid, plagued with mosquitoes and quite lacked the charm of Delhi. Even the food was worse than it need have been, with yams figuring large on the menu.

On the 21st I flew down to Penang by Dakota with a Warrant Officer Taylor as pilot, who kindly let me act as second pilot and get the feel of the aircraft. Penang was full of colour and vitality, of exotic scents and wonderful cooking smells, of music, and above all of ceaseless chatter as Malays, Chinese and Indians went about their business. It was my first glimpse of Malaya, and the beginning of a love affair with the East which was to last throughout my service. The next day, again with the same accommodating Warrant Officer Taylor, we flew on to Seletar in Singapore, where I was soon to spend nearly four years.

Singapore was the end of my legitimate business and I should by rights have turned for home. However, as a Transport Command staff officer, I had priority travel on any Command aircraft to wherever I wanted to go and no questions asked. So I decided to go to Java, and if necessary Sumatra, to try and find Sylvia's brother, who was an officer in the Dutch colonial service, and his wife and child, and Sylvia's elder sister together with her husband, a Dutch tea planter, and their two young children. The Red Cross in Singapore thought that the brother was in Batavia and that the sister was in Medan in northern Sumatra. So on the 25th I flew, again by Dakota, to Kemajoran, the airfield for Batavia, refuelling at Palembang in southern Sumatra en route. In Batavia I could find no trace of my brother-in-law but found instead that No 32 Squadron at Kemajoran was commanded by an old friend, Brian MacNamara, a seconded Royal Tank Corps officer who had been second in command of 614 as a squadron leader when I had been a flight lieutenant flight commander. I subsequently discovered from a photograph in Mike Carver's autobiography that he and Brian had been two of the seven junior officers forming the 1935 intake to the Royal Tank Corps.

No 32, known unsurprisingly as MacNamara's Band, were a high spirited lot equipped with Dakotas, and as Brian was happy that I should fly with them I managed to get in four operations in two days. On the 26th with Brian as captain we dropped supplies to the garrison at Ambarawa, then being besieged by Indonesian insurgents. On the 27th I flew as co-pilot to Squadron Leader Whiting and we dropped supplies to the cut-off women's camp at Bandoeng and went on to land ammunition at Sourabaya, then under shellfire. We then carried reinforcements from Sourabaya to Semarang and, in the final sortie, evacuated wounded from Semarang back to Batavia.

It was an exciting few days as the situation on the ground was extremely unstable with, I think, one Indian division trying to hold down the insurgents and with the Japanese, still under arms in places, having to be called on to help as guards. The insurgents were an extremely ugly rabble and, just before I got there, had cut the heads off a crew that had crash-landed on the far side of the airfield. Nobody quite knew what to expect next and when we had to drive through Batavia we went fast by Jeep, with one driving and one riding shotgun with a Sten gun at the ready.

My only vivid memory of the Japanese is ludicrous rather than frightening. Where I can't remember, but I had got out of my Jeep to have a pee in a bush, and was so engaged when a platoon of Japanese came marching by and gave an extremely smart Eyes Right. I have often acknowledged a salute with a sword in my left hand but this was the one and only occasion when I was forced to do so with a sword substitute.

On the 28th I said goodbye with reluctance and flew back to Singapore. The next day I flew to Medan via Padang on the west coast of Sumatra. There, still in a camp, but free and awaiting repatriation to the Netherlands, I found Sylvia's sister and the husband and children I had never met. I had not seen Maidie since she was a schoolgirl and it was quite an emotional reunion, the more so as for their part they had no idea I was still alive, let alone in Sumatra. We celebrated with the best that the Hotel de Boer had to offer — the universal corned beef and cheese followed by tinned peaches.

Two days later I flew back to Singapore via Padang, again by Dakota. We took-off from Padang in the afternoon with the cloud building up all around us at a faster rate than we could climb. It was obvious that at some stage we were going to have to abandon this circular climb in clear air and penetrate the thunder cloud. Some instinctive feeling that all was not well led me to go up into the cockpit where I found a very unhappy warrant officer pilot who was fighting the turbulence and continuing to climb virtually on the stall. He was pouring with sweat and, before I could make the suggestion, he asked me to take over. It was a pretty horrid ride through the sort of cumulo-nimbus cloud that had been known to take the wings off Dakotas, but I felt a great deal happier in control of the aircraft than I had done as a passenger.

Two days later I flew by Sunderland of 205 Squadron from Seletar to Koggala, the flying boat base in the extreme south of Ceylon. From there I went by road to Colombo and on the next day to Karachi by York. Take-off from Karachi for Shaibah seemed to go on for ever, even though it was at night in slightly lower temperature. We pressed on that night and through the following day to Cairo where, for some reason I no longer remember, we were delayed for four days. On the 10th we flew to El Adem in a BOAC Dakota piloted by a Pole who was totally unsafe and thence, providentially with another captain, to Hal Far in Malta. Next day, still by BOAC Dakota we flew back to Hurn via Istres in 8 hours 35 minutes, another long haul in a pretty primitive passenger aircraft.

This tour of inspection enabled me to write a report in which I recommended a reduction in the establishment of Intelligence Officers from 112 to 16. I also, over-egging it a bit, suggested that the post of CIO could come down from wing commander to squadron leader. I was too inexperienced to know that this would be quite unacceptable and was also motivated by a desire to get a new job as I felt I had done all that needed doing at Transport Command. I succeeded in moving on at the end of March and, shortly thereafter, the establishment went up to 20 and the post of CIO was upgraded to group captain. I learnt something from that.

The short seven months I spent at Transport Command Headquarters taught me a number of things. It was the first time I had had to handle a staff, all older than me and all more experienced in the job. They were all wartime officers and most loyal to and — that most horrible modern phrase — 'supportive of' the young regular officer who had been visited on them. Two of them — Ned Gourlay, a very rich Canadian businessman, and Henry Grazebrook, something big in the City and equally well-to-do — became and remained friends for some years.

As soon as petrol rationing eased a little Henry went out and bought a 1938 Bentley tourer and took me for a ride in it. To me, whose car ownership to that date had been confined to a 1928 Austin Seven and, at that time, to an MG sports that could not better 60mph, this vehicle was an absolute eye-opener and gave me a taste for fast cars that I was not able to indulge until very much later in life. Henry had a friend, also in Intelligence, who had been present when the Berlin archives were being examined and had, quite illegally but probably with a nod and a wink from a superior officer, pocketed one of 25 copies of Operation Sea Lion, the plan for the invasion of England. Henry, now in possession of this document, felt it was too hot to handle and offered it to me. It was an absolutely superb production, drawn up for the Führer's eyes, all the maps hand drawn and the General Staff signatures in full, the whole in mint condition and of enormous historical interest.

I determined to risk the Tower, or, whatever other penalty might be involved, and accepted it to gloat over rather as a millionaire art collector might gloat over a stolen Old Master that he knew he could never bring to the market. I was always conscious that I was in illegal possession of a document of historical importance but I had never even considered its financial worth, as an attempt to sell it would no doubt have exposed me to court martial and prosecution. Now, retired for 20 years, I might, if I still had it, be negotiating a sale through Zurich or Geneva for somewhere between £2 million and £3 million. Unfortunately, or perhaps fortunately for my conscience, it was thrown in a quarry along with other believed worthless papers in the frenzy of clearing out attics which often accompanies a death, when my father-in-law died in 1963.

The second lesson that I learnt during that period had to do with public relations, then in its infancy. During the autumn and winter of 1945 every effort was being made to 'bring the boys home'. Ex-POWs and servicemen at the top of the demob list were clamouring to get back to Britain and every aircraft that could carry passengers, whatever the crew's background or experience were pressed into service under the aegis of Transport Command. There were a number, indeed a large number, of fatal accidents, and every one made headlines in the tabloids. The poignancy of these deaths was undeniable — these were men who had been POWs for most of the war or who had served for five years or more in Burma, India or elsewhere overseas. Someone had to be a whipping boy, and the prime candidate was Cochrane. A huge press briefing was arranged and the journalists, some of whom were less than attractive, were lushed up with cream cakes and other normally unobtainable delicacies. This did nothing to mollify them and only widened their suspicions that, in addition to incompetence, they were now confronted by corruption. I learnt that day that once the press has made up its mind no amount of logic will shift it.

Cochrane, who conducted the briefing personally and with great persuasiveness, had all the facts and figures on his side — the accident rate was minuscule in relation to hours flown, and was much lower than the civil aviation rate prewar — but none of this made an iota of difference. Our boys were being killed on their way home, and that was that. The lesson, which I attempted to observe for the next 35 years, was to have nothing to do with the media if I could possibly avoid it and, under no circumstances, to do anything which could possibly be construed as seeking to influence them.

The third lesson was a continuation of what I had been learning for the last six years — the nuances and different styles of command and what a great influence they had on the individual. My first experience had been the prewar Commandant of Cranwell, Air Vice-Marshal Jackie Baldwin, immensely remote from the cadets and appearing infrequently and impeccably garbed on a horse; my second the air commodore at Old Sarum, whom I saw only once, who was benevolent and forgiving when he should properly have been more stern. These were distant figures who had no direct impact but, for a lesson in the dynamism of leadership, I was privileged indeed to be able to observe Laurie Sinclair. He had, to start with, the advantages of height, good looks, a facial scar, a broken nose and a George Cross. He was intensely public school, and conducted his briefings in public school terms — always ending with the exhortation 'Now let's go and give the Huns one up!' — seemingly unaware that many if not most of his audience were from grammar or secondary schools. He was the epitome of enthusiasm, of leading from the front and of disguising his true feelings if they would not be helpful to morale. Only once, towards the end of the Bisley debacle did he drop the mask when viewing yet another burning wreck and permit himself to exclaim, 'Thank God, that's another of the bastards gone.' He was one who led by enthusiasm and example, something admittedly not open to more senior commanders of whom so far I had been able to observe only a limited number.

I now had Ralph Cochrane perhaps to learn from, but before him had been the famed Harry Broadhurst, AOC Desert Air Force. I had looked to him as a role model and had been sadly disappointed. I have always felt that AOCs should know not only their station commanders but also their squadron commanders and this Broadhurst failed to do. Commanding a squadron under him, I was never once summoned to meet him and received only one letter from him, which was less than felicitous, during my time in command.

This letter was preceded by one from Desert Air Force, signed by a flying officer for AOC, instructing me to accept and crew up a certain flight sergeant who had been dismissed from the squadron before my time for LMF (lack of moral fibre), had since spent a year in the hands of the psychiatrists and was now reported as being fit for flying once more. There were two snags: the first was that I would have to break a crew in order to absorb him; the second and more intractable was that my NCO aircrew knew this chap and were not willing to accept him and, if he were forced on them, would send him to Coventry. I duly reported this to Desert Air Force, hoping that the fact that the letter had been signed by a flying officer might indicate that the AOC had not had the opportunity to consider the matter, and asked that the flight sergeant be posted elsewhere. I received a single sentence letter in reply signed by Broadhurst personally. It read, 'Either you accept Flight Sergeant so and so or you go.' It was I suppose leadership of a sort, in that he was backing up a junior officer who had made a bad decision, but I felt it was an example of how not to exercise command. And I had now got the same feeling from Cochrane — in nine months I saw him only once; I felt that he and Broadhurst had been too remote and that there must be a better way of commanding.

On 1 April 1946 I was posted to the Allied Staff College as one of six squadron leaders who were to be syndicate leaders, godfathers, interpreters and in general agony aunts to an otherwise all foreign course. These foreigners had all been carefully selected as having the potential to become heads of their own air forces, and in due course many did so. A number of them had operated with or alongside the RAF during the war. On that particular course, which was the second of its type, French, Dutch, Belgian, Norwegian, Danish, Polish and Czech officers fell into that category and one, an Iraqi, had briefly operated against us at Habbaniyah. With the chaos going on in their respective countries, the position of the Poles and the Czechs was delicate in the extreme. Both Poles were communists and were recalled before the end of the course. Of the two Czechs, one was a communist and continued in the Czech Air Force. The other, a wing commander who had fought with the RAF during the war, was strongly pro-Western. Against all advice he insisted on returning to his homeland, counting on his war record to protect him. He was stripped of his uniform and put to work on the roads. After six months of that course I was promoted acting wing commander once again and appointed to the Directing Staff, in which capacity I learned a great deal more than I ever did as a student. Those first two courses were the only ones made up entirely of foreigners, and the next four courses were fifty/fifty foreigners and RAF.

The main RAF Staff College had moved to Bracknell, leaving the Allied Staff College initially at Bulstrode Park and, from 1948, at Andover, the original home of the Staff College in the 1920s and '30s. The symbol used to denote that one had passed the Staff College course was for many years psa, held by some to mean passed Staff Andover and by others to mean passed Staff Air, before we fell into line with the Army and all retrospectively became psc, passed Staff College.

The college went from strength to strength, attracting Egyptian, Portuguese, Greek, Swiss, Argentine, Thai and Chinese students. It was an extremely good shop window for our aircraft firms, the major ones of which we visited every course, and all of which seemed to be doing well at that time. It is tragic looking back to those days when De Havillands, Hawkers, Bristols, Avros, Handley-Page, English Electric, Shorts, Westlands, Supermarine, Armstrong-Whitworth, Glosters, Vickers, Miles, Percivals, Faireys and possibly others that I have forgotten were all in the market place. And not only our aircraft firms. We showed these foreigners our car manufacturers, our shipyards, our steelworks and our coal mines, then still world leaders but now sadly all gone, partly, if not mainly, through mismanagement and trade union intransigence over the years.

The college was undoubtedly extremely cost-effective if viewed in national terms but, unfortunately, civil servants, no doubt under instruction from the Treasury, raised the cost to foreign governments year after year until, eventually, they priced us out of the market. I have, in parentheses, wondered over the years how much of our economic decline can be laid at the door of the Treasury. It is to me an extraordinary paradox that a great department of state, staffed at the top as it always has been by the best minds in the civil service, can so consistently get it wrong, with abysmal lack of vision, with chronic and determined short-termism and with an arrogance undented by serial disaster.

Bulstrode in those days was a very happy ship, first under Togs Mellersh who went on to be AOC Malaya, Commandant-General of the RAF Regiment and finally Air Officer Administration (AOA) Bomber Command, and then under Arthur McDonald who sailed dinghies in the Olympics and who ended up an Air Chief Marshal as Air Secretary. Togs was a wonderful chap, full of bravura and bonhomie, and Arthur, though quieter, was a wise operator held in respect by all. The Directing Staff were an unusual bunch. Most of us were extroverts, most were characters and God knows what the foreigners made of us. Ranks were all over the place at that time and led to some strange anomalies. I was at that time a war substantive squadron leader, an acting wing commander and a peacetime flight lieutenant. When faced with instructing peacetime group captains this could give rise to delicate situations. One such student, a pompous little man with no war record, who subsequently and undeservedly in my view, reached the rank of air vice-marshal, found it very difficult indeed to accept instruction from a junior whilst another, Tubby Vielle, who retired as a group captain and made a fortune writing novels that were made into films, always claimed that I had set him on the road to success by teaching him to write. I may say that I am still waiting for a share of the profits!

I made two lifelong friends at Bulstrode: Eric Beverley who had been in 13 Squadron in the Bisley days, and Tony Trotter who had been a Sunderland pilot before losing his flying category and transferring to the Secretarial Branch. Eric could, I am sure, have ended up on the Air Force Board but elected to retire as a squadron leader and reached the higher echelons of the British Aircraft Corporation. Tony was brilliant in many ways and had stood for Parliament in the Liberal interest in 1945, narrowly escaping being elected. His father had been a major shareholder in a large coal merchant's business with warehouses in Oxford, Reading, Aldershot and Newbury. When his father died Tony obtained Air Ministry permission to go on the board to look after his mother's interests provided he only worked on Saturdays. By applying Staff College methods he revolutionised the firm, taking them out of coal and into furniture removals and storage. When he found he was making more money on Saturdays than he made from the RAF on the other five days put together he retired, became chairman of the board and in due course by exploiting the potential of his storage areas became a millionaire a number of times over.

For me that Staff College period was a great experience. It came at exactly the right time when the Air Force was in relative turmoil, reducing from a wartime strength of many hundreds of thousands to a more modest initial peacetime figure of perhaps 250,000. New aircrew non-commissioned ranks were introduced as was a new officers' uniform with gold wings and no belt. There was a let-out clause on the uniform regulations to the effect that you could wear out your old pattern uniform before buying the new. All my generation, unwilling to dress themselves as band leaders, immediately voted with their cheque books and bought a new uniform of the old pattern. This silent revolution succeeded and the new pattern uniform was withdrawn, to the satisfaction, so we understood, of the King who had grave doubts about the New Look and had only approved it against his better judgement.

Against the background of upheaval and change it was the perfect time to be locked away in the academic world. For me it was the equivalent of a university degree course. I learnt at least the theory of how to use one's brain to best advantage, how to think logically, how to analyse, how to be concise yet persuasive at the same time, how to write effectively and the do's and don'ts of speaking in public. The most pleasurable part of it all was that I found great satisfaction in teaching other people and in seeing their dormant abilities come to life.

Anyone who has read R. V. Jones' book *Most Secret War* will know that as Chief Scientific Adviser to the Air Ministry he rendered great service to the country during the war. They may also remember his account of the 'mutiny' at Bracknell on the first postwar course. Apparently two senior group captains presented the unfortunate commandant with a round robin signed by the entire student body and detailing their various discontents. Professor Jones goes on to claim that he defused the situation and got the whole course with him by his inspired opening remark, 'I sometimes think that strategy is nothing but tactics talked through a brass hat!' He then records how 30 years later I told his daughter in Belize that I had been one of the group captains concerned and how well I remembered the occasion. I did indeed speak to his daughter in Belize but otherwise there is not a word of truth in it. Apart from the fact that I was not a group captain student at Bracknell at the time but rather a wing commander instructor at Bulstrode, and the perhaps minor fact that I consider his 'inspired' statement to be fatuous, I am sure his account can be relied upon!

Throughout my time at Staff College I did little flying. As pilot I did a little local flying from time to time and made several visits to Guernsey, once by Proctor but mostly by DH Rapide, or Dominie to give it its RAF name. As a passenger in June 1946 I flew some 12 hours in a Dakota viewing the bomb damage to German cities. This was a flight specially laid on for the DS and the six syndicate leaders. We spent a night in Berlin and another in Hamburg. I later saw the destruction at Hiroshima but this horrific view of what Bomber Command had done to the Third Reich, at the cost of 55,000 aircrew lives, made a much more lasting impression. It was a strange macabre world with people living after a fashion in the ruins with no heating, probably no roof other than a tarpaulin, water from a standpipe and food hard to come by. Money had ceased to count as all transactions were conducted in cigarettes which, being so valuable, nobody smoked. As a rough guide in the currency of the day 20 Players that cost about 2s 6d (12.5p) in England were worth £5 to £10 in Germany in terms of goods or services. Two memories in particular remain from the kaleidoscope of that visit. One was that the lift operator in what remained of our Berlin hotel had been a Ju88 night fighter pilot, and was glad of the job. The second was the eerie sight of Cologne Cathedral standing alone and undamaged in acre upon acre of total devastation.

My flirtation with the academic life came to an end in September 1948. I had been asked by the postings staff, in a very civilised manner, what I would like to do next, it being common ground that it would be a flying job of some kind. These days, when training costs are so high, it is very unusual for any pilot to fly in more than one role. Once you are streamed into whatever it may be — fast jet, transport, maritime, helicopter — that is where you stay for the rest of your flying life. In the 1940s, and indeed through the fifties and sixties and well into the seventies, it was not like that. There was perceived merit in widening pilots' experience, and re-roleing was normal, particularly for regulars who might be in the running later for high command. It was therefore not all that unusual that, when in September 1948 I enquired about the possibility of a Sunderland squadron, 'P' Staff readily agreed and said that I could have 209 Squadron at Seletar in Singapore in August 1949.

The author (centre) beneath a Lancaster's bomb bay at Kinloss.

6. Far East — First Tour: October 1948–March 1953

At the beginning of October 1948 I started the long process of retraining and conversion. I was posted first to No 1 Pilot Refresher Flying Unit at Finningley and given some 15 hours on Oxfords before being put on to Wellingtons for about 10 hours. I liked the Wellington for the few hours that I flew it; it felt somehow right, though very heavy on the controls, almost though not quite as heavy as the Whitley, beyond which there can have been no heavier aircraft ever put into service.

I began to realise that things had changed in the training world since my biplane days; a great deal of emphasis was put on instrument flying and in particular instrument take-offs. The peril of instrument error on take-off, which I had never even heard of, was explained to me and I was made to spend what seemed like long hours on limited panel. When not on limited panel one was on one engine and sometimes one was on limited panel and one engine at the same time, and it was not your modern day 'one throttled back ready to be brought in in an emergency' but the full-blooded fully feathered no-turning-back type of landing. This practice of carrying out single-engined landings for real, whilst concentrating the mind, proved too expensive in terms of accidents and was eventually stopped throughout the service, I think in the early fifties.

From Finningley I was posted to the Maritime OCU at Kinloss and flew a Lancaster for the first time on 1 December. The course lasted until mid-March and entailed about 100 hours on the Lancaster which, with no bomb load, was a very nice aeroplane and surprisingly light on the controls for its size.

The weather that winter was good. It was cold, with quite a bit of snow but often a fair amount of sunshine by day and good clear nights. The flying, most of which was over the sea, took in some interesting places such as the Shetlands, Fair Isle, Rockall and the weather ships. I remember in particular the satisfaction of seeing Rockall come up dead ahead after 4 hours 10 minutes flying and of seeing the bird-packed cliffs of Fair Isle for the first time.

Ten days after leaving Kinloss I reported to Calshot for conversion at long last to the Sunderland. The course lasted six weeks and opened up a whole new world of water handling, of buoyage, the effect of wind on tide and many other aspects of seamanship and maritime lore. Every sortie ended with the challenge of picking up one's buoy first time to avoid the humiliating and time-consuming business of going round again. The technique was to close down the two inners and then very slowly, judging the effect of wind and tide, to bring the buoy snug up under the port bow, with all way off the aircraft for long enough for

A Shorts Sunderland in all her glory.

the bow man to make fast. One had drogues that could be streamed in particularly difficult circumstances, either to slow the aircraft up or to assist a turn to port or starboard but, crucially, one had no means of stopping or of going astern. It could be a difficult manoeuvre and gave a great sense of satisfaction if skilfully carried out.

I loved this whole new experience and, above all, I loved the aircraft. It was unbelievably light on the controls for its size, considerably lighter even than the Lancaster, yet at the same time stable and docile. There was, however, one technique which seemed unnatural and took a bit of getting used to. Because, in a calm sea, the aircraft could be set down so smoothly that the impact was virtually undetectable there had been accidents at night through pilots cutting the throttles at 50ft or so under the impression that they were on the water. So the standard technique was devised whereby, at 75 mph and in a slightly nose-up attitude, one set up a rate of descent of 300ft per minute and allowed the aircraft to sink like a lift until it hit the water with a resounding and unmistakable thwack. It was simple enough and undoubtedly safe but one had to hold an uneasy feeling at bay that somehow this near-vertical descent was not quite right.

From Calshot I went to Northern Ireland to the Joint Anti-Submarine School at Ballykelly. Here, as part of the then practice and belief that one should as it were see how the other half lived, I spent what seemed near eternity boxed up in a submerged submarine. This experience, together with my memory of coming under shell fire near Longstop Hill and again at Sourabaya, confirmed me in my strongly held view that I had been wise indeed to choose the Air Force in preference to either of the other two services.

Ballykelly behind me, my refresher training and re-roleing was complete and it was a matter of embarkation leave and packing before embarking for Singapore in the trooper *Empire Ken* in August. This was an experience indeed. Prior to receiving embarkation instructions I had gone to Movements in the Air Ministry to find out what was happening, only to discover that Sylvia and our two children were on one ship whilst I was on another. I remonstrated with the WAAF squadron officer who told me that it was ministry policy to send the husbands out separately so that they would arrive fresh and rested and ready to take up their duties. I said that, whatever the policy might be, I wished to travel with my family. She proved totally intractable to the point where I began to suspect that it was not Air Ministry policy at all, but some rule of her own. Eventually, after I had insisted on seeing her group captain, sanity prevailed and she was forced to give way, although with no very good grace.

I had cruised in the White Star liner SS *Homeric* in 1934, crossed to Canada and back in 1937 in one of the crack Canadian Pacific Railway ships and trooped back from Algiers in

1944 in a P & O liner so nothing had prepared me for my first glimpse of the *Empire Ken*. I do not know what tonnage she was but she seemed unbelievably small and more fitted to cross-Channel work than to a long sea voyage. She was a German ship, seized as part of war reparations, and had been built for the Baltic so that the whole of her promenade deck was glassed in, hardly ideal for the Red Sea in August. She was run by the New Zealand Shipping Company and her captain, a bluff old number who relied heavily on the bottle, proclaimed openly that she was not fit to carry immigrants, let alone service personnel. The conditions were in fact ludicrous, made no better by an elderly Army OC Troops who had his laid down rules and was not prepared to exercise his discretion whatever the circumstances. Thus in the Red Sea in an evening temperature of more than 110° Fahrenheit and humidity knocking 100%, he insisted on the men wearing mess kit and the ladies long dresses for dinner each night. Showers or baths were salt water, so you were sticky anyway, and by the time you had your shirt on for a matter of seconds you were soaked through once more. It was all so stupid that it was laughable.

The wives were at one end of the ship and husbands had to have a pass to penetrate that area. Sylvia, with two children, shared a cabin with another woman with two babies who not unnaturally cried quite a lot. I shared a cabin which had an outside porthole and a washbasin with seven other officers. It was considered one of the best in the ship, possibly because, being on the port side, it satisfied the first half of POSH. Port Out we certainly were, but whether we could be Starboard Home we would not know for nearly four years. If the condition of the officers was bad, that of the men was far worse, cooped up below decks as they were. Looking back on it now the conditions were absolutely scandalous, but no one complained. All were, I think, imbued with a sense of adventure, all were delighted to be escaping from the gloom and austerity of postwar Britain, particularly the dreariness of food rationing.

We passed Gibraltar, with its memories of 1942, in beautiful weather and our first port of call was Port Said. There the children were entertained by the *gully-gully* man who came on board one afternoon and did some seemingly impossible things. One of them I witnessed at first hand as he called me out of the audience to be his assistant, or victim, for a particular trick. I was wearing a pair of shorts with an open-necked short-sleeved shirt tucked in. He was wearing the usual Arab robes but I distinctly remember that his arms were bare and that I was watching him and not conscious of him touching me in any way. I suddenly felt a warmth and movement inside my shirt and found that I was harbouring perhaps a couple of dozen day-old chicks. That sort of a trick is impressive enough just to watch, but when you are part of it, it becomes a quite extraordinary experience.

The journey down the Red Sea was notable only for the heat and we were glad to disembark at Aden for the day and to swim inside the shark net. The passage to Colombo was memorable, with flying fish by day and a magical luminous wake by night. Colombo was crowded with shipping, almost all wearing the Red Ensign and reminding us that we were still the greatest maritime power in the world. There I made tracks once more for the Galle Face then, as probably now, an admirable hotel and introduced my family to its delicious duck curry.

Twenty days out of Southampton we arrived in Singapore, its rich smell of raw sewage, durian, rotting fruit, fish, spices and cooking smells starting five miles out and increasing mile by mile. We disembarked and were taken to the Grand Hotel in Katong. There, Percy Hatfield, the departing CO of 209 Squadron, came to welcome us and to take me to Changi to call on the C-in-C, Hugh Pughe Lloyd ex-Tiger Force, and AOC Malaya, Togs Mellersh ex-Staff College.

Percy was unmarried and lived in the Seletar Mess but, as a married squadron commander I was entitled to an ex-officio married quarter and our stay at the Grand was short, much to the chagrin of those who had been waiting for quarters for many months. We had a long handover as Percy did not leave until the 21st, but on the 8th we moved into a prewar warrant officer's quarter, far superior to the officers' bungalows then being built. Percy, a very experienced and respected flying boat pilot, was very helpful and personally conducted me round the immediate geographical area starting with Cocos & Keeling Islands, then Kuching, Brunei, Labuan, Jesselton and Hong Kong.

On the visit to Cocos we carried AOC Malaya, Togs Mellersh and AOA (Air Officer Administration) Far East Air Force, Air Vice-Marshal Bobby Blucke. We were met on the jetty by young Clunies Ross in shorts, shirt and sandals looking rather wild and unkempt and with a dagger at his waist. In some ways he was a near tragic figure, heir to an anachronistic inheritance, isolated and no doubt lonely he lived half-king half-castaway, hard by the graves of his ancestors. He was destined to be the last of the island's rulers. Queen Victoria had granted his great grandfather the island in perpetuity and the old man had knocked down, shipped out and rebuilt stone by stone his Scottish castle so that there was the strange anachronism of a Scottish castle standing in this tropical island. The arrangements were entirely feudal. The work force was paid in tokens which were acceptable only in the island shop, which was owned, stocked and run by the Clunies Ross family. Any islander was free to leave Cocos for Singapore or Java or Australia, or anywhere else but, once having left the island he would not be readmitted and would remain a permanent exile. But few even thought of leaving. Such a happy and tranquil arrangement was undoubtedly out of step with the times and was bound to fall victim to the Colonial Office of a socialist government anxious to divest itself of colonial responsibilities.

The Brookes of Sarawak, who had also been ceded that territory by Queen Victoria, had been prevented from returning to Kuching after the war and had been summarily stripped of their land, titles and possessions. Princess Pearl of Sarawak, the daughter of the last Rajah, caused quite a stir at the time by marrying Harry Roy the band leader at the Savoy Hotel. Clunies Ross was about to suffer the same fate of dispossession and exile. Whether the Brookes or Clunies Ross were compensated at all I do not know but, if they were, I would think it certain that the figure was derisory as they had no bargaining counter with which to oppose the legalised piracy of the Attlee government.

Percy left at the end of the month after a lengthy handover involving 39 hours flying and which contributed equally to his enjoyment and my education, with enjoyment as a bonus. The Malayan Emergency, as the campaign against the communist terrorists was known, had been in existence for a little over a year and was to last for another 11. I was to see a great deal more of it, though of course I had no inkling of that at the time.

In 1949 the squadrons available to AOC Malaya could do little, other than drop supplies, that was of immediate practical help to the Army as at that time we had no helicopters or short take-off and landing (STOL) aircraft which would later be used to such powerful if not decisive effect. No 209 Squadron's role in the campaign was, on occasions when a communist terrorist (CT) position was thought to be known with some accuracy, to carpet bomb on but mainly behind that position with the intention of driving the CT towards our own troops waiting in ambush. It was not a very satisfactory role because we usually had little or no idea of its effectiveness. We suspected that, because of the dense jungle canopy, many of the 20lb anti-personnel bombs that we were dropping would explode before reaching the ground and we felt, in our gloomier moments, that we were just bombing the trees.

The Sunderland bomb racks, which had to be winched in and out, could carry only 16 bombs at a time and, as our full load was 340 bombs, these operations took so long that we decided on a short cut which effectively took us back to RFC days. Over the target the bombs were manhandled from their crates in the aircraft wardroom down a line of four or five crewmen, the last man removing the safety pin and dropping the bomb by hand. I took the Command Armament Officer on one operation to view this procedure at first hand. He was pretty horrified as it was no doubt contrary to a great number of regulations, but it had the merit of working and, so far as I remember, he did not to his credit veto the practice.

Apart from these rather unsatisfactory anti-bandit operations (we still called them bandits, and had not, I think, appreciated the gravity of the threat which they posed) 209 had a wide variety of tasks. Up until that time the squadron had been carrying mail to Borneo on a regular basis and I personally carried mail from Hong Kong to Borneo as late as March 1950.

Regular commitments included exercises with the Far East Fleet and with ships of the American fleet based in the Philippines. I remember one such exercise vividly. We were detached to Subic Bay, the flying boat anchorage near Clark Field in the Philippines and, knowing that there would be formal entertainment, had brought mess kit. This in itself impressed our American counterparts but what impressed them much more was the show put on by HMS *Triumph*. *Triumph* had not only a Royal Marine Band embarked but also that of a Scottish regiment, I think the Gordon Highlanders, and the Beating the Retreat that night was the most impressive and memorable that I have ever seen. It was a beautiful tropical night with a full moon, and the whole display was superbly stage-managed with the use of floodlights and the forward and after lifts, with one band disappearing in darkness and the other simultaneously appearing, brilliantly lit, at the other end of the aircraft carrier. The pipes, in that setting, gave a very special air to the occasion and the effect of the massed bands at the culmination of the ceremony was little short of magical. I was proud to be British and especially proud of the Royal Navy. One American, standing near me, said to another, 'Gee — we could never put on a show like this!' and on that occasion at least it was true because their return hospitality was a barbecue which, enjoyable though it was, lacked the panache of the night before.

I have another cause to remember that same exercise, equally if not even more vividly. My regular second pilot Stan Wright, a charming Canadian, was ill and I inadvisedly agreed to take a Polish NCO in his place. This pilot had been in 60 Squadron on Spitfires and had been taken off as unsafe. Presumably it was thought that he could do no harm as a co-pilot on Sunderlands, but whoever thought that was in error. We were to position for the first part of the exercise at Hong Kong and flew there via Jesselton (now Kota Kinabalu) and Labuan. This took some 13 hours but the weather was good, requiring little if any instrument flying, and we made the transit at 8,000ft without incident although the Pole was rough on the controls with a marked tendency to over-correct. We left Kai Tak at dusk the following day on what was to prove to be a 16 hour 10 minute sortie, the longest I have personally flown in any aircraft, 11 hours of it at night. Our task was to search for and shadow the US fleet and, once in the area, we were to keep at 300ft or below because of their night fighters.

Although the Sunderland had a primitive form of automatic pilot it was not very reliable even at altitude and could certainly not be used at low level. Equally, the radio altimeter was somewhat dodgy, so flying at 250–300ft at night required quite a lot of concentration and smooth handling of the controls. Fortunately I had been to the heads before we let down, as I was not to visit there again for more than 12 hours. One of the many charms of flying Sunderlands and, I imagine, Catalinas was the nautical terminology used. As well as heads we had a wardroom and a galley and a flightdeck, rather than a cockpit. After an hour or so at low level I handed over to the Pole only to take back control in a matter of minutes. His rough handling at altitude by day had, by night at low level, become potentially lethal. He could not hold altitude within 100ft and he could not hold course within 10°. Added to that he had his own version of 'unusual attitudes' which, at low level, were somewhat over-stimulating. That part of the exercise had us landing back at Hong Kong and the second part of the exercise which involved HMS *Triumph* and a stop at Subic Bay took place two days later. It involved night exercises with a US submarine, again at low level, and again I had my Polish second pilot. When we eventually returned to Singapore I was greatly relieved to be shot of him after some 66 airborne hours in his company.

During that time in Hong Kong I met an old school friend, Bill Gwyn-Williams, then a Royal Marine captain and on leave in the colony from his unit in Penang, and was able to show him a bit of the South China Sea on our return flight to Singapore. We flew from Hong Kong to Jesselton on the first day and took up 13 local officials the following morning for a couple of hours to view their territory. We stopped that night at Sandakan and did the same thing the following day with 21 officials. After a second night at Sandakan we flew the Resident, Mr Sykes, to Tawau near the Indonesian border before returning to Seletar via Labuan. Just recorded factually it all sounds rather dull, but in practice it was anything but. British North Borneo (as it then was), Brunei and Sarawak were still totally undeveloped and unchanged from the days of Somerset Maugham. Tarmac ran out a few hundred yards from the main towns and facilities were fairly primitive, bathrooms consisting of a large stone-floored room with a drainage channel, huge Ali Baba-type jars of water and a scoop or ladle with which to douse oneself. If hot water was required it would be heated in a vast copper. Accommodation for visitors was normally in the government rest house, though one might on occasion be invited to stay in the Residency or in a private house.

The rest houses were pretty standard, usually on stilts with wooden floors, *atap* roof and outer walls on a wooden frame, windows a hole in the wall which might have shutters or just a chick blind, one large dining-cum-sitting room, a number of thinly partitioned bedrooms with *charpoy* beds, large ceiling fans suspended from the rafters, and a very large verandah which was the focal point, particularly at sundowner time. Food tended to be plain and rather dull, if in the European tradition, but could be delicious if one was fortunate enough to strike a Malay, Chinese or Indian day. There was something not only relaxing but also extremely satisfying about sitting on a verandah either at sunset or in the cool of early dark drinking one's *stengah*, the long weak whisky and soda, or perhaps a Tiger or Anchor beer brewed and bottled in Singapore. There was no sense of change or even of impending change. India had just gone, with frightful loss of life, but here in Borneo, in Malaya and in Singapore we were still needed. Here, the Empire still lived.

Working westward from Tawau, little more than a large village and the haunt of Filipino smugglers and pirates, one came to Sandakan. Sandakan was a tranquil town cut out of the jungle, as they all were, and its main interest to a flying boat pilot was the alighting area, a large shallow lagoon filled with dangerous outcrops of coral, beautiful from the air but always an anxiety. Next was Jesselton, the most developed town in Borneo — which was saying very little — dominated by the spectacular Mount Kinabalu. A short flying time from Jesselton was Labuan, an island with the best flying boat anchorage but little else going for it. The few roads were dirt tracks and it had a very jungly rest house, redeemed by the staff who served the most delicious local fish. The most incongruous and moving thing in this poor and unkempt island was, and I am sure still is, the vast cemetery holding Australian dead, most beautifully tended under the auspices of the War Graves Commission. Further to the southwest was the little enclave of Brunei with its primitive fishing village on stilts contrasting with the magnificence of the Sultan's palace. Lastly, Kuching with its interesting buildings, comparative wealth of history and, in common with Labuan, possessing a usable airfield.

Singapore during this period — 1949–53 — was little changed from when I had first seen it in 1945. In addition to its being one of the busiest ports in the world and a thriving commercial centre it was also the major military base east of Suez. The Navy, in the form of the Far East Fleet, was a sizeable force which always included one carrier and was to increase in size and importance once the Korean War started. The Army had its headquarters and major infrastructure on the island but the great majority of its formations and units were in Malaya. The RAF had its three major airfields on the island. Tengah, to the west near the naval base, was the main operational airfield with Spitfires, later Vampires and Hornets, and Brigands, later Canberras. Seletar, with a relatively short runway, was the maintenance base and home to No 81 PR Squadron, with a mixed establishment of Spitfires and Mosquitos, and the Far East Training Squadron which acclimatised new pilots before sending them on to their squadrons. Seletar was also, importantly, the maritime base, initially with 209 Squadron on its own but soon to be joined by 205 from Ceylon and 88 from Hong Kong to form Far East Flying Boat Wing under command of a wing commander, initially Dudley Burnside, who, though he was a charming and experienced officer, must have felt at some disadvantage in that, by one of the strange vicissitudes of 'P' Staff, he was not a qualified flying boat pilot. Changi, the most easterly of the three stations, housed Headquarters Far East Air Force and Air Headquarters Malaya which did not move up to Kuala Lumpur until later. It was also the home of the transport squadrons, then Hastings, Beverleys and Valettas, and also initially housed the first three helicopters in the theatre — Westland Dragonflies — perilous machines, indeed, as I was to discover.

I made several flights to Sibu, a small town in Sarawak on the banks of the Rajang river, deep in Dyak country. The first of these was in tragic circumstances. I received word late on 3 December 1949 that the Governor of Sarawak, HE Mr Duncan Stewart, had been stabbed by a would-be assassin whilst on a visit to Sibu and that he was to be flown out. We took-off with a medical team at about 0300 on the 4th and, after a path clear of logs had been swept in the river, touched down about an hour after dawn. The Governor was ferried on board and the doctor told me that he had been stabbed in the stomach, that his condition was very serious and that I should try and make the flight as smooth as possible and stay below 1,000ft.

This was a tall order as the weather low down was pretty dirty but we flew round the blackest bits, adding about 1 hour 30 minutes to our journey, and kept the turbulence to the minimum possible. Mr Stewart was conscious and cheerful on arrival at Seletar and thanked me most courteously. Very sad to say, he died in Changi Hospital a few days later.

My second trip to Sibu a few months later was a different matter altogether. I was tasked to carry HE Mr Malcolm Macdonald, the newly arrived Commissioner-General for South-East Asia, Air Marshal Sir Francis Fogarty, the new AOC-in-C, Lady Fogarty and two staff, Major Gilliat and Mr Rayner. I had taken a certain amount of trouble in preparing for this flight. Sylvia had made covers for the plain bench-type seats and curtains for the portholes in the wardroom and we covered the small amount of deck, I think with fitted carpet, but it may have been mats. I ensured that there was a good supply of spirits and of coffee, tea and biscuits and put good crockery and glass on board. I raided the squadron silver for the centrepiece, a very large solid silver cigarette box. We put on a bit of pomp and ceremony with the crew, in white overalls, manning the hull and breaking out the Union Flag as Malcolm Macdonald stepped on board.

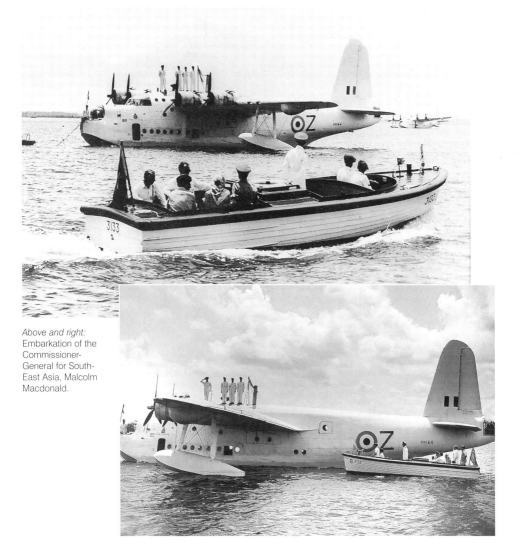

Above and right:
Embarkation of the Commissioner-General for South-East Asia, Malcolm Macdonald.

A long-boat race on the Rajang river at the Sibu Regatta.

The weather was kind and all went well on the outward flight. The visit was planned to coincide with the Sibu regatta and to give two nights and one full day in Sibu. On regatta day word came that the Commissioner-General would like us to take up some of the locals for a short flight. There turned out to be too many for one flight so in the event we made two 10-minute trips. The first of these was for fifteen Dyaks, longhouse dwellers only one step removed from headhunting, who had never been in a motor vehicle, let alone an aircraft. Just after take-off I went below to see how things were going. It was like an exceedingly out of hand charabanc load; they had raided the cigarette box and were all smoking furiously, stamping on the deck and shouting with enthusiasm and wild excitement. Unfortunately, in some instances excitement won out over bladder control to the disadvantage of the next party of fifteen which, though containing some Dyaks, was predominantly made up of Malays and Chinese and was, in consequence, somewhat more orderly.

The local *dhobi wallah* responded to the emergency and with a bit of on-board spit and polish all was returned to normal in time for the passengers' embarkation for Singapore the following morning. To this day I don't think that Malcolm Macdonald, who was notoriously besotted with Dyaks, ever realised what pandemonium he had caused. He was a curious man, immensely informal by the standards of the day. When, before air-conditioning, people sweated uncomplainingly either in a white dinner jacket or in a long dress he caused a terrific stir, immediately after his arrival, by removing his jacket at some evening function. Such a break with custom, no doubt designed as a signal of a more relaxed approach in the political field, went down well with the locals but horrified the Establishment who felt that this new fellah simply didn't know the form and was going to let the side down badly.

At about that time air/sea patrols were introduced to intercept CTs coming in from Thailand and I flew the first one of these in conjunction with HMS *Cockade*. These patrols may well have acted as a deterrent but so far as I know never yielded anything concrete. To fly, they were no more exciting than bombing the jungle, which went on steadily, sometimes with 500lb bombs if we had a pinpoint, or thought we had a pinpoint, on a CT camp. On one such occasion disaster struck whilst bombing-up. An error was made in the course of testing the circuit and a 500lb bomb fell from the port bomb rack and exploded on impact, killing

Flight Lieutenant Kearney who was checking the circuit. It destroyed the aircraft, which sank at its moorings, but mercifully did not set off a sympathetic detonation which could so easily have destroyed another three aircraft and resulted in further loss of life. That was a 209 Squadron aircraft and 88 and 205 also had fatalities.

The 205 aircraft concerned got off course whilst flying from Okinawa to Hong Kong in bad weather and flew into a mountain in Formosa with total loss of life. The 88 Squadron aircraft ran out of flare path whilst attempting to take off from Seletar on a hot and windless night and ploughed into one of the numerous small uninhabited islands in the Johore Straits. The pilot was Flight Lieutenant Birrell who had been crewed with me at Kinloss and later at Calshot. The aircraft was a write-off with the lower half of the hull destroyed and everyone below decks being killed. Those crew members on the flightdeck survived, at least initially, but could not free Birrell whose left leg was trapped under the control column. His situation was desperate as what was left of the aircraft was lying on its port side in this patch of mangrove swamp with his face close to the water on a rising tide. To add to that the fuel tanks had been ruptured and some electrical equipment was arcing so that there was constant and imminent danger of fire or of an explosion. In these perilous circumstances and in near total darkness the Station Medical Officer, Squadron Leader Woolley, amputated Birrell's leg and got him out of the aircraft alive. Unfortunately Birrell did not long survive the shock of the crash and of the amputation and died later that night The SMO was awarded the George Medal. The court of inquiry found that the aircraft was above maximum all-up weight and, from then on, proper attention was paid to this factor which previously had been largely ignored.

When heavy, the Sunderland in the tropics took a very long take-off run if it was hot, as it invariably was, and if there was no wind. In these conditions it was difficult to get 'on the step' — a precondition to getting the necessary acceleration to take-off speed — and take-off in hot and still conditions could last as long as three minutes. These protracted periods at maximum power put a lot of strain on the engines, which were in any event not in their first youth, and engine failures were not infrequent. I had to make five landings with one engine feathered in two years and I would think that was about average. A three-engined landing presented no problem, provided there was sufficient water, as at a certain height and speed one was committed and could not overshoot and go round again. Of my five three-engined landings two were at Seletar, one at Glugor, the alighting area for Penang, one at Labuan and one at Hong Kong. It was only the Hong Kong landing that presented any difficulty as the wind coming off the island necessitated a very steep approach down the mountainous Kowloon side into a restricted patch of water, but all was well and we touched down in exactly the right spot.

On 10 July 1950, with the Korean War in the offing, I set off on what was to prove a somewhat embarrassing journey. With OC Flying Boat Wing on board we night-stopped at Kai Tak and then, on the next night, on Okinawa before flying on to Iwakuni on the Inland Sea, not far from Hiroshima, which I saw for the first time. It resembled Hamburg where, in the big raid which created firestorms, loss of life to conventional bombing was comparable to that caused by the atomic bomb, first at Hiroshima and then at Nagasaki. We spent a day in Iwakuni, which would be our likely base if we were to take part in the looming Korean War, before flying on to Yokosuka, the naval base near Tokyo.

Here we made fast to one of the buoys that had been especially laid to hold the US Mars flying boat, a massive aircraft and by far the biggest and heaviest flying boat ever to be put into operation. I felt that my aircraft was totally secure and with an easy mind moved into Tokyo, where we planned to spend three nights as Dudley Burnside had business in relation to our probable deployment. These were still days when Japan was an occupied power and BCOF, British Commonwealth Occupation Force, had a simply wonderful hotel in Tokyo, the name of which I forget, run by the Australians. Apart from accompanying Dudley on his calls I had no duties and made two exceptional buys of beautiful objects that, for their price, must have fallen off the back of a Japanese lorry. I still have them today.

In the late morning of the third or fourth day I was sitting in the hotel with a gin and tonic on the table in front of me when two things happened in rapid succession. The first was an earthquake and, never having been in one before, I did not immediately realise what was happening. For perhaps a few fractions of a second I watched the gin and tonic spill out of my glass and felt the floor seemingly lift up and sway before I realised what was happening. No sooner had the tremor passed than I was called to the telephone. It was not clear precisely what had happened, but in the heavy seas which accompanied the earthquake my aircraft had broken free and was pounding itself to pieces on the Yokosuka jetty. On arrival at the scene I found that the aircraft was still made fast to the buoy but that the buoy, meant to withstand many times the strain to which it had been subjected, had broken free from its anchorage. This was disaster. Not only were we thousands of miles from our base with all the attendant complications that entailed, but there would inevitably be a court of inquiry which would ask all the politically correct questions suggested by hindsight — did you, as captain of aircraft, personally supervise the testing of the Mars buoy, as required by Section A, sub-section B of some unknown publication and why, as required by that same publication, did you not mount an anchor watch? I felt that any fair court would not in the circumstances press either of these questions but there was the immediate embarrassment of returning to Seletar without my aircraft.

The first leg, to Kai Tak, was in the ignominy of a passenger in a 205 Squadron aircraft. A fellow passenger was Air Vice-Marshal 'Bones' Ragg, SASO (Senior Air Staff Officer), Far East Air Force, himself an old flying boat man, who cheered me up a bit by saying, 'Don't worry old, chap, I've lost three in my time'. From Kai Tak I was flown, with further humiliation, in an RAAF Dakota to Changi via Saigon. About a month later the court was convened under the presidency of Wing Commander Lombard, the SASO of Air Headquarters, Hong Kong. I flew up to Hong Kong but as the 'Accused' or 'Prisoner at the Bar' it was not felt right that I should fly the party to the scene of the crime and accordingly we flew to Tokyo and thence back to Hong Kong six days later in a 205 Squadron aircraft. Lombard was a very experienced wartime Sunderland pilot and, fortunately, was able to distinguish quite clearly between seemingly inapplicable regulations and the dictates of common sense. After this long drawn out affair I was happy to return to Seletar, once more in my own aeroplane, knowing that I was not about to face a court martial charge of 'hazarding my aircraft' or whatever other nautical charge might have been laid.

Ten days later 209 set off for the Korean War, the first of the three squadrons in the wing. I was not inclined to take it too seriously, and viewed it as just another campaign, until at 06.00 we were seen off by a posse of padres, no doubt rightly concerned with the state of our souls. My mind was further concentrated that night in Hong Kong by the news that America's most prestigious carrier had been sunk. This news, though totally false, made one wonder whether Korea was just the opening act of World War III, seeking to lure the US and the UK to operate on exterior lines far from what was to be the decisive European theatre. This could well have been the view taken by the government of the time who were less than generous in their military contribution to what I suspect they wished to see as a strictly American operation. The major part of the Commonwealth Brigade — some ships including a carrier, one RAF flying boat squadron and three or four RAF pilots flying on exchange with US fighter squadrons — might be held to fall short of whole-hearted commitment. There was even an element of hand-washing, of uncertainty as to whether we really wanted to be involved, which found its fullest expression a few years later in Vietnam.

I became aware of this in a strange way. We were operating, as I shall describe, under the operational control of the US Navy and were therefore, on the precedent of World War II, entitled to the routine honours accorded their own forces. On this basis all my pilots were entitled to the Air Medal, most to the next one up, I think the Silver Star, and some to the DFC, again awarded on the basis of number of operational sorties. Though they were all put forward for these honours, approved by the Americans, they were vetoed in London. I have always felt that this decision, motivated by petty political considerations, was a disgrace.

We arrived in Iwakuni on 11 September 1950 and immediately had to fly back to Okinawa because of an expected typhoon. Back in Iwakuni, two days later, I was able to take stock for the first time. It was a very strange set-up. Iwakuni was an RAAF base with an RAF squadron as a lodger unit which was under operational control of Fleet Air Wing 6 of the US Navy. Perhaps unsurprisingly it worked well, unusual arrangements invariably working because personalities

Above: Jack Slessor inspecting No 209 Squadron.
Crown Copyright

always triumph over lines drawn on a chart. The RAAF group captain station commander was a charming host who made no demands on his lodgers, and the captain USN commanding Fleet Air Wing 6 from his seaplane tender anchored offshore exercised his operational control with great tact so that I normally received my orders in the form of a request. It had all the elements of an independent command and I thoroughly enjoyed the feeling.

Air Marshal 'Boy' Bouchier was based in Tokyo as British Chiefs of Staff representative at the US headquarters, and he tried to establish his right to give me orders as the senior RAF officer in

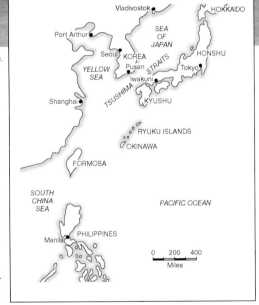

Above: Korea and neighbouring countries.

the theatre. I referred him to my AOC in Singapore and heard nothing further so I have no doubt that Togs Mellersh told him to stand clear and mind his own business.

Iwakuni was a fine station and an agreeable place to be at that time. There was a large mess run by the RAAF but staffed by Japanese who all but fell over in their desire to please. Drinks were ludicrously cheap, whisky for example being the equivalent of 3 old pence for a double, accommodation was in houses that had been intended as married quarters, and the food, if you could eat it all, was quite outstanding — I particularly remember the traditional pre-operations flying meal of a vast steak and however many fried eggs you felt you could manage. By way of entertainment there was a very fine officers' club, again Australian run, with a great variety of menu and with a high rolling craps game which few of us felt bold enough or rich enough to take a serious hand in but which was at times fascinating to watch.

The flying was interesting but largely unrewarding in that one saw no verifiable results for one's efforts. My first sortie was a long 12 hour 45 minute patrol of the Yellow Sea at night covering Port Arthur and Dairen. Our radar picked up nothing. This was followed two days later by a Yellow Sea and Inchon patrol by day, again with no visible results, and then three days later by a 12 hour anti-submarine cover, again in the Yellow Sea, of carrier refuelling. On the 25th I did the first Tsushima Straits patrol extending to Pusan, this time looking specifically for mines. We carried on with these long patrols throughout the late autumn and early winter, mostly anti-submarine cover for carrier refuelling, and the most challenging element was the weather. It really was cold during that winter, and the Sunderland had no heating. For a pre-dawn take-off you kept your pyjamas on, put on trousers and two sweaters and Irvine trousers, submarine stockings and flying boots, Irvine jacket, silk inner gloves, outer gloves and a silk scarf and could still freeze.

On the night of 22/23 November I had been patrolling off Vladivostok preparatory to giving anti-submarine cover to carrier refuelling off the east coast of Korea when a crew member brought me a mug of tea from the galley and set it down between me and Flight Lieutenant Crane, my second pilot. I was not long distracted but when I came to take a sip I found that the tea had frozen over. I have never known temperatures like it, except perhaps when duck shooting in Turkey, and hope that I never will again.

Hector Procter brought 205 up to relieve us in mid-December and the squadron flew to Hong Kong on the 18th and on to Seletar on the 19th. The middle of March saw us back in Iwakuni again to relieve 205 — what part 88 played in all this I cannot now recall — and it seemed as though we had never left. This time the detachment lasted only about a month and was broken up by a flight to Hong Kong on 18 March carrying Admiral Sir Guy Russell, C-in-C Far East Station.

On 9 April I again flew to Hong Kong, this time carrying witnesses for a court martial. About three hours out of Hong Kong listening to the radio it was obvious that the weather there was bad and rapidly getting worse and I expected to be diverted to the Philippines, the nearest alternative anchorage. Time went on and no diversion order came, not even the permissive 'divert at captain's discretion', and I came to believe that the weather must be better than the 'actuals' were giving.

About an hour out I let down below broken stratus with a ceiling of about 1,000ft. There was some rain but visibility wasn't too bad and I flew on buoyed by a false optimism that it was not going to be too difficult after all. Once funnelled in to the northern approach one gets hemmed in by mountains, and there comes a point, perhaps 10 minutes out, when you are committed. We reached that point with a 300ft ceiling rapidly lowering in pouring rain and a high wind which, mercifully, prevented a complete clamp and gave us a few hundred yards visibility.

Alec Barrell the squadron nav leader, and my navigator for this flight, did a magnificent job of map reading with few features to go on and in very limited visibility. It was a full emergency in which any error on his part would have been fatal for us all. During the last few minutes before we made the turn in to Hong Kong harbour the cloud came down almost to the water and just after we had turned I had to go up momentarily into cloud to avoid hitting the mast of a large junk. There was no question of turning into wind and it was a matter of putting her down straight ahead in the first stretch of water clear of boats. We were across wind in a nasty chop and she dug in to port, wiping off my float on that side. Enough crewmen manned the starboard wing to keep us on an even keel and we taxied in rather bedraggled, immensely relieved and, in my case, very angry.

Whilst picking up our moorings I listened to the last transmissions of a civil Dakota that was trying to follow us in. Originally bound for Hanoi it had been diverted to Hong Kong thence back to Hanoi. Hanoi clamped before it got there and it had no option but to try Hong Kong again. Down to 100ft it ran out of fuel and ditched. No one survived.

Back in Singapore later in April we fell into the routine of the east and west coast patrols and bombed targets in Johore and Selangor. In early June the squadron moved to Japan once more and started operating from Iwakuni on the 14th. The weather was fine and throughout the rest of the month we flew anti-submarine patrols of some 12 hours' duration. On the 17th the sea state became such that there was no possibility of picking up a periscope and I abandoned the sortie and returned to base after 9 hours 35 minutes. Had I been an American

Fleet Air Wing 6 tender at Iwakuni.

I would apparently have been in trouble as US Navy pilots, certainly at that time, did not have that degree of discretion; a 12-hour patrol was a 12-hour patrol and that was that. That was one of only two surprises that I had whilst under operational control of Fleet Air Wing 6. The other was earlier, in the winter of 1950, when the US 1st Marine Division with remnants of the 7th got cut off in the area of the Chosin Reservoir north of Hungnam. This reservoir was big enough for flying boats to use and, for some three or four doom-laden hours, 209, together with its sister USN boat squadron, was under orders to fly in and evacuate the beleaguered Marines.

Eventually sanity prevailed and the order was rescinded, but I was surprised that the sacrifice of two squadrons — because that was what it would inevitably have entailed — had even been considered. It illustrated, I thought, a side of the American character where, more perhaps than in any other nation, pride in the Flag and loyalty to one's comrades can transcend almost any other consideration. Fortunately in this case, and at the 11th hour, it did not.

On the evening of 30 June I was in the mess at Kai Tak en route for Seletar when the orderly officer came in calling for Wing Commander Le Cheminant. I said that I was Squadron Leader Le Cheminant and he said, 'No sir, you're wrong. You are Wing Commander Le Cheminant. I have here a signal with the half yearly promotions taking effect from midnight.' As it was past midnight he was correct, and the announcement cost me dear. It was in some ways the happiest day of my life in purely service terms. Although admittedly I had been an acting wing commander on and off since the age of 22, I had not expected to get substantive rank when just 31 and the news came as a complete surprise unlike any of my subsequent promotions.

The downside, and it was virtually an immediate one, was that I had to give up 209. Originally No 9 Squadron, RNAS, during World War 1, it had been credited with the shooting down of the Red Baron and on the formation of the Royal Air Force had taken a red eagle diving earthwards as its squadron crest. In common with all ex-Navy squadrons it was renumbered in the 200s. By chance it happened that both the squadrons I commanded were ex-RNAS, 223 having been originally formed in Kenya in 1917 as No 23 Squadron, Royal Naval Air Service.

Giving up the squadron was a wrench but was made much less painful by my new job as Wing Commander Flying, RAF Seletar. Looking back on it I suspect that the post was invented, as 'P' Staff would have known, as I did not, that a new group was to form at Seletar in six months' time and that I was earmarked to go on the staff. It seems almost certain that this was so because, when I was posted in January 1952, I was not replaced.

But all that was in the future. In the meantime as Wing Commander Flying I had two highly experienced and competent squadron leaders under me, of whom one, Jimmy Morgan, the CO of 81 PR Squadron, operated virtually as an independent baron as he was

One of the last of the Spitfires.

tasked directly by Command. He would have resented any of what he would have seen as interference by me in his little empire, and indeed no such intervention was necessary as Jimmy knew his business inside out and ran a very efficient squadron. The other unit in my wing, Far East Training Squadron, had a syllabus to follow and was staffed by experienced QFIs so, there again, my supervisory role was a light one.

My main worry was unserviceability which was a constant threat to 81 and FETS meeting their monthly targets, and I held endless meetings with the Wing Commander Tech, a real old-timer called Tim Falloch who had served in the Sudan and on the Frontier while I was still at prep school. He was a wonderfully lugubrious character who became a family friend and who unknowingly lent his name to any outrageously strong measure of spirits, usually but not exclusively whisky. A three or four finger measure, whether poured accidentally or with intent is to this day known as a Falloch, a beautifully onomatopoeic word. We had a delightful station commander at that time called Dick Shenton, who also went back a long time and had been on armoured cars in Aden. He was something of a professional station commander, Seletar being his eighth, and he ran me with a very light touch.

Apart from the occasional accident as Seletar had a short runway and we were still idiotically required to teach single-engined landings with one feathered, life was not only tranquil but extremely good. Every aircraft coming out of the Maintenance Unit had to be air-tested so I could legitimately indulge my passion for flying new types. I started off with FETS and flew the Buckmaster, the trainer for the Brigand, which I found heavy, under-powered and generally unattractive. Then I had 45 minutes dual on the Meteor T11 before soloing and next day getting off solo in the Vampire. Flying the Vampire in particular, immediately after the Sunderland, was a huge transition. Instead of being perhaps 10 or 12ft above the water you were 2-3ft above the runway, and instead of considering yourself short of fuel if you had less than three hours remaining you had to adjust to landing with as little as five minutes fuel left. And of course there was one cardinal change to get used to immediately: whatever aircraft I was flying I had to change my pre-landing checks to include 'undercarriage down, three greens' instead of the 'all hatches and watertight doors secure' to which I had long been accustomed.

I suppose that for pure enjoyment, and certainly variety of flying, that time at Seletar must rank high in my experience. There was a Mk XVI Spitfire, not on inventory, left over from the time before 60 Squadron re-equipped with Vampires, and the ground crew kindly kept it serviceable for me. I flew the Mosquito again on a few occasions, but not after I had flown the Hornet which made the Mosquito seem like a London bus in comparison. Effectively a light, single-seat Mosquito, it was possibly the finest piston-engined aircraft ever to enter service. Very nearly as fast as a jet, it was a joy to fly.

There was a Hornet squadron in Hong Kong at that time, No 28 I think, and AOC Hong Kong, one-eyed, one-armed Bonham-Carter used to fly one in spite of his handicaps. On one occasion he flew one to Clark Field, near Manila, to pay an official call on the US commanding general there. Approaching the Philippines he was intercepted, as he expected he would be, by US fighters. They came in from astern and slowly overhauled him at full throttle. When they finally drew level they found to their astonishment that Bonham-Carter, who had been watching them in his rear mirror and had chosen his moment to perfection, had one engine feathered. In their estimation the Hornet 'sure as hell was one ship!' When not using the Spitfire I used the Harvard as a hack, and grew to like it in spite of its tendency to swing, but I did more hours on the Dakota, carrying freight to Butterworth and Kuala Lumpur than on any other type.

One-offs were the Auster, the Tempest, the Beaufighter, the Devon, the Valetta and a Bristol Freighter of the Royal Indian Air Force loaned in exchange for a ride in a Meteor. Perhaps because of the contrast in size and power, I was surprised to find that the Auster was the only aircraft that I found at all difficult, though I scared myself half to death in the Tempest by taking off without having wound on the rudder bias that was necessary to counteract its fierce torque. The result was that as soon as I was airborne I found myself in an uncontrollable turn to starboard which I converted into a climbing turn to starboard in time to miss flying into the hangar, the roof of which I cleared by a few feet. By the time I'd sorted things out I was in a muck sweat and felt that not only was it not my day but that the Tempest was not my aircraft either. I never flew it again.

One particularly interesting sortie, and the only operational one that I flew during those six months, was a PR sortie in one of 81 Squadron's Spitfires. It was a line overlap between two points in the jungle, themselves very difficult to identify. The procedure and the vertical camera sight were familiar from my Lysander days but, whereas the Lysander was extremely stable, the Spitfire was skittish by comparison and I don't think the end product was very good.

Later on in the year FETS lost three Hornets en route to Hong Kong. The flight was led by a senior flight lieutenant QFI, the most experienced Hornet pilot we had at that time, and he gave a full route briefing and a Met briefing for the first leg which was to be Seletar–Kuching–Labuan for a night stop then Labuan–Manila for another stopover, and finally Manila–Hong Kong. The CO of FETS attended the briefing but I did not as I was flying at the time. All three arrived safely at Labuan but disaster struck the next day. With hindsight they should not have taken off in the weather prevailing but they did, and all three were lost. I don't remember the details now, or even if we ever found any wreckage, but it came as a very nasty shock that this could have happened on a routine flight.

'Bones' Ragg had been replaced as SASO by Charles Hawtrey, an old Etonian who was rather a strange man and not an aviator of note. He was determined to find a culprit and I found myself cast in that part. He held strongly that, as Wing Commander Flying, I should have been at the briefing, and by some queer mental process seemed to have convinced himself that, had I been there, the course of events would in some mysterious way have run differently. He got quite a bee in his bonnet about the affair and drove over from Changi to confront me and give me an Old Etonian version of the third degree. Fortunately his ADC had neglected to inform the station commander, Dick Shenton, or the base commander, Air Commodore Bill Opie, of Hawtrey's intentions so that they were both irritated to find him on their territory without due warning and defended me with greater spirit than they might otherwise have done. I don't believe that Hawtrey was entirely convinced by their joint affirmation that as Wing Commander Flying it was not incumbent on me to attend routine briefings and that I was perfectly within my rights to elect to go flying instead, but at least he backed off and I heard no more about it. It had been an uneasy few days because, in a way, one could see what he was getting at, however illogical his reasoning. Something had gone badly wrong within my organisation and, as the commander, I could be held to be ultimately responsible on the Truman principle of 'the buck stops here'.

In February 1952 I was posted to the newly formed 230 Group, soon to become Air Headquarters Singapore as SOA, Senior Officer in charge of Administration. This was to be my one and only administrative post in 41 years of service and, as I promised in my opening paragraph to eliminate the boring bits, I shall not dwell on it. The lasting impression I was left with was that administration, so far from being a black art was in fact not very demanding and that the difficulty of being an SOA or an AOA had been greatly exaggerated. You had under you experts in every field — Org, Manning, 'P' staff, Works, Medical, Education, Establishments — and all you had to do was to interject the occasional question to keep them at peak performance. I have, on the whole, happy memories of that year, and in particular of the example set by the AOC — Air Commodore W. M. L. Macdonald, later to become Air Chief Marshal Sir William Macdonald. Bill Macdonald was possibly the most charming and certainly the most short-fused senior officer I have ever served under. He came, I think, from the Embry 'rule by terror' school, but softened by a little Irish magic.

The only claim to fame I can make for that year — in fact probably the only positive achievement — was to have set the Maintenance Base in turmoil by sending them a letter — purportedly signed by Group Captain Org HQ FEAF, whose signature I had forged — asking for a report on the performance of the Watts cooking machine, a device designed to heat the airmen's bath water at the same time as it cooked their food. A secondary demand was for a graph plotting the olfactory index against degrees Centigrade. Nobody rumbled it and, in the end, the AOA was demanding results from the base commander.

Mercifully I was tour-expired in the nick of time and we set sail in the *Empire Windrush*. She was on one engine most of the way and on her next homebound journey burnt to the waterline off the Algerian coast. No lives were lost but all baggage was a write-off. That was a great pity as, apart from the unreliability of her engines, she was a good ship.

Altogether I trooped four times, once on the *Empire Ken* as already mentioned, this one journey on the *Empire Windrush* and twice on the *Empire Fowey* which was by far the best of the troopships, being bigger and more comfortable. The first journey we had on her was in 1952 from Singapore to Hong Kong and back on what was known as an indulgence passage whereby one travelled at no cost other than one's messing. These indulgence passages were very popular and were readily available from Singapore as the ships would be half empty on the onward leg to Hong Kong and, again on the return leg, as the bulk of the homeward-bound passengers would embark in Singapore.

The *Empire Windrush*.

7. First Interval: March 1953–June 1955
Middle East Team of Joint Planning Staff

My posting, after disembarkation leave, was to the Middle East team of the Joint Planning Staff. We were sited in the old Cabinet Office building in an office with bare boards and with one grimy window giving onto an inner court. The Mrs Mopps were not allowed to clean above shoulder height, so it was pretty dusty and altogether rather Dickensian. Each team consisted of a commander RN, an RAF wing commander and, perhaps because promotion came at a later age in the Army, an Army major.

The task of each team was to write papers for the Chiefs of Staff Committee and ours, as our title indicated, were mainly though not exclusively concerned with the Middle East. I had an additional single-service job which I inherited from my predecessor Peter Fletcher — later Air Chief Marshal Sir Peter Fletcher — which was on occasion to draft lecture scripts for the Chief of Air Staff and for the Vice-Chief. The Joint Planning Staff had been set up by Churchill during the war and, along with the Joint Intelligence Staff, was a fine machine. I think anyone who was selected for it felt honoured. I certainly did and found my two years there challenging and enjoyable in a masochistic way — as we worked any and all hours — and very educational.

There was a requirement up until, I think, about 1957 for all staff officers in receipt of flying pay to do 20 hours a year as pilot. In 1953 I did mine on Oxfords and in 1954 on Chipmunks, Harvards and the Prentice. When working in Whitehall this was a time-consuming process which served no worthwhile purpose and I think everyone was pleased to see the back of it.

The highlight of those two years was a 10-day tour of the Middle East in March 1954. We flew in a Hastings from Lyneham to Fayed in the Canal Zone, refuelling at Luqa in Malta, in just over 12 hours in the air. The next day we did a tour of the Canal Zone by Devon, piloted by Tubby Vielle, my old Bulstrode student. Two days later we flew by Valetta of 114 Squadron — a great comedown from Bostons — from Fayed to Aqaba and thence to Amman where we saw something of the Arab Legion before flying on the next day to Jerusalem in an Arab Legion Devon.

After some sightseeing in Jerusalem, swimming in, or rather on top of, the Dead Sea and visiting the impressive Roman ruins at Jerash we flew on to Habbaniyah where the temperature was 130° Fahrenheit and the headquarters had stood down. I found that AOC Iraq was the same Charles Hawtrey who had made me his target in Singapore and who now took umbrage at my not attending his cocktail party. He unfortunately chose to interpret it as a deliberate slight on my part whereas in fact I had a high temperature and had taken to my bed. I was glad that I never served under him but I was none the less sad that he died, I think of a heart attack, whilst on his way home from Iraq.

From Habbaniyah we flew, again by Valetta of 114 Squadron, to Mosul and Kirkuk and did a reconnaissance of the Zagros mountain passes through which any Russian attack on Iraq via Iran would have to come. The next day we flew to Baghdad and from there on to Nicosia to have a look at Cyprus as it was recognised, greatly though Churchill opposed it, that an alternative to the Canal Zone as our major base might soon be required. I do not remember the occasion but on our last night in Nicosia we were inveigled into drinking far too much with the result that our meeting with the Commanders-in-Chief, Middle East, in Fayed next day took on a form of minor nightmare. Stricken with hangovers of epic dimensions we could barely utter and cannot have done anything to change the C-in-Cs' doubts about Whitehall's competence and understanding.

We flew back the next day by charter York to Stansted, again refuelling in Malta. One of the advantages of the Joint Planners was that the erratic hours gave one time to oneself. I started to do a bit of writing on the side and, at opposite poles, put together a children's bedtime book, mainly for parents, and won the Royal United Services' Institution (RUSI) Trench Gascoigne Gold Medal essay prize for the first time.

A flavour of the book which is mostly in doggerel can be given by my venture into the Arabian Nights scenario when having dealt with Abdul the Bore, El Ramadan the Rude, Omar the Munificent and Suleiman the Sit:

> Who spent an uneventful life
> Entirely free from stress and strife
> Resting his generous bottom on
> A rather vulgar ottoman

I came to my favourite character Akbar Khan, known as the Hug:

> The Khan who really cut a rug
> Was Akbar Khan who gave a hug
> To everyone who passed his way.
> Sometimes his hugging went astray
> He hugged a her, an it, a him
> On Holy Days a Seraphim

And so on, for two more verses.

I was also fascinated by the bizarre names of some of our ambassadors at that time, in particular Gladwyn Jebb, Alvery Gascoigne and Ivone Kirkpatrick and wrote a bit of doggerel about the importance of first names starting with 'If you've an Ambassador still in his pram'. It went on for a few verses, only one of which I remember:

> And there in proud serene array
> Stand Gladwyn Jebb and Gascoigne A
> Oblivious to this life's rough game
> Clothed in the magic of their name

It was circulated within the Foreign Office anonymously and was probably followed up by a far wittier in-house version.

The Joint Planners tour was pretty much exactly for two years so that I could expect to be posted, hopefully to a flying job, in early 1955. Towards the end of 1954 I was rung by Al Deere, the distinguished New Zealand Battle of Britain pilot, then in charge of wing commander postings and told that I would be getting a Canberra wing. This was most exciting news as the Canberra was still pretty new and a world leader. A week later he rang again to say that I would not after all be getting a Canberra wing as C-in-C Bomber Command, Harry Broadhurst, had vetoed me on grounds of insufficient jet experience. This, though perfectly proper, was very disappointing and was a different version of *Catch 22* — if you haven't got enough jet hours you can't go onto jets, so you'll never have enough jet hours to go onto jets.

Al was very sympathetic and bent on giving me something I would like by way of compensation. Misguidedly thinking that because of my Sunderland experience I might like to continue in the maritime field, he offered me a Shackleton squadron in Coastal Command. I turned that down flat and asked him what else was available. When in the next breath or two he came up with Wing Commander Flying, Kuala Lumpur, I told him to go no further and that that would suit me fine. In fact, knowing that, thanks to Broadhurst, I was not going to get on to Canberras I could not think of any job I would rather have. It meant going back East once more; it meant going back onto operations as the Malayan Campaign was in full swing; and it meant learning to fly helicopters as I would have three helicopter squadrons in my wing.

There were very few helicopters in the Air Force in early 1954 and no training organisation. Accordingly I was sent to Westlands at Yeovil for five weeks where I did 40 hours on the Dragonfly and then on to Bristols for 15 hours on the Sycamore. It took me 13 sorties and a total of 4 hours and 5 minutes before I went solo. In common, I suspect, with most people starting on that ancient breed of helicopter I went through a period of feeling that I was never going to cope with the Dragonfly — that some people might be able to hack it, but that I was not one of them. It of course had no linkage between the twist-grip throttle and the collective lever so that one was in a constant sweat about keeping the rpm within narrow limits, and it was a swine to hover. However, after about three hours of near despair I was over the hump and just about able to cope. After that it got better and the Sycamore, though it had problems of its own, was an improvement.

With this short notice posting to Malaya — we had two weeks between the end of my helicopter conversion and embarking in the *Fowey* — it was necessary amongst other things to find a boarding school for our eldest daughter. I hoped to get her into Cranborne Chase, then just becoming known, and made an appointment to see the headmistress, landing a Dragonfly on her hockey pitch on the assumption that this bit of panache would sway her in our daughter's favour, although she had warned me that she was full. I failed to persuade her to take just one more and suffered the first of what was to become over the years a series of defeats at the hands of various headmistresses, a steely and terrifying breed. One of the happiest days of my life was when our youngest daughter left school and I knew that I would no longer have to traffic with these masterful women.

Digger Kyle (left) and Francis Fressanges (right). *Crown Copyright*

8. Far East — Second Tour: June 1955–November 1957

We arrived in Singapore in mid-June after a very enjoyable three weeks in the *Fowey* and took the overnight train to Kuala Lumpur. Sylvia had been born in Sumatra and spent her early childhood there; we had spent nearly four years in Singapore together; and now we were back again in a part of the world that we loved. It seemed almost too good to be true.

The new C-in-C was Sir Francis Fressanges, not a particularly well-liked commander, but AHQ Malaya had now moved up to Kuala Lumpur and the AOC was Digger Kyle, then an Air Vice-Marshal but later to become Air Chief Marshal and Governor of Western Australia. He and his wife Molly were great and he was a fine commander.

The station commander was Group Captain Peter Broad, to be succeeded later by Philip Warcup. Peter Broad could be charming but could also be difficult. I think that, in turn, he found me a difficult subordinate as I had been a wing commander for the best part of 13 years and thought myself quite capable of running his station, let alone my wing. Our relationship was never easy. I found him rigid and exacting but I respected him and learnt a lot from him.

Digger Kyle obviously thought that with a variety of types and roles, OC Flying was a demanding post and had arranged for me to have a month's handover from Bill Williams, my predecessor. It was far longer than necessary but Bill and I got on well and flew all over Malaya by Sycamore taking Digger with us on two occasions. I used that month also to familiarise myself with the other main types in the wing — the Whirlwind, the single-engined Pioneer and the Pembroke — and flew on two Valetta supply-drop sorties and one Dakota 'Voice'

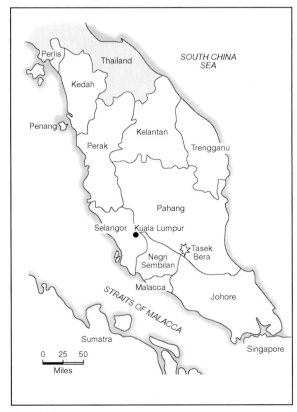

Above: Malaya.

operation, exhorting the CTs to give themselves up. The downside was that we had to spend that month in a hotel waiting for Bill and Kitty to move out of what was to become our married quarter.

Kuala Lumpur was the hub of the air effort which was of most help to the Army: troop-lift, supply either by air-drop or air-landing, and casualty evacuation mostly by Sycamore. Stationed at KL for these roles I had the Sycamore squadron, No 194, two Whirlwind squadrons, No 155 and a Royal Navy squadron, No 848, a mixed fixed-wing squadron of Pioneers and Pembrokes, No 110, and a 'Voice' flight of a Dakota and an Auster. There was also a station flight of a few Dragonflies. I also had operational control of the Valettas and a New Zealand squadron of Bristol Freighters detached to KL for supply-drop sorties.

More theoretically I had operational control of the Army Air Corps flights stationed in

Malaya. The Army Air Corps was on the brink of independence and, in practice, the AAC flights ran their own show and I was involved only when, not infrequently, they had an accident. Counting in the AAC Austers, but not counting the supply-drop aircraft, whose numbers varied, I had operational control of 103 aircraft, a heady responsibility for a wing commander.

If I had the chance of reliving any of my postings in the RAF, I think I would choose those two and a half years from June 1955 to the end of 1957 that I spent as OC Flying KL. The flying was very exacting but also very satisfying in that one could see tangible results. Night stops away were not very frequent, so family life was more settled than in many jobs. As the airfield was close to the town, social life tended to centre less on the mess than on the 'Dog', the lovely old club on the Padang which, I believe, is still operating.

We, of course, worked on Saturdays in those days but our Sundays were usually spent at the Selangor Club which had two 18-hole golf courses and a splendid pool. The usual arrangement was for the men to set off early for golf and meet the wives and children later in the morning at the pool, often for lunch. On those Sundays when the children were hived off we used to go to Kassims, a very basic curry house, so basic that the men's loo was an extension of the kitchen, where the Malay-style curries were unsurpassable.

Our married quarter was just below the mess, near the top of the only hill on the station and so was cooler than most. The station had only started to be built in 1950 so it was a fairly new bungalow, gable end on to the road leading to the mess and separated from it by a wide ditch spanned by two girders set a car's width apart. These girders were not very wide, two tyres' width at the most, and had a sobering effect in the early hours of the morning. Our car, which crossed that potentially lethal gap many times in the two and a half years, was a 1949 Rover, built to the 1939 design, not as dashing as the wonderful old 1934 Sunbeam with right-hand crash box I had run in Singapore, but more practical and also a quality car in its day. The bungalow was built to a simple plan with three bedrooms and a bathroom opening off a single corridor which ran along the back of the house from the sitting room. This room gave directly through large double doors on to the verandah and was itself the long arm of an

The Rover about to cross the bridge.

A Sycamore in its natural habitat.

open plan L, the short arm being the dining room which gave on to the kitchen which in turn led to the servants' quarters.

The servants, as in Singapore, were Chinese, a cook boy and an *amah* who doubled as a part-time baby *amah* and was devoted to our small son. There was no *kebun* as there was not much garden to speak of, just coarse grass with bougainvillea and frangipani bushes. The grass was kept under control by a Tamil 'swing sister'. The large covered verandah was the focal point of the house and we furnished it with long chairs, the sort known as planters' chairs, made of rattan. These were designed for comfort and I doubt if the design had changed since the 19th century. They had a hole for a glass in each arm rest and two small protuberances to either side which could each just have seated a small woman. Without knowledge of their true purpose we chose to think the worst and called them conc, or concubine, seats.

From this verandah a great number of steps led down directly to the main road running through the married patch so that we had a commanding view of comings and goings. The married quarter nearest us was occupied by a group captain and his wife. He was on the Joint Headquarters Staff and, working long hours in that climate, was pretty bushed by the time he got home in the evening. She, having been lazing at home all day, invariably insisted on going to the 'Dog' and he allowed himself to be dragged there nightly where, after dinner, he would go off to sleep on a long chair while she lived it up at the bar. He was a nice chap who should never have taken her on and was reduced to taking pep pills by day and sleeping pills by night. She, though of good lineage, was decidedly rough and made two notable scenes that we were witness to. The first was in our house when he went to sleep over the soup and the second was a sort of Custer's Last Stand when, no doubt pushed beyond endurance, he summoned up the courage to lock her out. When she returned from a no doubt nefarious tryst — she was rumoured to be no better than she should be — and found she could not get in, the night was enlivened by a few interesting observations, all transmitted at maximum volume.

Also on that Joint Staff was Lloyd Joel who had commanded 55 when I was CO of 223. He had been a great friend of Bill and Kitty Williams and became a great friend of ours, becoming godfather to our son. Other close friends were Hugh and Dawn Chater who lived opposite us on the other side of the main road. I am godfather to one of their daughters and he and I see each other to this day. All in all, it was a pleasant tranquil background against which to operate.

Flying over the jungle, what is now called primary rainforest, day after day one became totally familiar with the environment and quickly learnt important landmarks. Southern Malaya was becoming relatively clear of CTs by the end of 1955 and most of our operations were to the north of KL. After a year I could have flown anywhere in Malaya, except Johore,

A Sycamore coming out of Ulu Langat. *The Aeroplane/Crown Copyright*

Whirlwinds setting off for a troop-lift.

without a map — I carried a map but seldom looked at it — and in Johore you could hardly go wrong as both coasts were not far distant and in the middle you had the railway running south from Gemas, in Negri Sembalan, through Segamat to Johore Bahru and Singapore. Most of our operations were in Pahang and Kelantan, though troop-lift operations in Perak, Kedah and Perlis to stop the CT infiltration from Thailand were not infrequent.

My first task before I could play a useful part in troop-lift operations was to become competent on the Sycamore, a small helicopter in which I had already flown 15 hours. So, though I soloed on the Whirlwind in the first 10 days, it was late in September 1955 before I flew my first troops into the jungle. By that time I had flown a further 56 hours on the Sycamore and 12 on the Whirlwind and had got used to the always difficult and sometimes frightening operating conditions. The essence of the problem was that both helicopters with their old piston engines were under-powered, and the invariably hot and often high conditions meant that for take-off and landing they were frequently right on limits. Sometimes, up on the Thai border for example, one could use natural clearings, usually in *blukar* or secondary jungle, which had open approaches, but more usually the lifts were to small artificial clearings cut by the Sappers in deep jungle.

The canopy in general was anything from 150 to 300ft above the ground and the descent into a landing zone (LZ) was very steep, normally on to a small platform built of logs. Before you were cleared for troop-lifting you had to 'pass out' by flying in and out of Ulu Langat, a small clearing near the airfield which although not particularly high, perhaps no more than 100ft, was extremely tight. We used it not only for training but also to demonstrate to visitors from Command Headquarters or Whitehall the degree of precision required for these operations where rotor blade clearance was frequently only a matter of feet.

Looking back on it, troop-lifting in Malaya in those early Whirlwinds really was quite a hairy business. The engines, all adapted and reconditioned from fixed-wing aircraft, were not infrequently older than the pilot flying them, and you had no reserve of power for emergencies. At altitude, say in the Cameron Highlands at about 4,500ft, you could take off normally if light, but with a load you needed a running take-off.

On one occasion at Frasers Hill, practising a running take-off from the *Padang* (every town or *kampong* had its 'padang', or village green), I was heavier than I thought and ploughed through the power cables before picking up full flying speed by plunging down the mountainside. The aircraft, remarkably, was little damaged but the hill resort was without power until the next day. It was not one of my more popular moments.

When it came to the number of troops to be carried it was not practicable to lay down hard and fast rules and everything had to be left to the pilot's discretion. Numbers varied according to temperature, altitude, fuel load and, not least, which troops were being carried. As a very rough guide you might expect to carry eight Gurkhas, six British troops, five Australians, four King's African Rifles, or three Fijians. In addition to British and Commonwealth troops we regularly carried units of the Malay Regiment and of the Police Field Force. There were a lot of soldiers in Malaya in the mid-fifties, I think rising to six brigades at peak and I personally lifted troops of some 12 different units.

The Whirlwind loads were not always troops. We frequently lifted tractors, broken down into loads, for use in making airstrips at the growing number of jungle forts; we casevaced Sakai, the Malayan aborigines, on occasion; and we had two more exotic loads: a young elephant whose mother had been shot and a tiger that, I believe, became the mascot of the 1st Royal Hants but, I presume, was excused parades. I have been convinced all these years that I personally lifted the elephant but can find no evidence in my Log Book to support that fancy.

Considering that the Whirlwind was being flown to its limits, and sometimes beyond, the accident rate was good. There were a number of minor accidents but only three fatalities during my time at KL. One of the most dangerous roles was supply-dropping and there had been a number of fatal accidents before I took over from Bill Williams. The basic trouble was that the dropping zones tended to be low down in a valley, often near a river bed with mountains rising steeply all around. The Valetta could get down to the DZ but unless its escape route was plotted with great care it was at risk of being unable to clear the immediate high ground as its rate of climb was poor. I did two of these drops as a co-pilot during my first 10 days at KL, one on Fort Brooke and one on Fort Sinderut, both easy by local standards, but I was struck by the low speed, lack of manoeuvrability at low altitude and, above all, lack of climb of the Valetta and could readily appreciate the dangers of dropping on more exacting DZs.

We were so seized of the dangers, after previous accidents, that the greatest of care was taken at every briefing to plot the escape route to be taken after the drop, and this worked well until November 1956 when we had our first fatal. It was the classic case once again. The DZ was in Kelantan, beside a river running down from the western slopes of the central mountain chain not far from Ipoh. There was no exit that did not involve a climb out so it was essential not to drop too low and to get power on immediately. The pilot failed in one or both of these vital actions, the aircraft stalled in the climb and pancaked in. All seven crew members were killed on impact.

The SAS, for whom the resupply had been intended, set about cutting an LZ near the crashed aircraft and were ready to accept a Whirlwind next day. A fresh supply-drop was necessary and Peter Broad and I flew as passengers in a Valetta piloted by Squadron Leader Hague. After the drop, which was successful but scary, we landed at Ipoh and I flew a Whirlwind into the crash site LZ with Flight Lieutenant Burke as co-pilot and carrying Major Baxter the CO of the KL Air Supply Regiment and Flight Lieutenant Darvell, a medical officer.

The scene on board was gruesome. I remember in particular a torso severed at the waist and with no head or arms, and the skin of someone's face, all that was left of the head that had been forced back onto a metal pillar on impact. The MO satisfied himself that there were in fact seven bodies and we loaded them into the Whirlwind in due course and flew them to Ipoh.

The president of the court of inquiry, the CO of the Royal New Zealand Air Force Bristol Freighter squadron, was somewhat critical in his findings. Ironically, and sadly, he himself was killed some three weeks later in similar circumstances high up in the Cameron Highlands. I did a reconnaissance of the crash site by Sycamore and was quite satisfied that there could be no survivors. For some reason that I do not now remember — perhaps the length of time it would take to recover the bodies — it was decided to hold a memorial service, and this was duly done, with the service sheet naming each of the crew.

Soon afterwards word came in confidence from the SAS who had been parachuted in to the crash site that a hide had been found close to the aircraft and that there might after all be a survivor. This was incredible, and embarrassing, news which turned out to be true. The man himself, an RASC air despatcher, had no recollection of what happened but came to, the better part of 100yd from the crash. He was obviously thrown clear, but how he survived on impact and why he was not even injured are questions that defy a rational answer. Finding all his companions dead, he built himself a shelter for the night and set off walking downhill the next day, following the course of a stream. Acting on the SAS report, a patrol set off on what they judged would be the reciprocal track of any survivor and, perhaps surprisingly in jungle with a multiplicity of streams, found him within three days.

Something similar had happened in December 1955 when an Auster had set off from Ipoh in bad weather and just disappeared. Searches either side of the intended track were made with no success. This was hardly surprising as, for some reason known only to himself, the pilot was a good 40° off course when he crashed high up in the Cameron Highlands. He, too, survived the impact and set off walking downstream, to reach civilisation eight days later.

The end of 1956 and the beginning of 1957 was a very bad patch for fatal accidents. We had lost the Valetta on 14 November, the Bristol Freighter on 13 December, a Whirlwind on 3 January and yet another on 6 March. All these accidents and a number of minor ones also, notably from the AAC squadrons, counted against Flying Wing KL and therefore against me. I used to think that this was a bit unfair so far as the AAC and the supply-drop squadrons were concerned, particularly as, although they used my ops room, the COs of the Valetta squadrons with whom the expertise lay, insisted that the briefings should be given by their own nav leaders or flight commanders.

After the bad run of accidents I expected an inquisitors' visit from the Accident Prevention Branch of HQ FEAF but surprisingly it did not happen until June. A Wing Commander Mackenzie and a Squadron Leader Duckenfield, who was the father of my future son-in-law, came up for a two-day visit. They had been very critical of my accident rate over the previous two years and seemed to hold to the view that there was no excuse for supply-drop accidents and that accidents should never happen with 'safe' aircraft like the Auster and the Pioneer. Without actually saying so, they managed to imply that all our talk of operating the helicopters, and indeed the Pioneers, to the limit was little more than excuses.

In a way I was sorry for them as they were in a difficult position in that they were not helicopter or Pioneer pilots and had no experience of our operating conditions. We set out to remedy this. We started them off on Ulu Langat, our very tight training LZ, and I think then sent them on a Whirlwind troop-lift with a typically steep approach in primary jungle. This would also have demonstrated the operational need for frequent small refuellings from Jerrycans with the engine running, a practice which they deprecated.

A Sycamore over Ulu Langat. *Crown Copyright*

The single-engined Pioneer.

Above: Approaching Fort Legap.

Right: Fort Legap.

My personal contribution was to fly them both in and out of Fort Legap, the tightest and most impressive of the strips. The approach to Fort Legap had to be learnt by heart as there was only one way in. It started at 2,000ft at a particular flame of the forest or jacaranda tree which stood out above the canopy. From there you started a let-down following a river bed, taking care to keep left where the stream divided. You needed to be at 100ft at the last recognition point, another distinctive tree. A tight turn to port around this tree and Fort Legap was dead ahead with the strip of perhaps 150yd beginning just the other side of a fast-flowing stream. There was, of course, no possibility of overshoot and the only way out was the reciprocal of the approach, climbing hard all the way. I used to visit Legap as often as opportunity offered as I found it so satisfying. It may sound overstated but that steep descent, throttled right back and with little noise, slipping past giant trees with lush foliage below them and with only the occasional hornbill, with its bright colour and huge yellow beak, as representative of the living world, produced in me a tranquillity and awe such as I have only otherwise experienced in an empty cathedral.

Either by persuasion or by terror they seemed to recognise what we were up against and that we couldn't cross every 'T' and dot every 'I' if we were going to get the job done. Almost certainly by chance and coincidence the accident rate improved for the rest of 1957. Maybe they congratulated themselves on their visit having done the trick.

The jungle forts played a very important part in the eventual defeat of the CTs. They were built at or close to aboriginal settlements. These aborigines, the Sakai, with their unrivalled knowledge of the jungle and of local geography became, once won over, valuable allies in the struggle against the CTs. Apart from their use as centres for controlling the Sakai, the jungle forts acted as bases from which infantry and Police Field Force patrols could operate. There were a number in operation in mid-1955 with more under construction, and by the end of 1957 there were nine completed and fully functional. It was a major achievement on the part of the Sappers and I have never seen it recognised as such in any book or journal. Every bit of material, apart from timber, needed to build the airstrips and the living quarters and to make them secure had to be flown in by helicopter, as did the plant such as bulldozers, diggers and earthmovers.

The forerunner of the chain of jungle forts that was to follow later was a primitive strip built by the Semilai, a small Sakai tribe, under the direction of Jock Neill DSO, ex-1st Airborne Division and, in 1949, Assistant Superintendent of Police. This strip was at Tasek Bera, a large reedy lake in South-Eastern Pahang on the Johore border. The government

A Sakai posing.

Troop-lift to or from a Malayan jungle fort.

View from below at a Malayan jungle fort.

knew that Tasek Bera was a communist-dominated area with a number of camps and was a CT communications link between Pahang and Johore. They therefore mounted an operation with 1st Seaforth Highlanders to penetrate this then unknown and remote area, protected by perhaps the densest jungle in the whole of Malaya, to drive out the CT, establish a base which would become a police post to protect the Semilai and enlist their aid against the CT.

The strip was built entirely by hand, the great trees being felled and their stumps blown out by explosives, the undergrowth burnt away and the holes filled in and the ground roughly levelled by the Semilai under Jock Neill's direction. The strip proved usable by Auster — the Pioneer had not yet arrived — but for some reason the police post was abandoned in 1951.

In 1953 a new strip and police post was built nearby. This was Fort Iskander and, from a pilot's point of view, by far the easiest of the jungle strips in that it had clear approaches from either end. When a Pioneer pilot was judged to have reached jungle fort standard, he was always started at Fort Iskander and graduated from there. Fort Langkap in Negri Sembilan was the next easiest with a steep curving approach but clear exit. Fort Legap has already been described and Fort Chabai was not far behind in terms of challenge. The top of a small *bukit* or hill had just been cut away and levelled so that you had a clear approach from either end but

Fort Langkap.

the challenge lay in the fact that it was a small hill and that its flattened top could provide only a very short strip of perhaps 150yds. It was more a mental than a practical problem in that it looked daunting but was perfectly safe provided one was at the right height and speed in the last few yards of the approach. In between in terms of relative difficulty were Fort Dixon, Fort Telanok, Fort Kemar and Fort Shean. There were also two forts that could be reached only by helicopter — Fort Sinderut and Fort Brooke. With the exception of Fort Iskander and Fort Langkap, all these forts were in Northern Pahang or Kelantan on either side of the central mountain range.

Anyone stationed at a jungle fort would no doubt have a different view but, for a pilot visiting for an hour or so, they had a certain romance. Each fort had its Sakai settlement and these were, after all, extremely primitive people who hunted by blowpipe, had animist beliefs and had until the coming of the forts, been almost entirely cut off from civilisation. Now, perhaps, on many Mediterranean beaches one would be surrounded by bare-breasted women, but in the 1950s it was a rarity. The Sakai women would cluster in groups curious to see any aircraft arrive, and one would be confronted by a variety of breasts ranging from bananas, through oranges to water melons. Unfortunately the whole effect was lost and spoilt by the fact that they were far from Gauguin's Pacific beauties, being small, malnourished and uniformly ugly. This bare-breasted scenario did not, I think, long survive my day and by the end of the fifties the Aboriginal Department, no doubt dictated to by the Church of England, had kitted them all out with brassieres, the missionaries' second biggest export following the Bible.

Everything, including the women's substitute for jewellery, was made from rattan. Artefacts that interested me were the long sticks they made from vines, bent over at one end to form a handle and lashed in that position, again by their rattan, until the curve was permanent. I assume their use was for gathering fruits of some sort that grew at a certain height. I saw that, cut down, they would make admirable walking sticks and I have a number to this day, expensively tipped by Swaine and Adeney of Piccadilly.

Teddy Hudleston and Air Vice-Marshal Hancock RAAF, Digger Kyle's successor as AOC Malaya.

The jungle forts and the Sakai were part of any armoury we might need to deflect possible Whitehall criticism of our accident rate which by any normal yardstick was quite high. Any potential critic was charmed and frightened during their visit: charmed with a fort and frightened with Ulu Langat. Any VIP visit was orchestrated and I remember in particular flying Teddy Hudleston, then VCAS, and later Air Chief Marshal, into Fort Langkap where amongst other mementoes he was presented with a blowpipe, so useful if you live in a London flat.

Teddy was to be my boss later when I became DD Plans 1 as a group captain and I have, in common with very many others, always held him in the highest regard. He was a splendid officer who should with hindsight perhaps have been Chief of the Air Staff — legend has it that he ruined his chances by putting his arm, in a protective and fatherly way, around the Queen's waist. That story may or may not be true but he was certainly revered by a Frenchman — perhaps a unique distinction — who was his personal staff officer (PSO) during his last job as COMAIRCENT in Fontainebleau. Freddie Fuchs, a very old friend of mine and a Free French Spitfire squadron commander, was then a général de brigade aérienne and he held Teddy second only to Général de Gaulle in his esteem.

The other high points I remember about that tour were various important visitors. We had a full-scale Royal Visit from the Duke and Duchess of Gloucester, which entailed much rehearsal, and a fleeting visit from the Duke of Edinburgh, during which he piloted his own Whirlwind and disregarded his wife's regulations by refusing point-blank to wear a Mae West for the short sea crossing from Penang to Butterworth. Another visit of moment was that of General Sir Gerald Templar who came to stay with his successor as High Commissioner.

About that time two Canberras flew in from Hong Kong, one piloted by Air Chief Marshal Sir Dermot Boyle, Chief of Air Staff designate, on a self-briefing tour of the overseas commands before taking over. He had given me my wings test in 1939 as Squadron Leader D.A. Boyle AFC, and vaguely remembered me, which was nice. What was not so nice, indeed rather dispiriting, was his clear view that what we were doing was peripheral to the task of the Air Force proper which he saw almost exclusively in terms of nuclear deterrence.

The senior visit that was the most fun was that of the new C-in-C, Paddy Bandon. Paddy's first visit to KL took place in Peter Broad's time, who drank little and could be counted on to follow a programme to the letter. Paddy could not lay claim to either of these attributes. Trouble started when, halfway up the hill to the mess, Paddy demanded to know what that building was on the right-hand side. On being informed that it was the sergeants' mess, which should arguably have been included in the itinerary anyway, he expressed a wish to call in there. Half an hour or so and several gins later we arrived at the officers' mess where Paddy, thoroughly enjoying himself by now, felt that more gin was the order of the day. Lunch, which had been ordered for a precise hour, was steak and was already in cinders. A complete new lot had to be cooked, which suited Paddy just fine as he chatted to everyone and consumed yet more gin. We all — other that is than the station commander, the PMC (President of the Messing Committee) and the cooks — loved it. He was such a breath of fresh air after Francis Fressanges and such a dynamic personality that everyone warmed to him and, half drunk ourselves, looked to him to overthrow yet another pillar of convention.

We did not have long to wait. There were to be no speeches, so Peter Broad had not planned to, and did not, welcome the new commander-in-chief who proceeded to welcome himself. He stood up, red-faced and cheerful and puffing the inevitable cigarette and said, 'Thought you'd like to just take a look at me', and then proceeded to ramble on about how he'd been with Mountbatten and ready to come ashore at Port Swettenham when the Japanese surrendered. What he said was immaterial, but the light-heartedness of his approach made a great impression; we knew his formidable record and yet it was as though for a brief period an amusing and dashing wing commander had suddenly put on air marshal's uniform. Slightly disreputable and half tipsy as he may have appeared on that day, he was none the less an earl and, although his castle in Ireland might be falling down, he had great personality and qualities of leadership to which we instinctively responded.

Not exactly a high point, in fact perhaps the exact opposite, was the only serious clash I had with Peter Broad who took it into his head that I was flying too much, to the detriment of

Paddy Bandon and the Templars. *Crown Copyright*

what was going on in my wing on the ground. As evidence of this he adduced, correctly, that I did not know that a new bog had been constructed in 155 Squadron's area. I felt that he was being unreasonable and told him that I had to keep absolutely on the top line on the Sycamore, the Whirlwind and the Pioneer and keep my hand in on the Pembroke and occasionally fly the Dakota and could not possibly do all that on 15 hours a month, the figure to which he wished to ration me. His reply was that I should concentrate on one type each month. I felt that this was an improper order which I was not prepared to accept and, much though I loved my job, I was prepared to go rather than be told as a Wing Commander Flying how much I should or should not fly on any given type in any given month.

I was probably arrogant and certainly stubborn and put in to see the AOC with a view to posting, the last thing I really wanted. I learnt a lot from the way Digger Kyle handled things. He refused to see me, and thus have to take formal notice of my request, but instead invited me to play golf. Nothing was said until the 18th fairway when he said, 'I hear you're not getting on too well with the station commander, but stick it out, you'll be all right in the end.' He must, I think, have told Peter to lay off, because I heard no more and continued to fly as I felt the job demanded.

The Pembroke. *Crown Copyright*

Peter was an exceedingly conscientious station commander and kept everyone on their toes. A very private man and not an easy mixer, he kept himself very largely to himself, much as an admiral might keep to his

Above and right:
The Queen's birthday fly past.
Crown Copyright

own quarters in his flagship. Our temperaments did not mix and he cannot have found me an easy subordinate, something I vaguely recognised but failed to remedy.

He was succeeded by Peter Warcup who was CO for the latter part of my tour. He was an ex-Halton apprentice and a very practical straightforward person with a particularly keen interest in the airmen's welfare. I learnt from him as well and found him likeable and easy to work for. He for his part gave me a free hand with running my wing.

My tour coincided with the last days of colonial rule and saw *Merdeka* or 'Freedom', the granting of independence to Malaya. The last High Commissioner of the Federation of Malaya was Sir Donald MacGillivray, a charming man who looked every inch the part in his tropical full dress complete with plumed hat. The memory of him haunts me from time to time when I remember how close I came to disaster in his presence.

MacGillivray was taking the salute on some formal RAF occasion — probably Battle of Britain commemoration — and I was leading the march past. Perhaps 50yd short of the dais, on which were assembled the High Commissioner, the AOC and the station commander, I was suddenly joined by my younger daughter, then about 11, wheeling a bicycle and accompanied by my son, aged 3, running unsteadily to keep up, and our large mongrel dog. She was in terrific form and greeted me happily, apparently convinced that their presence would lend tone to the proceedings. Met with unexpected hostility in the form of a venomous 'look' and a loud hissing noise she peeled off, very hurt and in the nick of time, and in today's climate would no doubt have sought counselling.

The next time I saw Sir Donald was on the occasion of his formal departure which was by air in a Britannia, then just in service and a really classic aircraft. I can remember looking at it and wondering whether its lines would ever be bettered. The departure programme had been drawn up with due protocol and the final farewell was to be made by the Tungku, the new First Minister, Tungku Abdul Rahman. He arrived together with his cabinet and we were astonished by the unconscious tribute to colonial rule which their dress represented. We had thought that they would wear sarongs, and this they did but over the white trousers of a governor's uniform. We also thought that they would wear some ornate and beautiful *batik* blouse or jacket, but instead they held to the colonial pattern formal white jacket, fastening in a high collar at 90° Fahrenheit temperature and similar humidity. On headgear we had been confident that they would hold to their traditional *songkok* but, to our utter disbelief, they turned up in pith helmets complete with plumes. It was Gilbert and Sullivan, but it was also a sort of half conscious 'thank you' for having saved them from communism and having delivered independence.

Not long after that my time was up. I learnt, not to my unadulterated pleasure, that I had been posted to JSSC, the Joint Services Staff College at Latimer, to join No 19 Course. Digger insisted on an immensely long handover, enjoyed neither by my successor or myself, the practical result of which was that we could not go home traditionally by troopship but, in order to catch No 19 Course, had to fly home. The only light-hearted moment I can remember from my handover was when my successor, who had, I think, five children and was pondering the safety of their future environment, enquired to what degree we felt threatened by snakes. I had just said something like, 'They're no problem at all, they're more afraid of you than you are of them and as long as you don't tread on one you might as well be in Balham High Street', when my cook boy came panicking in shouting, 'Tuan, Tuan, come quick, there's a snake behind the fridge.'

My successor was not enthused by this and I do not know whether his wife and family joined him or whether they elected that he could serve out his term unaccompanied. At all events the time came for us to leave which we did from the wonderfully Victorian railway station at KL. When we arrived in Singapore all was unbelievably sub-standard and probably unsafe. Trooping home was by Hermes, two of which had been lost over the South Atlantic and had been denied a civil licence in consequence.

In the two days I spent in this aircraft I could see nothing to support this ban other than a marked tendency to swing. Seated as I was near the rear of the aircraft and looking aft I was conscious of the tail swinging rather grandly from side to side. The flight times read oddly

The march past that nearly met disaster.

now. Singapore to Bangkok took 5 hours, followed by a further 6 to Calcutta and 7 to Karachi where one arrived at 04.30 local time, to leave at 04.30 the following morning.

The night-stop was at Madame Mindwallers, the biggest rip-off east of Suez, who either took the Government agency for a ride or, perhaps, bought their complicity. Either way it was a total disgrace. Karachi is in my experience, rather sadly, always a place that one is glad to leave, but never more so than in November 1957. The take-off, even in the pre-dawn comparatively cool conditions, seemed endless and it was a relief to be on our way to Bahrain for breakfast 5 hours later and then Ankara, 5 hours after that, for coffee, followed by lunch at Brindisi 4 hours later and final arrival at Blackbushe after 36 hours flying time. It was certainly no way to travel and very hard for mothers travelling on their own with young children, as many were.

The High Commissioner's farewell — with the Agong to the right, the Tungku to the left. *Crown Copyright*

The High Commissioner's departure, with the Britannia in the background. *Crown Copyright*

9. Second Interval: January 1958–August 1961 Latimer, Geneva and Deputy Director of Air Staff Plans

Back in the UK one was struck as always when returning from the East by how small and dark the rooms were and how pale everyone looked. On this occasion I had little time in which to regret my repatriation before starting at Latimer. I did not want to go there and felt that as an ex-Staff College instructor it had little to teach me, but to my surprise I thoroughly enjoyed it, making a number of friends in the other services and indeed in my own. It was customary at Latimer for anyone promoted on the course to stand Black Velvet in celebration. There were about sixty students and usually five or six promotees so the damage was not too heavy. When I was promoted on 1 July 1958 I had one other celebrant and, between us, we probably spent our year's increase in pay in one morning. My promotion caught the postings staff by surprise as coming earlier than they had expected, not a feeling I shared 16 years after first putting up wing commander's badges of rank. The end of No 19 Course coincided with a minor flu epidemic at Latimer so that I stayed on for a while as an instructor to No 20 Course.

Late in September or early in October 1958 I still had not got a posting but was told I was to be RAF representative on a multinational and multi-service team that was to meet with the Russians and their allies at Geneva in a conference to be called The Convention Against Surprise Attack. The line-up was impressive. The West was represented by the US, the UK, the Netherlands, Belgium and Italy whilst the USSR led the opposing delegation, 'supported' by Romania, Bulgaria, Hungary and Czechoslovakia. The UK team was nominally led by a recently retired general who had been C-in-C North and in retirement was Master Gunner. Sir Robert Mansergh was a bachelor, charming and dignified but perhaps more representative of an earlier, more mannered and more leisured age. He was supported by an Air Commodore Sheen, a blunt New Zealander, by a scientific adviser, and by the three single-service representatives, Captain Fanshawe RN, known in the Navy as Hornblower, an equally caricaturable Sapper, and myself. The whole team was held together and directed by a young and supercilious assistant secretary from the Foreign Office backed by an efficient secretariat and a Rasputin-like character in a long overcoat, a Russian speaker who doubled as interpreter and MI6 representative.

It was immediately apparent that, however it might be represented, this was effectively going to be the US talking to the Soviet Union, and this was made plain by our being summoned to Washington in mid-October. We travelled to Shannon by Viscount, then a world beater, and on to New York by DC7. However, the New York to Washington leg was by a mark of Lockheed that I have failed to specify in my Log Book. Total time in the air was 12 hours 30 minutes, still slow but appreciably faster than my 21 hours in 1944. We spent two weeks in Washington before flying back to London from New York by BOAC Britannia, again a pretty new aeroplane. The weekend we had free in Washington I borrowed the British Joint Staff Mission's Heron and flew down to Norfolk. We had been singled out for invitation to Washington partly because of the 'Special Relationship', which was still strong in spite of having been put under severe strain at Suez, partly because unlike Italy, Holland and Belgium we were a nuclear power and partly, I think, because the Americans genuinely thought that we, and in particular our bright scientist, might have something to contribute.

The American team was civilian-led, very strong on the scientific side, and we met not in the Pentagon but under the auspices of the State Department. I later was to become familiar, in fact all too familiar, with US staff procedures but this was my first experience of their methods and I was amazed at the sheer volume of the preparatory work which they had done.

The difference in the two countries' approach to staff work could hardly be more marked, other than in the purely mechanical field of issuing orders and instructions where there is not much room for difference. A typical British staff paper is short, well written, informative and/or persuasive and clear in its recommendations. A typical American paper on the other hand is, I regret to say, overlong, written in a form of jargon which, whilst using English words, concocts sentences which seem to be written in no recognisable language, and the meaning of which is all too often obscure. A typical paper is laden with facts and figures — in contrast to the British model which can be rather short on these — but seems unwilling to put forward any idea which is not mathematically verifiable. The measure of excellence seems to reside in the length of the main body and in the number of appendices rather than in the merit of any recommendations, which are often of a somewhat tentative nature.

The Convention Against Surprise Attack luckily called for position papers on the American model rather than the British as the raw materials were numbers and types of aircraft, of ballistic missiles and of missile submarines, their various performances and, critically, the warning time associated with each mode of attack. They took us through their thinking as to what was needed from the Russians if the West was to feel secure against surprise attack, and what could and could not be conceded in order to gain this security. It was an impressive body of work which allowed for a good deal of flexibility and elaboration if the Russian reaction were constructive. I have no doubt that the State Department was genuine in wishing to reach some form of understanding with the Russians. The same could not be said of the US military, and the Air Force in particular, who were deeply suspicious that the State Department might be willing to make militarily unacceptable concessions in pursuit of an agreement.

At the end of the two weeks we had established good working relations with the US team and had a fair understanding of their thinking. Early in November we flew to Geneva. Socially it was a delightful experience as we were treated as diplomats and put up at the Beau Rivage, then the best hotel in Geneva. The three of us each had a double room so that our wives were free to join us for the cost of their food alone, and the three of them in fact came out together for 10 days at the beginning of December. When not attending sessions of the Convention we worked, when there was work to do, in the Embassy compound.

The first meeting at the Palais des Nations was informal, a sort of dog sniffing meeting when the more senior members of the various delegations could meet one another while wandering around with a cup of coffee. It was then that I recognised the full degree of distrust felt by the US Air Force as CINCSAC and CINCTAC, the heads of Strategic and of Tactical Air Command and therefore the service's two senior operational commanders, were both present. CINCSAC was prepared for all eventualities and had the communications ability to launch Strategic Air Command from his Geneva hotel bedroom. He was a punchy and aggressive little man prepared to think the worst both of the Russians and of his State Department compatriots. I happened to be talking to him when one of those inexplicable hushes that sometimes fall over large gatherings occurred and the general was heard to be opining in penetrating and deeply felt tones, 'Gee, this cawfee tastes like rat shit.' That, so far as I know, was his only public contribution to the convention although I have no doubt that the US team was forcibly made aware of his views in private whenever something alarmed or irritated him, and that would have been on most days.

Proceedings were interesting at first because of the dignity of the surroundings, the air of importance lent by simultaneous translation, the interest of the media, and the knowledge that one was taking a small part in a new initiative. We were even naïve enough to think that just possibly we might succeed in easing the tension between East and West.

These thoughts did not long survive. It very soon became apparent that the Russians had no intention of agreeing to the one element that was essential to the success of each of the many proposals that were waiting to be put forward, and that was agreement to allow verification by the other side. It had been hoped that the acceptance of a few simple verifiable measures might lead to a gradual build-up of trust which in turn could lead to the introduction of a more sophisticated arrangement for mutual surveillance. But it was clear, virtually from the outset, that the Russian delegation had little or no discretionary power. Everything had to be referred to Moscow and, invariably, the answer was *niet*.

Had the delegations been made up purely from the military the convention would have been terminated in a matter of weeks. But because it was in the hands of diplomats, that was not even considered to be an option. They had been sent to Geneva to talk, and talk they were going to do. They had also been sent to negotiate and, although it takes two to negotiate, they were prepared to try a solo variant if necessary in order to keep the talks going. If the convention were to fail — and it was clear that it was doomed — it must be seen to be due to the intransigence of the USSR. And so it was the clear duty of the State Department and Foreign Office officials to talk on, however futile and time-wasting their efforts might be. In these circumstances, once the novelty had worn off, one's interest and initial enthusiasm waned rather rapidly and I began to hope that my next posting, which I understood was likely to be to Air Plans, would not be long delayed.

In fact I got so bored with proceedings that I attempted to brighten the lives of the Western delegation by drawing up a mock position paper featuring 'Natasha', a character of my unbridled imagination. She was tabled by the Eastern delegation in an attempt to subvert the Western side and I described her in some detail, crediting her, I recall, amongst other things with the 'heaving flanks of a Percheron mare and the flashing eyes of an Albanian Admiral'. She made an attempt on each team leader in turn, each encounter beginning with 'Pliz? watsit you say?' Natasha said, 'I don't spik good so come to bed.' I attempted to make the verdict of each delegation leader fit the individual and I don't think my general was too thrilled by his alleged reaction recorded as, 'How too, too, dreary to be so hairy.'

In the middle of December CINCTAC put his Skymaster at the disposal of his staff for the weekend and the three of us were kindly invited to go with them. A casual debate ensued as to where we should go. The favourites were Rome, Naples or Madrid and they finally settled for Madrid. We saw nothing of them in Madrid as they hived off to some expensive hotel while we settled for more modest quarters. We had a most interesting time, the highlights of which were the Prado, the School of Flamenco and eating suckling pig and *paella*. The convention broke up in time for Christmas, scheduled to return in the New Year to resume shovelling smoke. Mercifully my posting came through in time and I took up my appointment as Deputy Director of Air Staff Plans 1 in January.

That was a fascinating job that I was to hold for two years. Its basic responsibility was to set out the future size and shape of the RAF over the foreseeable years ahead and to do battle financially for the front line each year. The Plan, in my time it was Plan M, was subject to frequent change as in-service dates for new aircraft slipped and priorities changed. In 1959 the 'V' Force, the nuclear strategic bomber squadrons, were Priority 1 and set in concrete, so it was a matter of juggling the rest. The principal sufferer compared to its former glory was Fighter Command and its C-in-C, Basil Embry, was not pleased. As a group captain I did not of course have any powers of decision, but what I put forward as proposals stood a good chance of being accepted and becoming set in concrete in their turn.

I loved the job but hated the living conditions. We lived in married quarters at Northwood and I commuted daily, in the company of a number of good friends, but it was no way to live. Central heating for married quarters was more than 10 years in the future, and they were freezing. By today's standards they would not even begin to qualify as adequate council houses, but one put up with them as there was no affordable alternative.

I was tied to Whitehall for the whole of 1959 and the first four months of 1960, not even getting out occasionally to get the annual 20 hours in as that requirement had sensibly just been stopped. In May 1960 I was let out twice, once to the Paris air show and once as an observer of a 3 Div/38 Group exercise at Tmimi in the Libyan desert, 45 minutes by Beverley from El Adem. The 3 Div/38 Group relationship was close and was the Army and tactical aircraft element of what was meant to be a 'fire brigade' force, the forerunner of today's planned Rapid Reaction Force. The exercise was realistic and I think all the observers were favourably impressed by the speed and size of the deployment from the UK, by the air mobility within theatre, both by fixed-wing transport and by helicopter, and by the grip and 'jointness' of the two commanders and their staffs. The 3rd Division commander was Mike Carver, then a major-general, and AOC 38 Group was Pete Wickham, recently promoted from having been Director of Bomber Ops as an air commodore. It was quite a joke in the corridors that when Pete was D Bomber Ops, and deeply involved with the 'V' Force and all things nuclear, his wife took an active part in Ban the Bomb demonstrations in Whitehall, allegedly marching up and down carrying a placard.

After the travel famine of 1959, 1960 became a feast and on 1 June I found myself bound for Cyprus. Looking back on it, it was a slightly bizarre happening and came about in this fashion. The Air Staff was very large in those days, indeed vast in comparison with more modern times, but surprisingly did not include an Assistant Chief of Air Staff for Policy, a post which had existed previously and later was to become once more the cornerstone of the organisation at 2-star level. The Directors of Plans, of Joint Plans and of Air Staff Briefing answered direct to the Vice-Chief of the Air Staff (VCAS) although they and their staffs took care to keep the Assistant Chief, Operations (ACAS (Ops)), then John Grandy, informed at all times.

The VCAS was still Teddy Hudleston and he often sent for deputy directors rather than the directors, much to the latter's pique, so I was not surprised to be sent for by him late in May. I was however surprised as to the reason for the summons. He told me that the 50th anniversary of the formation of the Turkish Air Force was to be celebrated early in June and that he and his wife had been invited to attend as prewar he had done a tour in Turkey as a flying instructor and had taught a number of the now senior members of the Turkish Air Force to fly. He had accepted the invitation and proposed to take me with him as his PSO, and Squadron Leader David Ross, who was PSO to John Grandy, as his ADC. We would leave by Comet of 216 Squadron from Gatwick on the coming Sunday and, as Lady Hudleston was coming, we could bring our wives. Whether the fact that we both had very pretty wives had anything to do with it I am not sure, but it was terrific news and arrangements were made accordingly.

On Friday there was a coup in Turkey and the Prime Minister was hanged; Teddy was not going to allow a little happening like that to stand in the way of his planned few days in the sun and announced that we would leave on Sunday anyway, for Turkey if conditions allowed but much more probably for Cyprus. And so we arrived in Cyprus to the not totally unalloyed joy of the C-in-C who, at literally a few hours' notice, suddenly found he had the Vice-Chief on his hands for a full and unprepared-for working week. It was a slightly Gilbert and Sullivan situation in that Teddy wanted to do as little as he decently could, whereas the C-in-C felt it incumbent on himself to produce a full programme.

I was given the delicate task of trying to negotiate as much free time as possible without offending the C-in-C. By the greatest good fortune the C-in-C was Bill Macdonald who had been my AOC in Singapore and I was able to broker a deal acceptable to both sides whereby Teddy would tour the command by Sycamore on two mornings and the rest of the time would effectively be free, discussions between himself and the C-in-C to take place on the latter's private beach rather than in the headquarters. It was a great few days, marred only by an insufficiency of tonic to go with the gin on the flight back from Akrotiri to Gatwick, a matter of some moment which I had to take up with Transport Command.

Towards the end of the year I learnt that my next posting was to be to RAF Geilenkirchen as Commanding Officer in August of 1961. Geilenkirchen was right back on the Dutch border and one of the so-called 'clutch' stations of RAF Germany, the others being Wildenrath, Bruggen and Laarbruch and had three squadrons: two Javelin, No 5 and No 11, and one Canberra B18 squadron, No 3. I would need to be qualified on both types but had first to survive the All Weather Jet Refresher Course on Meteors at RAF Manby. Although I had flown Meteors and Vampires in Singapore for fun this was serious, and some of it was very demanding, particularly the asymmetric let-down and approach on limited panel. It was my first experience of 40,000ft and above and it opened a whole new world.

The Meteor course was thorough and lasted from mid-February to late March. I must then have had some leave because I did not start my Canberra conversion at 231 OCU, RAF Bassingbourn, until the third week in April. This was a three-week course of just under 30 hours, at the end of which time I felt quite at home on the Canberra B2.

In the middle of June I reported to No 228 OCU for Javelin conversion. It seemed very fast to me in those days — 535 mph at low level over the moors and an initial climbing speed of 400 mph as compared to the Canberra's 280. Going through the sound barrier was part of the course and, as the Javelin could not go supersonic in level flight or even in a shallow dive, this was achieved by half rolling and pulling through into a vertical dive at 40,000ft, going through Mach 1 at about 35,000ft and recovering at about 25,000. In some ways the Javelin was a strange aircraft. Nice to fly and a good platform for night or all-weather interceptions, it was not cleared for aerobatics as it could not be recovered from a spin, surely a unique indictment of a fighter aircraft.

At the end of May Desmond Hughes, the CO of Geilenkirchen flew in to Bassingbourn in a Canberra to pick me up. He put me up for a couple of nights so that I would have some idea of the station before taking over, which was a great help.

During this appointment, in 1959, I won the RUSI Trench Gascoigne Gold Medal essay prize for the second time. I was to win it later for a third time, thus beating Jack Slessor's two wins.

10. NATO — First Tour: August 1961–January 1964 CO RAF Geilenkirchen

July 1961 was spent on leave and in getting packed, and on 2 August we flew in to Wildenrath by Hermes trooper from Manston. There was a short handover during which we lived in a small hotel in the local village of Teveren and then Desmond and Pam left and we moved in to the CO's house. It was a very nice house and after the one-brick-thick structure at Northwood it seemed luxury indeed. The winters were very cold there, as we were to discover, but the Germans knew all about central heating and we had a quite excellent system which included the garage and was stoked by a handyman. After a Mrs Mopp batwoman at Northwood who was not allowed to clean above shoulder height we now had two young German girls, the elder of whom spoke good English and was intelligent. They were extremely hardworking and cheerful with it and between them managed the whole house including the laundry and the cooking.

To have command of a station in the sixties was, as it probably is now and always has been, the test as to whether you were going on to air rank or were to retire as a group captain. To have friends, or at least people well intentioned towards you, was not enough. I was well placed in that respect in that John Grandy was the C-in-C, Dim Strong the SASO and Freddie Hazlewood the Group Captain Ops, all people that I knew. The AOC was Edward Gordon-Jones, later Sir Edward, known universally as 'Taps' with whom I got on well and, at Geilenkirchen, I again had familiar faces with David Ross commanding 3 Squadron and Duncan MacIver, with whom I had done the Meteor refresher, commanding 11 Squadron. But friendly and familiar faces were not enough if the fates were against you, and I very nearly failed in my first few months.

Part of the requirement placed on the station — one might say the principal requirement — was to be able to despatch two Canberras armed with nuclear weapons within a laid down number of minutes and, to this end there were always two aircraft bombed-up and two crews on QRA, or Quick Reaction Alert, living within the barbed-wire enclosure with the American nuclear weapon custodians responsible for arming the weapons on receipt of the 'Go' code. This readiness, and indeed the response of the station as a whole to a sudden emergency, was tested annually by the NATO Tactical Evaluation Team. This team would arrive unannounced in the small hours, immobilise the telephones in the guard room and, with the correct code, gain access to the operations centre, order a general alert and the simulated despatch of the two QRA aircraft and then sit back and see how the station performed.

I had inherited a very good station from Des Hughes and I had every confidence in my operations staff. The thought that when Tac Evalled we might fail to meet the simulated QRA despatch time never even entered my head. It was the *sine qua non* of our existence, the very justification of the expense of maintaining one of NATO's nuclear strike bases. The chances were, if war started, that Geilenkirchen would be subjected to nuclear attack very early and, if we had failed even to get the QRA off, we might well all have died totally in vain.

The news when I arrived in the ops room, summoned by siren, that the QRA aircraft had not got away on time was totally devastating, so much so that I could scarcely comprehend it. It was as though one had been custodian of a Ming vase worth millions of pounds and had dropped it and seen it shatter into minute pieces. The Tac Eval report was kind in saying that the situation was gripped immediately and that, after the initial failure, all had run smoothly. But that was akin to saying that the accused, in other words me, was fond of children and kind to animals; it was almost irrelevant, and if the station were to fail a repeat check, Le Cheminant would undoubtedly, and deservedly, be relieved of his command.

Within minutes of the debacle I had found the cause: the duty ops officer, newly arrived and only very recently cleared to stand watch, had had a nervous breakdown when suddenly confronted by the Tac Eval Team. This might not have been so remarkable were it not for the

The AOC's inspection at Geilenkirchen. *Crown Copyright*

fact that this same individual had suffered a nervous breakdown in a Bomber Command ops room, had had a period of psychological rehabilitation and been passed fit — presumably fit to control the despatch of nuclear weapons. We had had no inkling of this man's past record as nothing medical is normally divulged, and I felt that rather than sinning we had been unforgivably sinned against. I have never been a particularly meek person but I was totally outraged by the fact that this clearly 'dodgy' ops officer had been posted to me without a warning label attached.

I proceeded to go on the attack and to castigate the Air Headquarters for a culpable error. That way you are unlikely to win friends. However, luckily for me I had a friend, a very good friend indeed, in the person of Freddie Hazlewood who, though not telling me when the next blow was about to fall, none the less gave me helpful hints as to a likely period. I have always been immensely grateful to him. When it happened it was perfect — probably the best Tac Eval ever — everything moving exactly as though it were a stately gavotte. The one in the following year was similar.

My two and a half years in command were full of incident but none so stressful as the Tac Eval drama, not even the Cuban Missile Crisis when Kennedy went to the brink with Khrushchev. That was a very curious occurrence when everything went quiet. We knew that there was a crisis but we were given no hard information and no orders. Instinctively the station commanders consulted together and took the first unobtrusive steps towards getting the families into their cellars with adequate food and water. I think the seeming paralysis in the headquarters was caused mainly by lack of information and lack of direction they were receiving in their turn but also, to a degree, by not wishing to cause what might prove to be unnecessary concern to the families. There was, in any event, an underlying level of concern inseparable from living on a nuclear base but the only outward signs of what would now be called stress was the very high consumption of tranquillisers, known only to the SMO and myself, and the tendency for parties to break out at the drop of a hat.

All the stations in RAF Germany at that time had their attractions but, rather naturally, I think Geilers probably had it by a short head. Gütersloh, the furthest to the east and furthest from the Headquarters by a long way, tended to be visited fairly frequently for that very reason. Laarbruch was in nice country and the most modern of the four 'clutch' stations but again it was subject to frequent visits, partly because of its lodger Signals and Radar facilities. Wildenrath, though nice, was the least attractive, being slap alongside Command and Air Headquarters and, as it was the arrival and departure point for all VIPs, the unfortunate station commander had to spend a lot of time meeting and greeting. Bruggen was charming, housing as it did the command golf course, but again this in itself spawned a lot of senior visitors.

Geilenkirchen, the furthest away from headquarters of the 'clutch' stations, ostensibly had nothing worth visiting and so was left largely unmolested, to the great content of the station commander. Taps was a very good AOC, riding his station commanders with a light rein but leaving them in no doubt that he expected a high standard. A tall good-looking man, he was at his most impressive when carrying out his AOC's inspection. He did only one of Geilers in my time and I gave him the works with a full old-fashioned ceremonial parade with the men carrying arms. I thought it had gone rather well until photographs revealed that Duncan MacIver had apparently been seized with paralysis during the march past. On giving the command 'Eyes Right' he correctly raised his sword to eye level but failed to complete his salute by bringing the sword down smartly in the prescribed manner and marched past staring fixedly at the AOC through the small window afforded by his hilt. Taps kindly pretended not to have noticed this, or any other imperfections, and congratulated me on the smartness of the parade, adding, rather depressingly considering all the rehearsals we had been through, that he would have preferred something less formal.

What he did think highly of was that his route throughout the day was lined with tubs of flowers. This was entirely due to the initiative of my Wing Commander Admin, 'Kos' Cosby, who had a series of trucks picking up the tubs the AOC had already passed and planting them on the route ahead to await the AOC's second coming. Kos, now sadly dead, was a great strength who could charm the dreaded Works and Bricks into making Geilers look immensely smart and, almost as important, 'bid the mighty ocean' in the shape of disaffected wives 'cease' — and cease they did. He was a fountain of stories and reminiscences, one of my favourites being his colourful description of how, as a very young Spitfire pilot during the Battle of Britain, he had no idea of which way was up during a coming together with the enemy and of how, immediately following the general mêlée, he suddenly found himself absolutely alone. After a few moments he was greatly relieved to spot what he took to be a formation of Spitfires and hastened to join up, only to discover as he slotted easily in that he was joining six Me109s.

Taps used to come to lunch occasionally and his visits were not always well timed. On one occasion I was escorting him into station headquarters when there was a loud bang and bits of what turned out to be a Javelin could be seen fluttering to earth in the middle distance. Luckily it turned out to be a visitor who, being cleared for a low run across the airfield on departure for the UK, determined to show 5 Squadron how a tight turn at high speed should be executed. Unfortunately he got it a bit wrong and the aircraft broke up over 5 Squadron's hangar.

On another occasion Taps contrived to make his visit coincide with a serious incident involving an 11 Squadron Javelin. The pilot, very experienced on Javelins, had been having an unauthorised dogfight with a German F-104 when he lost all flying speed in a tight turn and went into a spin at about 25,000ft. Pilots' Notes were quite unequivocal in stating that the Javelin could not be recovered from a spin and that, should one have occurred, baling out was mandatory. The pilot thought he would have a try at proving Pilots' Notes to be wrong and was still trying to recover when, at 16,000ft, his radar operator left him to it and banged out, taking the rear canopy with him. This changed the airflow so markedly that the pilot began to have real hope and stayed with the aircraft through 11,000ft, the minimum height for safe ejection in a spin, and eventually recovered to straight and level at about 5,000ft. My enthusiasm at this feat of airmanship was such that, initially at least, I tended to overlook the fact that he should never have got into that emergency in the first place. Not so the AOC who, no doubt mindful of his court martial warrant, was markedly more muted in his applause.

Sir John Grandy who was C-in-C Germany at the time and went on later to be Chief of the Air Staff (CAS) used to say that the Royal Air Force was run by its station commanders. Station commanders are apt to say that stations are run by the senior NCOs, and there is a bit of truth in both statements. Certainly as a station commander one can have more direct and immediate effect on the lives of one's officers and men than one does as an AOC or C-in-C. It is the last time that one has a sense of family and the last rank in which one deals directly with people as individuals rather than impersonally in the mass.

The Grandys' farewell. *Crown Copyright*

Perhaps partly by nature and perhaps partly because I was never a junior officer in peacetime I have tended to take the view that rules and regulations are for guidance rather than for slavish observance. I twice had occasion during my two and a half years deliberately to go against the book.

The first became a matter of policy rather than a deliberate one-off flouting. Desmond Hughes had had trouble with young officers dashing off to Aachen when the bar closed at 23.00 and killing themselves on the roads on their return journey in the early hours. I took the simplistic view that if the bar did not close they would not set off for Aachen and therefore would not kill themselves. So I deliberately set up a trial, illegal if you will, of leaving the bars open, to be closed by consent by the senior officer or senior NCO present. Similarly with the airmen I let it be known that, so long as their friends put them to bed, falling down drunk on the station would not be considered a capital offence. It worked like a charm and, so far as I know, no one ever took advantage of this relaxed routine which became permanent in my time. I would not of course recommend the flouting of regulations as being either desirable or commendable in the main — all I can say is that in that particular time and place it worked. Desmond Hughes had, I think, five killed on the roads and I had none. My successor, who was a book man and horrified by my relaxed routine, closed the bars at 23.00 and had six people killed on the roads in his first six months.

The second occasion on which I deliberately took the law into my own hands involved a degree of personal risk. One of my airmen was a West Indian who, it transpired, had been subjected to racist taunts over a long period. Eventually his control snapped and he assaulted his tormentor so satisfactorily that the latter ended up in hospital. The West Indian appeared before me on a charge which was beyond my powers to deal with and which required trial by court martial. I was totally on his side and believed that natural justice demanded his acquittal. I also believed, however, that at court martial the facts were such that he would be bound to be found guilty and would be sent down. And so I dismissed the charge. I had calculated that this would cause uproar and outrage in legal circles, as indeed it did, but that I would survive the storm. Luckily for me I was proved right.

Flying at Geilenkirchen was a little difficult to come by as no allowance was made for station commanders and you were therefore poaching other people's hours. Because of this, and also because I was pretty busy, I managed less than 200 hours in two and a half years, most of them on the Canberra. The Javelin was nice to fly but I was not keen on its role of night/all-weather interception. They practised this endlessly in pairs and I frankly did not enjoy being solidly on instruments at 40,000ft in the pitch black at low speed flying to your radar operator's orders, until at last he would say, 'Look up', and there would be another Javelin just above the cockpit. I did only enough of those to prove that I could do it and understood their problems, and

Javelin G(AW) Mk 4 of No 11 Squadron, Geilenkirchen, 1960. *Crown Copyright*

otherwise flew the Javelin only occasionally so that 5 and 11 Squadrons would not think I had totally deserted them for 3.

The Canberra BI8 with which 3 Squadron was equipped was a really beautiful aircraft, by far the nicest mark of Canberra ever to come off the production line. It had a bubble canopy and felt like a fighter. Visibility from the cockpit was perfect and it was a delight to fly, standing to the B2 as a Jaguar does to a Ford.

The primary role of 3 Squadron was nuclear strike, and each crew had an allotted target which they studied for hours each week under secure conditions. Knowledge of the targets was on a strictly 'need to know' basis so that at station level the only individuals who knew the full targeting were the senior intelligence officer and the senior operations officer. Although I had no detailed knowledge of any of the targets, it was pretty obvious that in the main they were certain to be Soviet airfields which we believed to be nuclear bases. It was just as well that they were large targets as the method of delivering the bomb, known as the LABS manoeuvre, precluded pinpoint accuracy. LABS, or the low altitude bombing system, involved running in at 400 mph to a pre-determined point at which you pulled up into a loop at 4g and holding 4g all the way up released the bomb at a set

The beautiful Canberra BI8.

height of, I think, 5,000ft, before rolling off the top at about 6,000ft and diving full bore away from the explosion which would follow. This manoeuvre was flown entirely on instruments so that attacks could be carried out with confidence at night or in cloud.

Whilst the LABS pattern could be flown in Germany, actual practice bombs were dropped, or rather projected, only on the bombing range at Idris in the Libyan desert. No 3 Squadron's nuclear strike role required the aircraft to fly to their targets at low level so low flying was an important part of the training, both by day and by night along the low-level routes, known as link-routes, established over the more thinly populated areas of West Germany. Part of one route lay over a mountain plateau covered in pines which ended suddenly in a sheer drop of about 3,000ft. Suddenly launching the aircraft from tree-top height over this apparent abyss was a great sensation — rather, I should imagine, like launching oneself on a ski jump though without the abject terror that for me would accompany that manoeuvre. The squadron had the secondary role of low-level attack with conventional weapons and we used a local range for practice bombing and front gunnery.

I had a number of longish Canberra flights during my two and a half years but not as many as I should have liked.

In addition to the routine visiting of the squadrons when they were on armament practice camp — 5 and 11 in Cyprus and 3 in Libya — I flew up to Bodö in northern Norway to visit 11 Squadron when it was on exchange with a Norwegian squadron. This was in June 1962 and I stayed for four days, on one of which I flew up to the North Cape via the Lofotens and Hammerfest, returning to Bodö via Tromsö and Narvik. I was to return to that area some 15 years later.

This was to prove the first of several visits to Norway and it was by far the most spartan. The mess at Bodö had in some mysterious way fallen into debt and rigorous economies had been applied to remedy this situation. Breakfast was at 06.00 and consisted of cereals and milk and cold fish, none of which appealed to me. You were then expected to make cold fish sandwiches to take with you for lunch. This I passed on, which left the main meal of the day, which was hot fish, at 16.00. I lost several pounds during my stay but enjoyed it greatly none the less, particularly fishing at 03.00 in broad daylight.

I am afraid I was a great disappointment to my hosts in this matter of fishing. They simply could not believe that in waters swarming with fish an able-bodied white male with a public school education and able to fly many different types of aircraft could not land a single one of them, even though on his left hand and on his right hand they were constantly being reeled in. They took this inability as a challenge, and to remedy it was virtually a matter of national honour. Although my hook was properly baited they insisted on re-doing it, and although I could cast reasonably competently they insisted, in a final attempt at a breakthrough, on casting for me. All this was to absolutely no avail; fish continued to be landed to port and to starboard but not a one fell to me. My hosts were mortified and our return to the mess bore some resemblance to Napoleon's retreat from the gates of Moscow.

Had they had the gift of foresight they would have been of better cheer as this was but the first of a series of humiliations. I failed to catch any fish on a visit to Canada and in spite of living in Turkey for more than a year failed to catch a single trout. The closest I came to breaking this curse of the Pisces was when I hooked a beautiful salmon in New Zealand. Needless to say, it broke free.

In 1963 there was a return visit from the Bodö squadron bearing rich gifts. In addition to large quantities of fiery spirits they introduced us to two great delicacies, rotted fish and rotted sheep. I am not sure of the exact procedure but basically you take a perfectly good raw salmon and an equally good bit of raw lamb and rot them in straw buried under snow for about a year. The result is quite hard to enthuse about.

In addition to the Bodö visit I managed to get clearance for two longer flights known as 'Lone Rangers'. One, which followed the route Malta, Cyprus, Bahrain, Aden, Khartoum, Malta, Geilenkirchen, was uneventful but the other, to Harare in Zimbabwe (then Salisbury in Rhodesia), was a different matter. My navigator was Squadron Leader Bill Drake to whom the whole of life was one hilarious mirth-yielding occurrence, and I should have been warned. Duncan MacIver, the CO of 11, had a sister living in Salisbury, and I took him as a passenger. We set off on 17 March 1962 on the first leg to El Adem which we reached at about 18.00 after an uneventful flight of 3 hours 35 minutes. When we arrived at the mess a bit later on there was a large figure standing at the far end of the room. Bill and Duncan reacted as though they had just glimpsed a vampire, had forgotten their crucifixes and were a bit short of garlic.

One of them said, 'Good God, that's Big Daddy Sanderson, don't tangle with him, he'll drink you under the table.' That was not a very sensible remark and, several hours later, I would have judged that honours were even. I enjoyed Big Daddy's company but was somewhat dehydrated when we took-off for Khartoum early the following morning. It was exceedingly hot in Khartoum and everything moved at a snail's pace. After start-up we were held for 20 minutes in a temperature of 130° Fahrenheit before being cleared for take-off. No doubt to the alarm of Bill and Duncan I started to hyperventilate on the climb. I was not worried as I felt perfectly all right and knew it would pass off as soon as the temperature dropped, but hearing deep gasping noises emanating from their pilot can have been anything but reassuring to the others.

We night-stopped at Nairobi and flew on to Salisbury the following day. After about two and a half hours at 40,000ft we let down to 10,000 for the last 20 minutes or so and saw nothing but endless bush until suddenly a modern city appeared, a white and sparkling island in the ocean of green. After a day's rest in Salisbury we set out to retrace our steps. Arrived once more at Nairobi, Duncan and I said we would go and eat in the town. Bill said that as we had nearly six hours flying ahead of us the next day he would stay on the airfield and look up an old friend in married quarters preparatory to having an early night. Duncan and I were in bed before midnight and assumed that Bill had preceded us. Not so, in fact. A not well William was shakily present at breakfast and the story of the night before gradually emerged. He had duly looked up his old friend who had proved most hospitable. On his way back to the mess at about 01.00 he had been attracted by the sound of revelry which, on investigation, turned out to be coming from the sergeants' mess. It seemed to Bill that it would be a pity not to join them, and this he did in the guise of Squadron Leader the Rev Drake, the new C-of-E padre, just out from the UK. He made himself known to the mess president and was duly introduced to the assembled company by the words, 'Mind your language lads, this here's the new C-of-E padre.' Bill, who can impersonate a vacuous toothy parson to perfection, passed a happy hour or so during which, who knows, he may have contributed to the cure of a soul or two.

We passed through Khartoum without incident and were en route for El Adem, with nothing but desert for hundreds of miles in any direction, when we picked up the crew of a Vulcan chattering on their intercom. Bill gave them a quick transmission. Coming as it did in the remote stillness of the great Sahara and from some invisible source it could have had great impact, had the words been sufficiently moving or inspiring. Unfortunately the best that could be said for the message from on high, delivered in a strong antipodean accent, was that it had a certain air of divine mystery. The crew of the Vulcan were objured, 'Never kick a kookaburra, the bastard only laughs.' Not surprisingly, silence fell. Perhaps they were seeking enlightenment in their Bomber Command code books. Perhaps even now, as old men, they ponder the mystery of the voice that spoke over the Sahara.

Shortly after that we were informed that there was rising sand at El Adem and we were diverted to Akrotiri. A return to Germany via Cyprus and Malta seemed a small price to pay in order to avoid a second encounter with Big Daddy. We eventually arrived back on the 26th, nine days and 28 flying hours after departure, to be met by Bill's wife and mine on the tarmac, no doubt expecting rich pickings. Duncan was at that time a bachelor, I do not remember what I had brought, but Bill did not fare too well. He had excitedly discovered a record of 'Stranger on the Shore' which he knew to be one of Pauline's favourites. When he presented it to her it was found to be cracked, and in any event they already had a copy, a detail which he had overlooked. The story of our adventures grew with the telling and that particular Canberra came to be known as 'The African Queen'.

Geilers was a lovely station. There were a few 'mislaid' weekends along the way but only two 'lost' ones that I can recall. The first of these was known as Grandma's Day and lasted from Friday evening to the small hours of Monday morning. It was in celebration of the birth of our first grandchild. As Sylvia and I had got married when she was 19, and our eldest daughter had followed suit, 'Grandma' was a lively 40 and presided over events with enthusiasm. The second, which also lasted from a Friday to a Monday, was the occasion of a formal drinks party in the mess, supposedly from 18.30–20.00. The then CO of Wildenrath, a bachelor, was one of the guests and came back to our quarter after the party. In some mysterious way he was still there on the Sunday, having understandably been prevented from returning to Wildenrath by the fact that, somewhere along the way, he had lost a sock.

On the Saturday evening he had informed us that, with regret, he would have to tear himself away early on the Sunday as from about 11.00 onwards he had a series of VIPs arriving and departing that he would have to be on hand to meet, greet and despatch. The Sunday was a beautiful sunny day and the prospect of lying on our lawn sipping gin and tonics preparatory to a barbecue proved too much for him and he rang his duty officer and instructed him to meet the VIPs in his place. VIP was a fairly loosely applied term but it

Leaving Geilenkirchen, December 1963. *Crown Copyright*

became clear that he had at least one genuine article when at 11.00 he struggled to his feet and announced, 'Please be upstanding and drink a toast in honour of the Secretary of State, now arriving at Wildenrath'. This procedure was followed from time to time during the later morning and early afternoon as various ministers, generals and air marshals arrived at or departed from Wildenrath. Finally in late afternoon, worn out by his protocol duties, the station commander slumbered. We finally fired him off, back to Wildenrath, still in his mess kit and missing a sock, in time for breakfast on Monday morning.

Life at Geilenkirchen was not all one long party, though it sometimes seemed like it, and my allotted time was up all too soon. My full two and a half years would have taken me to February 1964 but I felt sure that I would be picked for the Imperial Defence College course starting in January as I was just the right age — 43. Instead, to my great disappointment, although it carried the acting rank of Air Commodore (which I held for one day as I was made substantive Air Commodore on 1 January) I was appointed on 31 December to be

Erratum slip
for page 104

became clear that he had at least one genuine article when at 11.00 he struggled to his feet and announced, 'Please be upstanding and drink a toast in honour of the Secretary of State, now arriving at Wildenrath'. This procedure was followed from time to time during the later morning and early afternoon as various ministers, generals and air marshals arrived at or departed from Wildenrath. Finally in late afternoon, worn out by his protocol duties, the station commander slumbered. We finally fired him off, back to Wildenrath, still in his mess kit and missing a sock, in time for breakfast on Monday morning.

Life at Geilenkirchen was not all one long party, though it sometimes seemed like it, and my allotted time was up all too soon. My full two and a half years would have taken me to February 1964 but I felt sure that I would be picked for the Imperial Defence College course starting in January as I was just the right age — 43. Instead, to my great disappointment, although it carried the acting rank of Air Commodore (which I held for one day as I was made substantive Air Commodore on 1 January) I was appointed on 31 December to be Director of Air Staff Briefing, working directly to CAS and VCAS.

11. Third Interval: January 1964–May 1966
Director of Air Staff Briefing

Those were the days of adequate staffs and I had a group captain and two wing commanders working for me. Thank the Lord they could all write well and all went on to higher things, notably John Nicholls who was my group captain and later became Vice-Chief of Air Staff. In those days the centre, consisting of the Chief of Defence Staff, the Permanent Under Secretary and supporting staffs was weak, and the real power was still exercised by the Chiefs of Staff who met weekly in Committee.

The Vice-Chiefs, whose decisions carried the same authority as those of the Chiefs, also met once a week in committee. It was our task to prepare the briefs for these meetings and my particular task to steer the principals through the briefs at their briefing meeting. Typically there might be eight items on the agenda which might with luck be known 24 hours before the meeting. As soon as they knew which briefs they were going to be responsible for, my workers would begin pestering the staffs concerned, often several, for their views and recommendations. They would begin to get these and be able to start writing by about 16.00 and I might get the first draft by 18.00. It was my task to edit these briefs, rewriting as necessary to give a consistent style. This often took until 21.00 and the typing went on until 22.00.

The typing pool, which was an impersonal and unionised organisation, shut at 18.30 so the success of the whole operation depended on the loyalty and willingness to work wartime hours in peacetime of my lovely old PA, Muriel Brown, who typed away mumbling strange plaintive oaths with a cigarette dangling from her lower lip. Without her the directorate simply could not have functioned.

I had a parallel job at that time as a member of the cabal advising CAS in his battle with the Navy over CVA 01. The Navy has been hostile to the RAF from its inception, constantly seeking not only to gain control of its own seagoing air power but also to take over land-based maritime air, notably in the shape of Coastal Command. In 1937 it partially succeeded when the formation of the Fleet Air Arm ensured that embarked pilots would be naval officers rather than RAF, as had been the case previously. It gave the Navy control of its own aircraft procurement thus enabling it to purchase the Skua, the Roc and the Barracuda, all disasters and the last being a death trap.

That said, the Fleet Air Arm built a great fighting spirit, did marvels during the war with its old Swordfish and in 1964 was desperately keen to upgrade from the small carriers of the period to a really large American-style carrier, designated CVA 01. The trouble as usual was costs and conflicting priorities. Denis Healey, on taking over as Secretary of State for Defence, had put through Cabinet the cancellation of the TSR2, a prospective world beater, on grounds of cost. This he was, of course, perfectly entitled to do but, in order to ensure that a Conservative administration could not in future reverse his decision, he ordered the jigs destroyed. Initially Healey had come with a great reputation and was alleged to have a first-rate brain, but the way he set the RAF against the Navy, and vice versa, hardly bore that out. Perhaps more importantly we came to doubt his integrity and eventually had no confidence that he would stand by his word.

The RAF was in dire need of a strike aircraft to replace its ageing Canberras and Vulcans and, TSR2 out of the window, had settled for the American F-111. The cost of re-equipping the RAF with F-111s and of building the CVA 01 were broadly similar — one or the other had to go. The CAS at the time was Sam Elworthy, a charming New Zealander, later Marshal of the Royal Air Force, Knight of the Garter and Governor of Windsor Castle, and he was a worthy champion in what was to become a life or death struggle. To help construct the arguments and counter-arguments that were to rage for a year or more Sam had ACAS (Policy), Peter Fletcher, who had trained as a lawyer and subsequently became ACM; Frank Cooper who was AUS (AS) (Assistant Under Secretary [Air Staff]) and would later become

CABINET TO 'AXE' CARRIERS TODAY

Headlines from *The Daily Telegraph*, 14 February 1966.

◆

WILSON UNMOVED BY THREATS TO RESIGN

PUS and was a very smart operator indeed; Splinters Smallwood who was ACAS (Operations) and subsequently became ACM; Air Commodore Andrew Humphrey who was Director of Defence Plans and subsequently became Chief of the Defence Staff (CDS); and myself. Digger Kyle, who was VCAS, was left to run the Air Force day to day.

Looking back, it could hardly have been a stronger team. The battle raged, stoked by Healey who enjoyed the intellectual argument and who seemed even more to enjoy watching the two services destroying one another. At one stage he brought into the argument Solly Zuckerman who wrote what was for him an uncharacteristically ill-argued paper in support of the Navy position. This we destroyed paragraph by paragraph. Specious argument was used on both sides, but the Navy team unforgivably put the First Sea Lord, Admiral Luce, in to bat on totally falsified information. When CAS confronted him with the facts in committee he resigned. It was all very sad and left a very bad taste. It was a Pyrrhic victory for the Royal Air Force. Healey told CAS that if he did not get agreement in principle in Cabinet on the Friday to an order of F-111s he would resign. On the following Monday he said he had changed his mind. I do not think Sam Elworthy ever spoke to him again other than when forced to do so by official circumstances. Certainly he had forfeited all respect. The Navy fared no better in the short term. They lost CVA 01 and it was ruled that carriers would no longer form part of the fleet. The Nelson Touch came into play and in very short order they had laid the keels of two 'through-deck cruisers' — carriers by another name.

At the end of the two years I was exhausted and was delighted to be sent as CAS's emissary to the Middle and Far East to brief the commanders and staffs at first hand on the result of the defence review, of which the carrier struggle was part. I spent 18–26 February 1966 doing this, starting off in Aden where Andrew Humphrey had just become AOC. Agnes helped me choose a watch for Sylvia — something I would never have bought had I been able to read the immediate future as I had to pay duty on it — and stopped Andrew and I from sinking into our chairs at dinner before Bishop Tickle, the Roman Catholic Bishop to the Forces and a fellow guest, had said grace.

It was a pleasant and brief interlude before I moved on to Singapore via Bahrain and Gan. At Far East Air Force Headquarters I met the commander, Air Marshal Sir Peter Wickham, whom I had known on and off over the years, and Air Vice-Marshal Hoot Gibson, RAAF, the SASO who, unbeknownst either to him or to me, I was replace in that job. During my time in Singapore I briefed Chris Foxley-Norris, an old friend who was AOC 224 Group on the review, and he offered me the job of COMAIRBOR, Commander Air Forces Borneo, which in spite of its being at the heart of the air action against Indonesia, in the so-called 'Confrontation', failed to attract me. It was an air commodore's command, and involved living unaccompanied in Labuan, and besides I had the feeling that there might be an AVM job in the offing. In the event it proved so, and as from 6 May I was authorised to put up AVM badges of rank preparatory to taking over as SASO, Far East Air Force.

SASO at No 8 Fairey Point.

12. Far East — Third Tour: May 1966–October 1968 SASO and Chief of Staff FEAF

On the evening of 11 May 1966 we had a family party at Lyneham preparatory to Sylvia, our daughter Joanna and I setting off the following morning for Singapore in our own Comet of 216 Squadron. We refuelled at Nicosia and reached Muharraq, the RAF station in Bahrain, that afternoon after just over nine hours in the air. We were due off the next morning but it transpired that we had a major engine fault which could not be put right on the spot and we had to wait for a replacement engine to be flown out and installed. This took two days so that we did not finally take off for Gan, en route to Singapore, until the morning of the 15th.

During those two days we were cheerfully hosted by the Millingtons — Spook was looking after the Gulf — and my abiding memory is of the flies. Even on the Sultan's private beach, meant to be relatively free, they were almost as bad as in the desert in 1943. Eating in the open air was a nightmare; we were invited to a picnic and trying to move food from your plate to your mouth without flies claiming it en route took practice which we lacked. Sylvia enjoyed the delay and became an habituée of the Souk, coming away several pairs of gold earrings to the better. On one of the days I took advantage of the opportunity to take part in a Beverley supply-drop: I can't now remember to whom but most probably the SAS.

The arrival in Singapore was exciting; we felt so at one with the Far East that it was like coming home, except that I was now an air vice-marshal rather than a wing commander and 'home' was a good deal more palatial. It was in fact No 8 Fairey Point, a lovely old house, the highest of five big houses that all overlooked the Johore Straits. From it you could see both the dawn and the sunset which constantly rivalled one another in beauty and dramatic splendour. Like many old Singapore houses it had its sitting room upstairs open to the breeze on three sides. Air-conditioning was just beginning to arrive in

Singapore but had not yet reached the services and we had chicks and shutters for our windows, rather than glass, and relied on big overhead fans for cooling. Its only disadvantage was that the dining room was downstairs alongside the kitchen. In practice this mattered very little as we were almost always able to hold our dinner parties or barbecues outside amongst the bougainvillea and frangipani.

My ADC was Flying Officer Tony Oliver. He was an amazing young man. A navigator, having failed as a pilot due to allegedly insufficiently fast reactions, he had all the dynamism of an outstanding fighter pilot, was a keen free-fall parachutist and a loyal supporter. I tried very hard to get him a second chance as a pilot but without success.

In defiance of insuperable odds we had inherited staff from Hoot Gibson by the names of Ah Pong, Ah Loo and Ah Wee. To these we were now able to add Ah Tone and, when our beagle Chaucer arrived by Blue Funnel, Ah Chauce.

The Air Staff, headed up by Geoff Newstead, an Australian, as Group Captain Ops, and Hugh Walmsley as Group Captain Plans, were, I believe, glad to see me. We were not entirely strangers as I had briefed them earlier in the year and any relief from Hoot was welcome. From what I saw of him he was a lovely chap but I could understand the staff's predicament as Hoot had a well-developed liking for the juice. He was a very ethnic Australian, who habitually drank his beer from cans and was seldom if ever strictly sober. His hand shook so much in the morning that he was incapable of signing letters until about 11.00 when his flask of lemonade, which was half gin, had taken effect. Then there was a window of about an hour during which he signed away like an author promoting a new book. Then he was into the lunchtime gin and lost to them so far as signing went for the rest of the day. Although his signing hand was a disability I never heard any other criticism of Hoot. His brain seemed to remain clear and no one ever had reason to question his decisions. He was an unthreatening Oliver Reed in RAAF uniform and everyone loved him.

At that time the Australians, certainly the RAAF, contributed a great deal to the theatre and they always had one AVM in post, either as SASO or as AOC Malaya, or 224 Group as it had become, so Hoot's sacking had political overtones and was hotly resented by the RAAF. To show their outrage and their faith in Hoot they appointed him to be AOC of their most prestigious command. I slunk in in his wake, taking little comfort from a dear friend's mystification as to why Air Ministry should have seen fit to replace one dipsomaniac with another.

In defiance of all its advantages of climate and geography, of large houses and numerous staff, Far East Air Force Headquarters was not a happy organisation in 1966 — Far East Air Forces as a whole may have been happy, almost certainly were — but the headquarters had problems. These really stemmed from Pete Wickham's discontent. He took the view, entirely justifiably I believe, that Air Ministry failed to recognise that he was on a war footing in the confrontation with Indonesia — his command was working seven days a week; they were working five. This had its culmination soon after I arrived and near the end of Pete Wickham's tour. A visit from Lord Shackleton, the Secretary of State for Air, had been mooted for some time with the dates constantly being changed. Pete Wickham's patience snapped and he sent a signal to Shackleton's PSO, a squadron leader, effectively saying I'm fighting a war out here, I'm tired of being messed around with constant changes of date, can't the S-of-S, for God's sake, make up his mind? By ill chance or the misplaced allegiance of the squadron leader, Shackleton read the signal in its original. He complained to CAS who in turn made his displeasure known to Pete Wickham.

So Shackleton's visit, when it finally took place, was never going to be a feast of geniality and goodwill, but it need not have been the exercise in studied insolence that it became. Pete Wickham did the absolute minimum that protocol demanded: he met him, he gave him accommodation in Air House, he gave a barbecue in his honour and he saw him off. When Shackleton visited Sarawak and North Borneo Pete flew himself by Meteor to Kuching to be on hand to meet him, but that was all. It was a demonstration of minimalist hospitality, and put the seal on Peter Wickham's future. He was posted to be Deputy Chief of Air Staff, a job on its last legs and about to be done away with, and as soon as he recognised that he had spoiled his chances of ever becoming CAS he resigned. It was a great loss to the Air Force. Peter Wickham-Barnes, as he originally was, was a man of outstanding ability. Entering the

Fairey Point House today — rear view.

Looking out from Fairey Point House.

service by way of a Halton apprenticeship, he had a fine war record and was recognised by his contemporaries as being of star quality. But he was at odds with the times. His wife was the daughter of J. B. Priestley and his father-in-law may have been influential in his becoming a socialist when to be one was virtually incompatible with being a senior commander. He hated the trappings of power and the social obligations of his appointment, and the wives of admirals and generals did not find him an agreeable dinner companion. And yet he had one of the best brains in the Air Force.

His replacement was Rochford Hughes whom I had never met. Far East Air Force, under his command, was extremely efficient, but every now and then he had some wild idea which could potentially have landed him in trouble. Instead of letting him get on with it I found myself opposing him in what I conceived to be his best interests. With hindsight this was a mistake on my part and put a strain on our relationship which, though amiable for the most part, was never warm.

One of Hughes' innovations, with which I agreed, was a major reorganisation of the command structure and of the senior staff posts. FEAF had the service's conventional three-prong organisation of a Senior Air Staff Officer, Air Officer Administration and Air Officer Engineering, all of them air vice-marshals. That was fine on the face of it but it had a unique flaw in that the AOA was also AOC of what was called the Far East Air Force Headquarters Group. This consisted of RAF Changi with the transport and maritime squadrons and one or two out-stations. The origins of this odd arrangement are not hard to guess at. With AHQ Malaya then being at Kuala Lumpur and with 230 Group/AHQ Singapore having no air staff, the formation of the HQ Group gave RAF Changi an AOC without the expense of an air staff as the AOA could call on the SASO and his staff. It was a cockeyed organisation which could, and did, give rise to anomalous situations. In spite of that it was workable, but what was quite unsatisfactory in the context of a war situation was the fact that AOC 224 Group, the old AHQ Malaya was now based in Singapore and had no control over the maritime and, more particularly, the transport squadrons. The simple solution was to put the Changi squadrons under command of 224 Group, and this was done. Hughes wanted to go further and introduce the army chief of staff system which he felt would be more efficient. His proposal was for a 2-star chief of staff and for SASO, AOA and AO Eng to revert to 1-star. This made a total of five stars against the original six and so appealed to the establishers. It also appealed to me as I stood to be Chief of Staff and would have a clear-cut position of authority when the air commander was away, which was quite frequently.

John Grandy, the C-in-C of the unified Far East Command, was not entirely convinced but viewed the proposal as a single-service matter and did not block it. And so in 1967 I ceased to be SASO and became Chief of Staff. This entailed moving from Sylvia's beloved No 8 down the hill to Fairey Point House, vacated by the homeward-bound AOA, Ian Spencer. Ian and his predecessors, at least in the last few years, had occupied Fairey Point House by virtue of their somewhat bogus status as an AOC. Now it fell to me as Chief of Staff. As its name implied, it was built right out on the Point with lawns immediately overlooking the Johore Straits and with private steps going down to the Changi officers' club with its large pool, almost always empty of people in the early morning. It was a large and imposing house with a carriage drive, and some fine trees including, outside our bedroom windows, some strikingly beautiful flames of the forest which were the home of golden orioles.

It had been built in the 1920s — and very well built, with the pantiles for its large roof being imported from Marseilles — to accommodate the Royal Artillery major commanding the coastal defence guns, and had now become the most prestigious house in Changi, a mark perhaps of the decline in standing of the armed forces. As it turned out I was to be the last but one RAF occupant, the last being Nigel Maynard who, as Air Commander, oversaw the final closedown of RAF establishments and our withdrawal from the Far East.

Somewhat against my better judgement — having always maintained that I would never return — I went back to Singapore in 1998. I stayed with Glynn Harrison and her husband Tony, a retired AVM and the British Aerospace representative in the Far East. Glynn was the daughter of Frank and Audrey Hyland-Smith who had succeeded us at No 8 Fairey Point and subsequently became our best friends in 1967 and 1968. In 1998 Audrey was staying with her daughter when I was invited out and, Tony having pulled a few strings, we all set off to explore what was left of RAF Changi and, in particular, to look at No 8 and at Fairey Point House. They were a sad sight. So far as we could ascertain they were being used, together with the other houses on the Point, as weekend retreats for senior civil servants of the Singapore government. Perhaps in deliberate contrast to the immaculate grooming and order of Singapore they had been left in a wild and overgrown state, only enough being done to the surrounds to render them habitable. In contrast again to the bright appearance of their green chicks and shutters whilst still in RAF occupation they presented, in 1998, a blind and dark appearance, the windows all having been glazed in tinted glass to allow full air-conditioning and to keep out the sunlight.

The author (centre) with Chris Foxley-Norris (left) and Ian Spencer (right).

But in 1967 that was all in the unimaginable future. Singapore was much as it had been twenty years earlier but change was beginning. The old civil airfield at Kallang had been replaced by a modern airport at Paya Lebar, a handful of luxury hotels had been built and more were building, roads were improved, land was being reclaimed at Bedok Corner and peasants were being forced out of their picturesque *kampongs*, where they typically kept ducks and a pig, into new high-rise flats. These concrete monsters were quite unsuited to the climate and quite foreign to their way of life. They must, before air-conditioning, have been hellish to live in. The suicide rate, always high, rocketed, with the unfortunates, mostly women, electing either to take caustic soda or to jump rather than endure these enforced conditions.

To go back a little to 1966. Confrontation with Indonesia ended in August whilst I was still SASO but not before I had seen a good deal more of Sarawak and North Borneo. From the air point of view, operations were similar to those carried out in the Malayan campaign — mainly troop-lift and air supply. Troop-lift was by modernised Whirlwinds with some naval Wessex; supply-drop was by Beverley and Argosy and communications within Borneo was by Pembroke and Twin Pioneer. The link with Singapore was maintained by Hastings and by Argosy. The aircraft involved were supplied and directed by two old friends of mine, Chris Foxley-Norris, AOC 224 Group, and Bill Pitt-Brown who, as COMAIRBOR with his headquarters in Labuan, was the Air Force commander on the spot.

It all worked very smoothly but I was surprised by how much in the troop-lift field seemed to have been forgotten in the six years between the two campaigns. There seemed to have been no proper consolidation and recording of the lessons learnt and techniques employed and, as a result, the Whirlwind squadrons spent some time re-inventing the wheel. On one of my visits to Labuan I flew to Brunei for talks with George Lea, then a major-general and COMLANDBOR. He was a charming man whom I had last dropped into the jungle in Pahang in June of 1957 when he was a lieutenant-colonel commanding the SAS in Malaya.

We regarded them as next door to insane as they dropped into the jungle canopy, which could be as much as 300ft above the ground, with a 60lb pack and reliant on abseiling to complete their journey. George became a good friend and I was to stay with him later in Washington where, as a lieutenant-general, he was head of the British Joint Staff Mission.

In December I went to Saigon and spent five days with the Air Attaché, Group Captain Mike Stanton. Mike was on very good terms with the Americans in spite of our refusal to support them in the Vietnam War and he flew me around the major airfields in the area of operations. Day one we spent at Da Nang, day two at Bien Hoa, day three at Can Tho where they let me fly a Huey gunship on the improvised range and loose off its cannons whilst the waist gunners sprayed all around giving a performance which combined the talents of a trapeze artist and a Chicago gangster. What the Foreign Office, which was highly nervous of any involvement with Vietnam, would have thought I hardly dare contemplate. So far as I know, I was the only RAF officer of air rank ever to visit Vietnam during the war. I suppose I must have got clearance from somewhere, but clearance or not it was a fascinating period rounded off on the final day by a visit to Vung Tau. I was received in a very friendly fashion wherever I went and felt particularly hypocritical on a South Vietnamese base where there was a welcoming arch reading 'Long Live Anglo-Vietnamese Friendship'.

There was no perception in December 1966 that the United States might lose the war but two things were already evident. The US Army had not profited from our hard-won experience in Malaya and were not securing the villages that they liberated from the Vietcong with the result that the village headman and some of the elders were all too often massacred on a return visit a few days later. The second was the political constraint being put on targeting. The subsequent spiralling effect of these two factors were in my opinion the main causes of the US defeat. The gradual turning away from the US on the part of the South Vietnamese was caused by fear of the Vietcong and could arguably have been prevented if the US Army had adopted a policy of protection which could have given the villagers confidence in their security. But the second factor lies squarely on the shoulders of the politicians. With targeting being done in Hawaii and in Washington and subject to crippling restrictions, the US Air Force commanders were fighting with one arm only. Had they been given a free hand, the Vietcong supply routes could have been cut, including the route from China, Hanoi could have been neutralised and the end result would almost certainly have been very different. Once politicians take a hand in the detailed direction of war the military are liable to end up in trouble. The Dardanelles in World War I is one example; Hitler's constant misdirection of his forces in World War II cost Germany dear, and some of Churchill's interventions, particularly in relation to commanders, were ill judged.

In the case of Vietnam, political control and interference led to disaster. Coming to more recent times in the UK, political rejection of military advice and Treasury insistence on the 'peace dividend' has left this country dangerously exposed and ludicrously overstretched. Even more recently the NATO bombing of former Yugoslavia, of which our Prime Minister was such an enthusiastic protagonist, will come to be regarded, I believe, as a political blunder. Almost certainly illegal, militarily ill conceived, largely ineffective in its primary purpose because of the political dictation of bombing altitude, it was little short of a politically generated disaster from start to finish which caused many thousands of additional and unnecessary deaths. We shall not know for another 30 years what military advice the Secretary of State for Defence and the Prime Minister received, but I would wager that it was advice which they saw fit to ignore or overrule.

Reverting to 1966, I got back from Saigon on 17 December, the same day that our son Peter arrived from the UK on a VC10. On the 18th the three of us set off for Gan, me to do the AOC's inspection and Sylvia and Peter to snorkel in the coral reef with its amazingly colourful marine life. It was a 9½-hour flight by Hastings and we ran through the Inter Tropical Front off northern Sumatra. We flew overnight and had bunks but it was so turbulent that Sylvia and Peter spent half the night sitting up. Peter has only just recently, at the age of 45, told me that he found that Hastings flight, coming on top of 18 hours in a VC10, pretty exhausting. Looking back I can well understand that, but at the time it simply didn't occur to me that a boy of 12 was capable of becoming tired.

Peter had a very good social life in the holidays, as indeed we all did. RAF Changi Golf Club and RAF Changi Yacht Club were on the doorstep, as was the officers' club with its large pool. We had a small locally built sloop called a Hong Lim, 14ft with a cubby up for'ard. It had an outboard engine, with which I could never come to terms, so we sailed without, a practice which caused our timing to be out when wind and tide connived against us. A safer and more reliable form of boating was a Sunday picnic on the C-in-C's launch to which we were invited from time to time, first by the Grandys and then by the Carvers. Hughie, who was a very keen and accomplished yachtsman, had an impressive yacht built in Hong Kong and, when she was complete, I had the use of the FEAF launch known as 'Lady Docker's Yacht'. We also had one or two exciting Naval occasions in HMS *Terror's* launch as the guests either of Roland Plugge, the captain of *Terror*, or of Teddy Gueritz — later to take over from me at Old Sarum — a born raconteur and holding the romantic-sounding post of Captain of the Fleet, Navy for SPSO (Senior Personnel Staff Officer).

In January 1967 I paid my first visit to Thailand where the air attaché, Group Captain Squires, had organised a first-rate programme which included a day trip to Chiang Mai to have lunch with the consul there and two nights at Siem Reap in Cambodia to explore Angkor Wat. The consul was a fascinating man, as was his house which stood unchanged from the last century, complete with the original cloth-type *punkah* and the *punkah wallah*, pulling it with his toe. In the garden was a life-size statue of Queen Victoria which, many years ago, had been brought in by elephant from northern Burma. At that time Chiang Mai was virtually an outpost, reachable by single-line railway. We saw no other Europeans during our day there but local hill tribesmen in their native costume were much in evidence.

Nothing very exciting in the way of visits took place in the first half of 1967 but I managed a good deal of flying particularly on the Andover. I added the Shackleton, the Argosy and the Hastings to my list of 'heavies' and flew the Lightning for the first time, recording Mach 1.6. The Whirlwind I flew frequently, flying myself to and from Phoenix Park for the C-in-C's twice weekly morning conference whenever Hughie was absent. One day, 30 August, is of interest in the light of subsequent events. I flew to Tengah by Whirlwind and then flew a Canberra captained by Wing Commander Mike Knight, later Air Marshal Sir Michael, to Labuan. From there I was taken bombing on Balambangan Range by Wing Commander Tony Skingsley, later Air Chief Marshal Sir Anthony, and I then flew a Canberra back to Tengah where I was met by the station commander Group Captain Phil Lagesen, later Air Marshal Sir Philip. I then flew myself back to Changi by Whirlwind. A day which held 5 hours 30 minutes Canberra and 35 minutes Whirlwind time in the company of three embryo air marshals was certainly unusual, though it seemed quite ordinary at the time.

In October I made a brief trip to Hong Kong, staying overnight with Birdie Wilson, the AOC. For reasons I cannot now remember I flew up by Britannia and back the following day by Caravelle via Bangkok. Six days later on the 19th I set off for Australia to call on the Air Staff in Canberra and to carry out an AOC's inspection of RAF units. I took an Andover, captained by Flight Lieutenant Sharples, though I did a good deal of the flying myself. Sylvia came, as did Dulcie Lagesen, Phil's wife, and we had a most fascinating 10 days.

The first night stop was at Bali where we stayed either in the Hilton or the Intercontinental. Whichever it was, the management had no feel for the surroundings — you might have woken up in any American city — and the food was equally uncompromising. In a very large à la carte menu there were only two native dishes, both of which I knew well. I ordered one of them and, when it came, it bore little resemblance to the authentic article. It was bland and lacking in chillies and essential spices, having presumably been modified to suit an imaginary standard Western palate. When I complained to a large figure, known predictably as the maître dee, and asked how it was that Balinese cooks could apparently not cook their own dishes, he indignantly informed me that he did not have Balinese or any other cooks but that he had chefs who were of outstanding reputation and came from the Bronx. We had all too little time there. Much of the island was probably still unspoilt but even then, over 30 years ago, the deadly virus of tourism was at work.

The next day we night-stopped at Darwin where many of the houses were still on stilts in the old colonial style. My main memories of Darwin are that a young kangaroo or wallaby fell passionately in love with Sylvia and that, very unexpectedly to me, the mayor was a Chinaman.

We flew on down the eastern seaboard, spending a night in Townsville. We overflew Sydney on our way to Canberra but it was unfortunately covered in cloud so we were unable to see either the bridge or the opera house. I had a friendly reception in Canberra in spite of the Hoot Gibson incident and the CAS provided a Mystère for us to fly on to Adelaide as the Andover was temporarily unserviceable. We stayed in the South Australia, then just like a good English country hotel of the 1930s with the maids in their white caps and aprons. My uncle by marriage was the resident vet at Roseworthy Agricultural College and he took us on an extended tour of the wineries of the Barossa Valley. Although Australian winemaking had not yet established itself within a country where Fosters had yet to feel its challenge it was clear that it had a great future, now realised.

My duties despatched, we set off back for Singapore with our first stop at Alice Springs. Flying up through central Australia, with virtually nothing between Adelaide and Darwin except Alice Springs, one became acutely aware of the vastness and challenge of that huge area. From 10,000ft the land seemed burnt dry by the sun; brown and scorched, it seemed inconceivable that it in fact supported thousands upon thousands of head of cattle. From Alice, very neat but failing to live up to romantic imaginings, we retraced our steps through Darwin and Bali, arriving at Changi with some Balinese carvings — not as good as the older ones — and a couple of nice Aboriginal paintings.

Previous to the Australian tour we had had a visit to Kuala Lumpur where Air Commodore Alasdair Steedman was CAS of the Royal Malaysian Air Force. Alasdair, later to become an air chief marshal and a good friend, was a perfectionist in all things and at the Presentation of Colours by the Agong, conducted with great dignity, he gave the main speech in Rajah Malay. Fluent in Bazaar Malay because of his appointment, he had gone to the considerable trouble of mastering its more formal variant especially for the royal occasion.

Early in 1968 the Argosys and Beverleys were replaced by Hercules, an aircraft that I came to like very much and to feel very at home in. I did a bit more Lightning flying, twice flying up to Butterworth with Ken Goodwin, the CO of 70 Squadron. On the first occasion the Australians let me fly one of their Mirages and, on the second, I flew a visiting Bomber Command Vulcan back to Tengah. Three other one-offs were the Belvedere, rather disappointing, and, by courtesy of the Army Air Corps, the Scout and the Sioux.

Sometime in July while Hughie was in hospital and I was acting Air Commander and we were reeling from the government decision to pull out from east of Suez, a delegation arrived led by a charmingly soft-spoken Welshman whom, I think, in retrospect, was later to become Lord Tonypandy. When I received him he informed me that, 'the captain on the bridge sends his greetings'. As the 'captain on the bridge' was Harold Wilson who, together with Denis Healey, had to be held responsible for the withdrawal decision, I found myself not only lacking in goodwill but asking whether the government really knew what it was doing. I took him to the window and made him look at what we could see of the well-ordered base and enquired whether they really meant to desert the Singaporeans against their wishes and before they could look after themselves; were they content to see the thousands of local workers who had served us so loyally just cast on the scrap heap, and so on. He was extremely uncomfortable and all but wringing his hands in embarrassment. He clearly shared our view but was unable to admit to it.

Officers in general had every sympathy with Lee Kuan Yew who felt betrayed and deserted. As guest of honour at Fairey Point Mess he had declaimed with great bitterness against the Wilson government, probably well aware that his hosts, although embarrassed by the vitriol of his denunciation, were privately wholeheartedly in agreement. We did not feel that the decision was wrong in principle and accepted that eventual withdrawal was inevitable, but we felt very strongly that the planned pull-out was grossly premature and militarily irresponsible. We would be leaving behind a Malaysia threatened by Indonesia and a Singapore threatened by both. And we would be sending a clear signal to the Russians who showed their understanding of events by immediately sailing a cruiser through the Straits of Malacca into the Indian Ocean.

Our disillusion and disgust was complete when Healey, who had proclaimed himself committed to an east of Suez policy, not only ordered the pull-out from Aden and the Persian Gulf but, when the Gulf States offered to pay to keep our forces in place, arrogantly dismissed their offer by saying that 'British soldiers are not mercenaries'. Healey, who had said he would resign over the F-111 issue, who had proclaimed himself wedded to an east of Suez strategy and who had changed his mind on both issues, had forfeited our trust. Those who knew the facts felt that we could no longer respect a secretary of state who seemed so lacking in integrity.

Life in 1968 carried on at a smart pace. The staff work was sad — making detailed plans for the pull-out. It was also an exceptional year in that it marked the 50th anniversary of the formation of the RAF and, indeed, of many of its squadrons. So there were many parades and fly pasts. The Air Commander naturally took the great bulk of these but, as an ex-CO, I took the 209 anniversary parade. Guest of honour was the West German Ambassador to Singapore, HE Baron von Richthofen, cousin of Manfred, the Red Baron, whom 209 had shot down in 1917. He and his wife were both charming and the squadron presented him with a model of a Fokker Triplane.

During our two and half years we took three local leaves, one in a hired VW Beetle up the then deserted east coast, staying in government rest houses, and two to the Cameron Highlands, staying first in the Sultan of Kedah's bungalow and the second time in a privately owned bungalow called Moonlight, next door to Starlight from which a prominent British merchant had disappeared, presumably abducted and murdered. No one knew quite why, but drugs were rumoured to be the cause.

Our one more far-reaching leave was to New Zealand and Fiji. Bill O'Brien, C-in-C Far East Fleet, gave Sylvia and I a lift in his Comet to Brisbane and on to Auckland. Arrived in Auckland, I attempted to hire a car only to find that my Singapore driving licence was unacceptable, even though it had only been issued on production of a British licence. The Licensing Office excused me a driving test but insisted that I take the written test, warning me that I needed a 100% result in order to pass. Just one error would destroy the whole of our holiday plans. This was serious stuff in a petty sort of way and I spent the best part of two hours making sure I would get it right. The answers were all numerical — which of these five numbers is correct? — and could immediately be checked by template. To my enormous relief I scored 100% and gained an on the spot New Zealand licence.

We spent six crowded days visiting two lots of old friends in North Island and in sightseeing and then flew civil from Auckland to Fiji, staying there a week before connecting with a FEAF Hercules on its way back to Changi from points east. Our first stop was Honiara in the Solomon Islands and we were served lunch in the air. Shortly before landing at Honiara a message came through asking Sylvia and I, much to our dismay, to lunch in the Residency. Protocol demanded that we accept and we did indeed have a delightful second lunch, eaten, I hope, with every appearance of relish.

I did the take-off from Honiara's rather short earth runway and the initial climb out took us immediately over Guadalcanal with its hulks of sunken ships testifying to the desperate fighting that had taken place there in 1942. We night-stopped at Port Moresby and on landing there and enquiring for a porter I was immediately reminded that we were on Australian administered territory by the reply of, 'You carry your own ports 'ere, mate.' And carry them I did in uncomfortably high temperature and humidity.

The flight back to Changi was long and became rather boring. We skirted West Irian where a few years previously Sylvia's brother had been the last Dutch governor of that same territory before the Indonesian takeover. He had formed a strong attachment to the Papuans and feared for their future under their new rulers. From there we avoided Indonesian Borneo and routed ourselves via British North Borneo, now Sabah, coasting in at Tawau and leaving Mount Kinabalu to starboard.

Within a few short months of that leave I became tour-expired and that terminal period passed in a flurry of last visits, including two AOC's Inspections, and farewell parties. It had been a memorable two and a half years which had seen our younger daughter's 21st at No 8 and her marriage from Fairey Point House. It had seen the end of Confrontation, the

Grandys go and the Carvers arrive and, dwarfing all else, the decision to leave Singapore. The consequences of that decision affected every activity and by October 1968 the atmosphere had become one of depression, with the end of an era only too clearly in view.

Sad though we were to go, it would perhaps have been even sadder to stay. On my last morning I called on Mike Carver to say goodbye, little knowing that in a few years I would be working with him again. At 21.10 we took-off for Gan in a UK-bound VC10. At Gan we transferred to a Britannia, landing at Nicosia in Cyprus the evening of the following day, there to be met by our daughter and her husband on leave from his Argosy squadron, then based on the station. We spent a hectic short leave with them, largely in Kyrenia, before flying on to Lyneham, again by Britannia.

One-time officers of the Khyber Rifles (or the JWE team in disguise?). *Crown Copyright*

13. Fourth Interval — Commandant Joint Warfare Establishment: November 1968–November 1970 Assistant Chief of Air Staff (Policy): May 1971–September 1972

My posting was to the Joint Warfare Establishment at Old Sarum as Commandant. I was initially not too thrilled as it seemed to my over-logical mind that the pull-out from east of Suez would spell the end of the British services operating together outside Europe and that in future we would all be part of an amorphous NATO. I did not foresee the Falklands War, then some 14 years in the future. I knew that Chris Foxley-Norris who, after a brief spell as an ACDS, had been sent to RAF Germany as Commander-in-Chief had tried to get me as his deputy but had been refused by the Air Secretary. I felt that I was being posted to a relative backwater which as often as not had proved to be a retiring job, but I was too hasty in my judgement.

It in fact turned out to be a fascinating appointment. I took over from Dick Keith-Jones, Major-General ex-Royal Horse Artillery, whom I had known in Malaya in the fifties. He left me a good team and a charming Georgian farmhouse, Ford House, just outside the airfield, but nicely tucked away with no other houses nearby.

I soon found out that though I was initially critical of JWE and of its *raison d'être*, I was very much in the minority. To some extent paid lip-service to and nodded to by the British armed forces, it was held in the very highest regard by foreigners. JWE was much in demand and lectured far and wide to Staff Colleges and other establishments of friendly nations who clearly thought the Establishment had a lot to offer.

In my two years I can recall JWE lecture visits, usually annually, to Canada, the US, Pakistan, Iran, Norway and Denmark and to US Marine Corps establishments at Quantico and Norfolk (Virginia). There was a special relationship between JWE and the US Marine Corps because JWE had absorbed the amphibious warfare know-how from Poole. As working proof of this common concern I had two Royal Marines on my staff together with a US Marine Corps lieutenant-colonel. Additionally I had Commandant to Commandant relations with my French equivalent and with the NATO Nuclear Weapons School at Oberammergau. Then there was the annual Shapex and the Paris Air Show. So from November 1968 until November 1970 I travelled a great deal. Some of the visits lasted no more than a week though the US ones, taking in a number of Establishments, ran for up to three weeks or so. The most popular visits were to Denmark and Norway as the hosts provided an aircraft and wives were included. On the Danish visit it was customary at the formal dinner to speak in verse, or as near as one could get to it. I remember only a very few lines. Towards the end of the first stanza in 1970 came

> Alone amidst this surging sea of change
> The Commandants still stand
> Rocklike unbending
> Calm and serene uncomprehending.

and later I set out our reinforcement commitments to the Northern Flank,

> Our minds made up our purpose clear
> We cannot see why you should fear
> Russian attack.
> If things come to extremes
> We'll send you one Commando Royal Marines
> One Commando at the best
> Northern Ireland claims the rest.

Nationally we were extremely busy. I was notionally responsible to VCDS through a Joint Warfare cell in MOD but in practice I was left to run the show on my own. Our bread and butter was the Joint Warfare Course which ran for two weeks virtually every month — there were 22 of them during my two years. We also ran Psyops courses, Junior Joint Warfare courses and FAC (Forward Air Controller) courses. Twice a year we had Joint Warfare Courses of foreign students only and there was an annual course for CENTO officers — a handful of Americans but mostly Pakistanis, Turks and Iranians.

There were lots of other seminars and closed discussion groups and we lectured at Camberley and Bracknell, but the three major events of the year were the Joint Services Staff College visit to us which lasted a week, the Joint Warfare Conference and the NATO Senior Officers Study Period. The JWC was for British officers of lieutenant-colonel to 2-star rank and was attended by about 100 officers, some 25 of them being air vice-marshals and major-generals in key appointments. The third occasion which was our showpiece and which attracted a wide audience was the NATO Senior Officers Study Period, held in December and also lasting a week. Deputy SACEUR routinely attended together with about 100 NATO officers, mostly from Central Region but with a fair smattering from AFNORTH and AFSOUTH. Many, particularly the more senior ones, brought their wives, and Sylvia was kept busy, as indeed she was most of the time, as there was a need for the Commandant to entertain a good deal.

Although I had not wanted the job, it grew on me and I became an enthusiastic proponent of 'Jointery', or more particularly of Army/Air co-operation. We were less concerned with the Royal Navy, our main involvement being with the assault ships and helicopter carriers which gave us an interface with the Royal Marines rather than with the Navy proper.

It was strange to be back at Old Sarum with very little apparently changed since 1939. It was still the same rolling grass airfield, the hangars were the same, the School of Army Co-op offices had become JWE offices and the only addition seemed to be the lecture hall. JWE was officially a lodger unit on the station but in reality JWE was Old Sarum as there was very little else there. The mess was from the 1930s or earlier, very solid and comfortable, and had a large and beautiful garden suitable for Beating Retreat on the last night of the NATO SOSP. Ford House was delightful apart from the heating system. Although central heating for married quarters was still over the horizon in 1968, the realisation had begun to dawn that commanders' houses, being generally on the large side, were as a consequence cold all the year round, and positively freezing in winter. And so we found that Ford House had Works and Bricks Mark 1 model heating installed. This was night storage heating of the period which, though better than nothing, was not a great success. It was quite expensive to run and was always running out of heat at critical moments, but the worst feature was the apparatus itself, vast white metallic boxes, not unlike large box freezers, which stood in the principal rooms and most definitely did not blend with the period furniture. The other oddity about Ford House was that it was haunted, but not malevolently, though I was pushed out of bed on one occasion, which was not the friendliest of gestures. Neither Sylvia nor I saw anything but our grandson aged 7 saw a man going up the stairs dressed, from his description, in Victorian clothes, complete with top hat. One of the guest bedrooms had a distinctive rather chilling atmosphere, rather like one of the bedrooms in the Old Parsonage at Frieth, which we had lived in when at Latimer, and we used it as little as possible.

The strangest thing that happened was after a guest night in the mess. I had two house guests, the family solicitor and an American general. Sylvia was in bed when she heard us come back at about one o'clock. She heard the front door open and then bang shut, loud and slightly alcoholic voices in the hall and then in the sitting room directly below our bedroom. She deduced that we were having a final drink and decided to join us in her dressing gown. She could still hear us from the top of the stairs, but when she came down the sitting room was empty. We in fact came back some half an hour later.

Ford House was our first experience of RAF house staff. We soon found that we had been spoilt by having German servants in one posting and Chinese servants in three. I assured Sylvia that now I was an AVM we would be bound to have first-rate staff. How ignorant I was. We had a nice local woman who did 90% of the cleaning and all the laundry, an efficient but extremely rude gardener who looked on the garden as his property to do with as he wished — we were just transients which, maddeningly, was true — and we had three uniformed staff. An elderly corporal steward who was amiable rather than alert, a pasty young corporal cook and a little rat of an SAC steward. The cook was fair as a cook, and in fact did well, but he was a great breaker of things and ruined a solid-fuel Aga and nearly burnt the house down by leaving it on full blast over a weekend when the house was empty. The SAC was slovenly, lazy and resembled a particularly shifty weasel. He also turned out to be a petty criminal. When Sylvia and I were on leave he brought his girlfriend into the house and occupied one of the guest bedrooms. He used my suitcases to carry things in and out, pilfered petty cash and, according to the daily woman, went through all our cupboards and chests of drawers. We were never quite sure what he had taken in addition to the money and some towels. He was duly charged and, as I being a lodger had no disciplinary powers, appeared before the station commander, Wing Commander John Whitlock, who as a flight lieutenant had been one of my navigators on 209 Squadron. I was confidently expecting that the SAC would get a month in the glasshouse, and was hoping that he would get three. He got seven days confined to camp. What yarn he spun and what came over Johnnie Whitlock I shall never know, but the insolent little swine was employed as a bar steward in the sergeants' mess within a month, and had the impertinence to grin at me when next I was invited there.

Flying from Old Sarum was rather limited. The only aircraft on strength was a Whirlwind which I flew occasionally and used when I had more distant visits such as Cranwell and Manby. We had a number of visits by American firms who thought we constituted a focal point for demonstrating their products which they believed had sales potential in the UK. Chief amongst these was the Huey Cobra gunship, then a very advanced and attractive aircraft. The demonstration was attended by Mick Martin, then AOC of 38 Group; by Terence McMeekin, GOC 3 Div; and by Major-General Pat Hobart, Chief of Staff Strategic

Command. Predictably the demonstration came to nought as neither the money nor the priorities were right at that time.

Then there was the giant Sikorsky heavy lift helicopter with its massive single rotor arm. Eventually it lost out to the twin rotor Chinook, still in service with the RAF and also demonstrated at Old Sarum. The third aircraft which was relatively cheap and unsophisticated but impressive in the ground attack role was the OV-10 Bronco. It was a good aeroplane but had no place in the NATO inventory.

I always tried to persuade the demonstration teams to let me fly their aircraft, albeit with a co-pilot. I was successful with the Sikorsky and the Chinook and flew as a passenger in the Bronco. I lost out on the Cobra but was allowed to fly one later in the States. My most exciting flight at JWE was from Linton as a passenger in the lead Gnat of the Red Arrows in April 1969.

We kept contact with the other Joint establishments and in particular with JATE, the Joint Air Transport Establishment, and JHDU, the Joint Helicopter Development Unit. Through the latter I was able to fly their little bubble canopy training aircraft Bell Augusta. Because JWE was the hub of so-called 'Jointery' and responsible for doctrine, we were invited to view at first hand anything which was actually or potentially of prime use in the land/air battle or in an opposed landing. Thus we were invited to Southampton for first-hand experience of the hovercraft and to Dunsfold to see the capability of the Harrier, then very much at the cutting edge of our business. We also visited Filton to inspect Concorde, for social rather than professional reasons.

Looking back on it, there was a wealth of talent at Old Sarum at that time. The key posts were rotational and on a strict timetable of two years virtually to the day. During my two years I had an Army officer, Brigadier Toby Caulfield, as Deputy Commandant; Group Captain Alec Blythe as Chief Instructor; and Captain Ian Robertson RN as Chief Doctrine and Development Officer. All were first rate in their jobs but, sadly, only Ian received further promotion. He became a rear-admiral after surviving a court martial resulting from HMS *Eagle* going aground when leaving port for the first time under his command, an occurrence which he compared to a cat losing eight of its nine lives in one go.

In June 1970 I led a small team to Singapore for Exercise Bersatu Padu. This exercise held on Healey's instructions was largely phoney and designed to promote a fiction, namely that the pull-out from Singapore and Malaya would not undermine their security as, if need be, we could readily return. Five nations were involved — Australia, New Zealand, Malaysia, Singapore and the United Kingdom — and the aim of Bersatu Padu was stated as, 'To train and exercise combined forces of the five nations under the conditions likely to prevail after the United Kingdom withdrawal and to practise the setting up of an organisation such as will be necessary to introduce, support and train forces from outside the Theatre.'

Bersatu Padu was a great success, if one discounted all the artificialities. Very limited forces were flown in from the UK and given time to acclimatise and train in jungle warfare, something that would not have happened in an emergency. The bulk of the units concerned, together with their logistic support, were in-theatre and their arrival was merely simulated as were naval reinforcements, represented by ships already on the spot. The exercise clearly failed to demonstrate what it set out to do but was nevertheless valuable to all those units taking part. I took passage in HMS *Bulwark* and witnessed a Royal Marine helicopter assault on the east coast of Malaysia — all good *Boys' Own* stuff that I thoroughly enjoyed.

Another incident towards the end of my time as Commandant which lurks uneasily in my memory concerned a lecture tour to Iran. On two previous occasions we had flown to Teheran with a refuelling stop at Rome. On this occasion in 1970, sitting in Heathrow at some uncivilised hour, the lieutenant-colonel in charge of the administrative arrangements came up and told me that we were routed not via Rome but via Moscow. I told him in probably colourful language to push off and not to try jokes so early in the morning. He duly retreated but soon after take-off it became apparent that we were, owing to the culpable idiocy of someone in Movements staff, indeed bound for Moscow. Our passports described us as civilians and there could have been a nasty diplomatic incident had the Russians so decided. I kept my staff on board the aircraft and we were duly cleaned around by the *babushkas*, the little women tied up in the middle by string, and were mercifully allowed to depart, unarrested and uninterrogated.

I had known when taking up the appointment that my tenure would be for two years, and I indeed handed over to Teddy Gueritz dead on time in late November 1970. I had had every confidence that my next appointment would be as a 3-star and had every hope of a major command. There were two falling vacant at the right time — Chris Foxley-Norris would be leaving Germany and Bob Hodges would be leaving Air Support Command at Upavon. I had heard it strongly rumoured that I was to get Germany, and this would have made good sense because of my Tactical background, my having worked closely with the army in a number of appointments, and because I had commanded Geilenkirchen and was familiar with the command set-up. It would also have been explained why the Air Secretary had refused to let Chris have me as his deputy. Furthermore, it would follow a logical progression. I had consistently been promoted at the right age to achieve high rank — wing commander at 31, group captain at 37, air commodore at 43 and air vice-marshal at 45 — now, just 50, I was the right age to become a C-in-C.

But it was not to be. At the critical moment John Grandy retired and Denis Spotswood succeeded him as CAS. I had never met Spotswood but, more to the point, he had never met me and I found myself literally out of a job. I never learnt who the other AVM was to fall off the Grandy plot but suspect that it was Gerry Wade. All that any of us knew was that Spots, on taking over as CAS, had exercised his prerogative to adjust the promotion list to include Mick Martin, of Möhne Dam fame, and Harry Burton. So Mick and Harry, who had already received posting notices to AVM appointments, found themselves suddenly elevated, Mick to Germany and Harry to Air Support Command. Although both were senior to me as AVMs I found it a very bitter pill to swallow, the more so as it was so unexpected. The whole fabric of my life seemed suddenly to have fallen apart — from relatively golden boy to unemployed was hard to take.

My first need was to establish some parameters, some fixed points on which I could rely. The first of these was how long I was going to be unemployed, the second what my next appointment would be, and I went to see Tubby Clayton, the Air Secretary. The first answer was up to six months, the answer to the second was Assistant Chief of Air Staff (Policy), a key appointment but yet another 2-star job. Depending on how long I stayed as ACAS (Pol) I would have been at least seven years as an AVM and in danger of toppling off the top of the list. So I asked Tubby if I could expect a 3-star job to follow. When he said that it would depend on how I got on with VCAS, who was Splinters Smallwood and not much senior to me anyway, I very nearly threw my hand in.

But, of course, I did not want to go. I had no doubt I could find a civilian job, and was arrogant enough to think it would pay a good deal more than an AVM's pay, but I could not imagine life outside the service which had been all I had known, or ever wanted to know. So, perhaps inevitably, I decided to stay and make the best of it. Those few months would be the only time Sylvia and I had had more than three weeks off at a stretch and the prospect, if not the cause of it, was not displeasing. We had for some time been toying with the idea of buying a house and had looked at a few. We now began to look in earnest. Having obtained an undertaking from the postings staff that I had some months clear, and would not be hauled in on some odd job or other, we settled on a house in the Cotswolds and bought it in time to move in direct from Old Sarum.

It was quite exciting as we were moving literally onto bare boards and camp beds. We had little furniture of our own and what we had was in store. We moved out of Ford House on 27 November and on 11 December, two weeks to the day, I was rung by P Staff to say that I was to head up a team charged with looking into our relations with industry in the procurement field and with making recommendations for improving matters. I reminded them of their undertaking that I would be left undisturbed, told them that men were coming to lay carpets in three days' time and said that I was simply not prepared to abandon my wife and move to London in these circumstances. They said that they were sorry but this important requirement had unexpectedly arisen, and there it was. I told them that I knew little about procurement and even less about industry and in any event had no intention of taking the job on. If they insisted, I would resign, and they were welcome to tell the Air Secretary that. I heard no more and we were not disturbed again as we went through all the business of setting up house for the first time.

Things began to move rather more quickly than I had expected and, towards the end of March 1971, I was called in for a briefing by the then ACAS (Pol) Alasdair Steedman, who had been CAS of the Royal Malaysian Air Force. As he was four years junior to me and I already knew everything there was to know about ACAS (Pol)'s job from having been DASB and, on occasion, acting ACAS (Pol), this did nothing to smooth my ruffled feathers. I did, however, brighten at the prospect of an overseas visit before taking up my new appointment which was to be on 1 May, just over five months after leaving Ford House. The visit was to Cyprus and Singapore and, more interestingly, to Oman. Singapore was very sad, with things the same and yet so very different, everything moving inexorably towards the end. I think Brian Burnett was still there as the tri-service commander but Nigel Maynard as Commander FEAF as an AVM had moved into Fairey Point House. I stayed there with him and Daphne and found it odd to be back in such changed circumstances.

The visit to Oman I found fascinating, never having been there before, and I loved the atmosphere at Masirah and particularly at Salalah where it was the nearest thing to World War II. Cyprus was another matter. My visit was primarily to Akrotiri, then commanded by Air Commodore John Stacey, later to be C-in-C Germany as Air Marshal Sir John and, briefly, to follow me at AFCENT. I had never met John Stacey before, although I had heard of him, and found him, and continued to find him throughout the years, somewhat unusual. Part of my programme was to view the base by helicopter, one would have thought a fairly low key item. However, as the aircraft was a Whirlwind and one was invited to sit in the open doorway with one's legs dangling over the abyss and not secured in any way, it was the equivalent of 'chicken' or 'last across the road'. You either had to state firmly that this was idiocy and you would have no part of it, or go ahead, terrified, trying to burrow into the metal of the Whirlwind's deck with the reverse side of one's wrists. The pilot must have been fully aware of his base commander's idiosyncrasies, and even more of the undesirability of having two dead air officers on his hands, because his turns to starboard were very gentle.

April 26 came and I found myself once more back at work and at one of the busiest jobs that the Air Force had at that time. Now that all power has moved to the centre and CAS is served solely by one ACAS it may seem hard to realise and to remember that at one time there had been a DCAS, a VCAS and no less than six ACAS. In 1971 this had reduced to VCAS and four ACAS, of whom Pol was the doyen and *primus inter pares*. I had my first meeting with Spotswood, who had changed my life so drastically, and with whom I was to work closely for the next eighteen months. I think he may have had an inkling of the degree of disturbance he had wrought because he muttered something about being sorry that I was going to have to wait. What he did not know and I did not know either was that in the broader scheme of things he had probably done me a good turn by causing me to buy a house before house prices took-off, as they did in 1972. In no time the value of my house had doubled and I eventually sold it at six times the purchase price.

Things were a bit edgy at first as I felt sore at effectively having been demoted and put to work on a level with people who had been up to four years junior to me and whom, in many cases, I had not even met before. Splinters, whom I liked immensely, was totally insensitive on this point and assumed that David Evans, as ACAS (Ops), with whom I would have to work closely, and whose office opened on to mine, was a contemporary and an old friend. I had to inform him rather sniffily that I hardly knew David as he was so much junior to me.

Gradually my soreness wore off as I came to accept that from now on I had a totally new lot of contemporaries, and that those who had been much my juniors were now my peers. There were some very good people on the staff. Alan Davies, who was Director of Plans, had been in post for some years and was calm, intelligent and very reliable. He was to succeed me as ACAS (Pol) and subsequently to make 3-star. DASB was Group Captain Peter Terry, the post having been down-ranked and brought under ACAS (Pol). He was soon made acting air commodore and brought in to be Director of Forward Policy, a new post created by Spotswood. He was later to become Air Chief Marshal and Deputy Supreme Allied Commander Europe and, ultimately, Governor of Gibraltar. He was succeeded as DASB by Group Captain Peter Harding, later to become CAS and finally CDS. When, near the end of my time in post, Alan Davies was due to go, I was offered Air Commodore Keith Williamson to replace him. I had never met Keith and knew nothing about him except that according to P Staff he had never served in the Ministry. I took the view that this would prove a great handicap and was reluctant to accept him, only being persuaded to give him a try by P Staff's insistence that he was absolutely first rate. He took the job in his stride and ultimately went on to become CAS. So we were certainly not lacking in talent.

I soon became immersed in the job which I knew of old to be a fascinating one in which you knew everything that was going on and were closely involved in whatever issues were concerning the Chiefs of Staff at any given time. The Navy and the Air Force were as usual often in disagreement and most of the problems were at least initially tackled in what was known as the 2-star Policy Group. This was chaired by ACDS (Pol) who was Major-General David Fraser and my Navy equivalent was ACNS (P), Henry Leach, who subsequently succeeded me as VCDS and went on to become First Sea Lord. Henry and I got on well personally but were seldom able to agree in what were often bruising and frustrating meetings. We kept our sanity and our personal relationship intact by always having a drink afterwards, either in his office or in mine.

The job was not what would now be called 'user-friendly', certainly as to working hours. There were not the very late DASB nights but it was 19.00 or 19.30 almost every night. There was little travelling, in fact I had only two overseas breaks of which one was to Washington with VCAS. The other was to Teheran where I was sent as head of a small team to try unsuccessfully to sell a grandiose mobile headquarters to the Iranians.

I came to work very closely with Splinters, stood in for him when he was away, usually accompanied him when he called on CAS and was present at most of his meetings with VCNS who at that time was Terry Lewin, whom I had known in Singapore when he was a captain commanding HMS *Hermes*. I had on occasion to take on the odd lecture in his place and lectured in my own right to Bracknell, Manby and the Senior Officers War Course at Greenwich. In July 1971 I had an experience which I was not anxious to repeat, that of appearing with AUS (AS) in front of the Defence Select Committee. They kept us waiting in what I considered a discourteous fashion and gave us a somewhat uncomfortable time. I cannot remember the substance of the meeting but David Owen, then an unknown back-bencher, asked particularly penetrating questions.

Another unique experience which came much later, on 30 January 1972 to be precise, was the laying up of the Queen's Colour for the Far East Air Force at St Clement Danes. I had spent nearly 10 years of my life in FEAF and although I had long since come to terms with the pull-out from east of Suez it was still a uniquely poignant and sad occasion. It fell to Nigel Maynard as the last commander to hand the colour to the Chaplain-in-Chief with the sombre words: 'Venerable Sir, I ask you to receive this Queen's Colour for the Far East Air Force for safe lodging in the House of God until such time as it shall pass to dust like those whose courage and devotion are enshrined in its history.'

The first year passed quickly with frequent meetings on the long-term costings with which I was only too familiar from my DD Plans days and, quite apart from endless single-service and joint staff meetings, more esoteric meetings with the Americans, the Australians and New Zealanders, the Canadians and on one occasion the French.

After almost exactly a year, when I had come to understand that I was likely to replace Splinters as Vice-Chief, I was summoned by CAS who told me he was going to send me to Turkey as the UK representative in CENTO. This was shattering news, except that it meant promotion to 3-star. This was the second time that Spots had intervened traumatically in my life; the first occasion had cost me over 18 months' seniority, and now he was proposing to banish me to a backwater.

I knew that Derek Hodgkinson was coming to the end of his time as C-in-C Cyprus and I asked Spots if I could not go there instead. He said no, he was sending me to Turkey for a short rest as he wanted me back in Whitehall as VCAS in about a year's time. He knew there was very little work attached to the post and urged me to make the most of the opportunity to get out and see the country. He didn't actually use the word but he was in effect telling me to go and have a good holiday. I was extremely frustrated and felt like a child drumming its heels on the nursery floor. I could see that my chances of holding a major command had become extremely slim if I was slotted to return to Whitehall after Turkey. However, there was precisely nothing to be done but make the best of it.

The annual CENTO visit to London was taking place on 11–18 May and we gave Jimmy Stack, who I was replacing in the CENTO job, and his wife Jennie lunch at Martinez — then a very much better restaurant than it is now — on the 17th to chat to them and get some idea of the job. They suggested that it might be a good thing, from the domestic side in particular, if we were to go and stay with them for a few days as and when opportunity offered. This turned out in the event to be 7–11 July but, before that two things happened: on Her Majesty's Official Birthday I was appointed KCB whilst still in the rank of AVM, and on 1 July, which I spent at Henley drinking Pimms, I was promoted to Air Marshal.

I did not hand over as ACAS (Pol) until mid-September, so for two and a half months my promotion placed me in a curious situation, made easier of course by the fact that we wore mufti. By the first week of August my appointment had been notified to the CENTO countries, and I paid calls on the Turkish Chargé D'Affaires, the Pakistani Ambassador, the Iranian Ambassador and the American Chargé D'Affaires. Later, in early October, I had an Audience of Her Majesty.

The second half of September and the first week of October were spent on packing and in general preparation for departure, including buying a new car. It was then that some of the hidden advantages of the appointment became apparent. Because I would be working from the British Embassy the post had diplomatic status and I was able to claim disturbance allowance at diplomatic rates. I knew from my experiences at Geneva that the treatment of diplomats and serving officers, however much overseas service the latter might have, was totally inequitable. The Diplomatic effectively made their own rules and, as a generalisation, were said to expect to live on their allowances, and bank their pay. Serving officers on the other hand had difficulty in keeping out of the red unless they had a private income. This matter of disturbance allowance nicely illustrates the difference, and worked to my unexpected and huge advantage. The RAF allowance in 1972 was a flat £80; the Diplomatic was six months advance of pay, interest free, repayable over one year. An air marshal's pay was about £8,000 so I suddenly found myself with a windfall of £4,000, a huge sum in those days, and the difference did not stop there; the discount on motor cars was very much more if you were a diplomat, and I was able to buy a BMW 2500 — the forebear of the present 525i — at two-thirds the market price or, in round terms, for £2,000 rather than £3,000. I find these figures quite interesting, representing as they do a depreciation of the currency by a multiple roughly of 10 over little more than 25 years, as today an air marshal's pay is roughly £80,000 and a BMW 525i roughly £30,000. I settled for a beautiful BMW in British Racing Green to be delivered to Air House Germany where we would stay a night with Mick and Wendy Martin on our way to Turkey.

14. CENTO — First and Only Tour: November 1972–January 1974 UK Permanent Military Deputy to the Central Treaty Organisation

We spent our last night in England at the RAF Club on 9 October and travelled to The Hague the next day via Harwich and the Hook of Holland. There we stayed overnight with Sylvia's elder sister and her husband and all our Dutch relations gathered for a party and to wish us bon voyage. The next day we took the train to Roermond and were made welcome at Air House. After, I think, two nights with Mick and Wendy we set off for Munich for the car's first servicing at 800 miles. It had been delivered from Munich in the first instance, so the mileage of 400 miles each way was exact.

The next day, restricted in speed by running-in requirements, we night-stopped somewhere north of Rome having crossed into Italy over the Brenner. From there, through Rome and Naples we branched off through Sorrento to the Amalfi coast and spent four nights in a charming hotel high above Positano.

From there we drove across southern Italy on lonely, largely deserted roads to Brindisi where we embarked on the small ship that would take us to Izmir. We were two nights on board, arriving in port to be met by the US Air Force general who was the local NATO commander. He and his staff eased us through the customs and immigration procedures, which would otherwise almost certainly have taken hours.

After a night in Izmir we set off on a somewhat adventurous journey, adventurous because we had nothing but a map, Fodors Guide, a phrase book and a dictionary. In 1972 unfortunately there was no such thing as a Turkish language cassette. Turkish is virtually a unique language. The Mongol hordes swept in in three separate thrusts ending up in Turkey, Hungary and Finland, and Hungarian and Finnish apparently have some common words with Turkish, but for most people this is not a lot of help, and neither is a knowledge of French or Latin. Until we arrived in Ankara some three weeks later we met no one who spoke anything but Turkish with the result that, to survive, we had to try and get along from day one in pidgin Turkish to the amusement and puzzlement of our hosts.

Driving south from Izmir we had lunch in a fairly primitive restaurant in Kusadasi which had excellent but expensive lobster, the best meal we were to have on our journey. From Kusadasi we drove to Pamukkale passing Ephesus on the way. The sign Efes was to become familiar as we passed it on a number of occasions whilst in Turkey. Each time we passed we promised ourselves that we would 'do' Ephesus next time, just as I used to tell myself when I was a frequent visitor to Hong Kong that I would visit Macao next time. Inevitably you run out of 'next times' and so we returned to the UK, to our great and lasting shame, 'Failed Ephesus'.

Pamukkale is a strange place with its hot spring and large pools of hot water and its 300ft waterfall in which part of the water has become petrified, forming bright white stalactites. We stayed in one of the motels that have been built there hard by the ruins of Hierapolis founded in 190BC and destroyed by earthquake in 1334. Parts still stand, including the theatre which it is claimed is unrivalled except perhaps by those at Orange or at Aspendos on Turkey's south coast.

Next day we drove south to Antalya, a charming city with many Greco-Roman remains including an arch built to commemorate the visit of the Emperor Hadrian in AD130. From there we visited Aspendos and drove the length of the south coast to Silifke, just short of Mersin. I have seen photographs of that coast as it is today, largely ruined and resembling the Mediterranean coast of Spain, but in 1972 it was totally undeveloped and was beautiful, particularly east of Alanya where the road becomes a corniche high above the sea with the coast of Cyprus just visible to the south.

At Silifke we found a campsite, beautifully situated right on the sea and, in November, virtually deserted. There we pitched our tent until it was time to leave for Ankara. The weather was lovely, warm and sunny, and the food was good. We had already become accustomed to the Turkish breakfast of olives, goat's cheese, jam and the wonderful bread called *ekmek*, handbaked in clay ovens three times a day, like the old-style French baguette, but even better. There was fruit in abundance, eggs, fish, salads and the inevitable frites. Meat in Turkey at that time was virtually inedible, consisting as it did of scraggy sheep or goat. The so-called *biftek* was an illusion, a product of myth or fancy, bearing no resemblance to its European counterpart. It was a beautiful, relaxed introduction to a wonderful country that we were to come to love. I soon came to realise that Spots, however much he might have impaired my long-term career prospects, had indeed done us a good turn by opening the door to this magical land.

Arrived in Ankara we settled quickly into the flat, or more properly two flats knocked into one, in Cankaya. This was the smart part of Ankara high up above the smog line and an area largely occupied by diplomats. The first few days were taken up by official calls, laying a wreath on Atatürk's memorial and getting to know the senior Brits. I had a very adequate office in the Embassy and a first-rate PSO in Lieutenant-Colonel Brian Pickford who together with David McTeer, my ADC, looked after me admirably.

The Central Treaty Organisation, originally formed in Baghdad, moved to Ankara after the revolution in Iraq. Its purpose was to demonstrate the solidarity of Pakistan, Iran and Turkey in their stance against the Soviet Union and the determination of the West, in particular the United States and the United Kingdom, to stand alongside them as a deterrent to any Soviet attack in that theatre. It was a paper treaty with no troops committed or even earmarked but the local countries attached great importance to its symbolism and to its perceived signal to the Soviets.

It had a Secretary-General, Nasir Assar, who was an Iranian career diplomat, a sizeable five-nation staff engaged in drawing up contingency plans and it had the five Permanent Military Deputies, all of 3-star rank. What the organisation lacked in teeth it did its best to make up for by maintaining a high profile throughout the region, and in this of course the PMDs were the leading players.

There was a major visit to each of the five countries each year and lesser visits to Iran and to various Army and Air Force Commands within Turkey, and also to the Turkish and Iranian navies. Additional to these regional visits we went each year to the Central and Southern regions of NATO. The Central region visit was to the US Army headquarters and the AFSOUTH visit was to the headquarters of CINCSOUTH at Naples. The most interesting part of the latter visit was being flown onto the USS *Forrestal*, at that time the flagship of the US Sixth Fleet. Apart from the annual UK visit, and the Pakistan visit when we travelled by Comet, we were flown everywhere in US Air Force transport aircraft fitted to VIP standard. Our wives had their part to play in keeping up the high profile and travelled with us on all the major visits. In keeping with this we stayed in the best hotels and, almost certainly counter-productive, we had luxury limousines and within the region a large motorcycle escort. In Teheran and in Karachi these police were quite ruthless and any traffic that did not immediately give way at the sound of our sirens was literally forced into the ditch to allow us to sweep past at high speed.

Getting to know the other PMDs and their wives was naturally a task which had to be tackled immediately and there was a flurry of cross-entertaining in which national characteristics were noticeable. The Turks never invited foreigners to their homes, only close Turkish friends being admitted, so Ihsan Göksel the Turkish PMD entertained in one or other of the Army messes. He followed the pattern set by the US PMD Earle Hedlund, a US Air Force ex-P-38 Lightning pilot, in giving drinks parties with substantial and difficult to manage food known as heavy hors d'oeuvres. The Iranian PMD, Mansoor Afkhami was the doyen when I arrived. He was an aristocratic and fastidious cavalry officer who was close to the Shah, and he and his wife favoured elegant dinners for small numbers, as did Akbar Khan the Pakistani PMD and his wife. Sylvia and I compromised by mixing largish drinks parties with small dinners and lunches. At the drinks parties the Turkish, Pakistani and Iranian women tended to herd together at one end of the room leaving the men at the other. At our

The PMDs and Chief of Staff with the Nato Supreme Allied Commander Europe (SACEUR), General Goodpaster.

first large party, in an attempt to get some of them to overcome what I thought was their shyness, I advanced into this female mass beaming jollity and goodwill. It was not amongst my most successful manoeuvres, in fact a lone wolf might have been received more warmly, and certainly with greater understanding, by a flock of sheep.

Our other early attempt at high-speed mixing, which was risky but in the event proved a success, consisted of entertaining the PMDs and their wives to Christmas lunch. Akbar, having served with an Indian Army regiment prewar as a Viceroy's Commissioned Officer, knew the form but to the others it was a divine mystery as to why the birth of Christ should be celebrated with crackers and paper hats and, to their palate, the no doubt barely edible but essential ingredient of the feast, the Christmas pudding.

Turkey in 1972 was calm on the surface but it was a volatile country, easily roused to violence. The modern forward-looking Turkey, the member of NATO and suitor of the European Union, sat uneasily with the proponents of the old religion and the old ways. The mullahs were powerful and had resisted the Atatürk reforms and in country districts Arabic script and Arabic numerals, theoretically no longer in use, were the norm. And with the Kurds virtually in revolt southeastern Turkey was a no-go area to foreigners. Any Turkish general ran some risk of assassination, and Ihsan Göksel carried a sub-machine gun in his staff car. The rest of us were, I think, perceived as possible kidnap victims. All PMDs had an army guard on their flat and we were issued with LS tear gas sprays guaranteed to cause temporary blindness. There was a Judas hole in the door of our flat, something which was to be repeated in London when, as VCDS, I was on the IRA hit list. It is a device that has never captured my enthusiasm as its use seems to me to be an invitation to the caller to shoot you through the eye.

All the PMDs spoke good English but, with the obvious exception of Elly Hedlund, this was not true of their wives. The Begum Khan, though middle aged, was only recently out of *purdah* and this was the first time she had left Pakistan. Named Zahoor, she was a sweet, shy person with little English, whose life had been blighted by the death of her son, a tank commander, on the last day of the Indo-Pakistan War. Betul Göksel was the mirror image of Ishan, short and round with a *koja popo* — a big bottom. Somewhat more serious than her husband, who had an infectious laugh and was always in high good humour, she was strong willed and probably managed Ihsan without him realising it. Madame Afkhami, whose given name maddeningly escapes me, was quintessentially feminine and fluttery and had probably been pampered and cherished from childhood without becoming spoilt. She was very wealthy and had brought vast estates to Mansoor on their marriage. Eleanor Hedlund, or Elly as she was known, was I believe from the east coast and a very cheerful, charming, family-orientated woman. Sylvia got on well with them all, particularly Zahoor, who formed a strong attachment to her.

The men were all easy to get on with. Earle was very sociable, fairly heavily into the juice in the form of Bloody Marys in the almost certainly vain hope that Elly would mistake them for tomato juice. He was a great enthusiast in all things, particularly goose and duck hunting at which he was an expert. Ihsan, as the host PMD, had probably been selected for his 'Jolly Good Fellow' qualities, and his sunny disposition was certainly a great asset to the group as a whole. Mansoor was highly strung, something of a worrier, but had great charm. Although he was a devout man the real object of his worship was the Shah who in Mansoor's view was a truly godlike figure. Although we saw Bhutto in Pakistan and saw General Sancar, who as Chief of the Turkish General Staff was probably the most powerful man in Turkey, many times, we unfortunately never met the Shah, so I was unable to form an opinion at first hand. And then there was Akbar Khan who was held by British Intelligence as the man most likely to take over from Bhutto in the event of an Army coup. He was an outstanding man who had a love-hate relationship with the British, the hate losing out quite heavily. The love stemmed from his days as a subaltern in the Indian Army, days which had bequeathed him an English sense of humour and an expertise at bridge.

Had we been able to foretell the future we would have been horrified at the fate in store for three of our group who we came to look on as friends. Ihsan was involved in an horrific car crash which left him permanently disabled, Akbar was banished to London as Ambassador when General Zia seized power and was shortly afterwards found dead at his desk, an unlikely and suspicious end for an exceptionally fit man of 58. Mansoor paid with his life for his loyalty to the Shah. He was shot by firing squad. I hope and believe that history will revile President Carter for his betrayal of the Shah and will be equally severe on the French for their harbouring Ayatollah Khomeini in the hopes of commercial advantage. Although the Shah's rule was autocratic and his officials corrupt huge improvements had none the less been made in the lot of even the poorest; now they are struggling once again to emerge from the dark ages. But in 1972 the dark fate that was to overtake Iran and the consequent break-up of CENTO were still some seven years ahead.

It would be tedious and repetitious to record all our visits in detail but some of them had an air of romance about them. In Iran we were frequent visitors to Isfahan and Shiraz; we saw Persepolis, drank pomegranate juice and were amazed at the silken pavilions standing in the desert as mute evidence of the Shah's celebration of the 2,000th anniversary of Persia's glorious past. North of Teheran we disported ourselves in the waters of the Caspian Sea and made a somewhat cursory inspection of sturgeons blast-frozen at minus 65 degrees. What remains in my memory as being most remarkable about that visit was the astonishing fact that north of the Elburz mountains leading down to the southern shores of the Caspian is a rice growing area, mile after mile of *padi* looking for all the world like the Far East.

Pakistan too had much to offer: the beauty of Lahore, the unchanging Britishness of Peshawar, and of the Khyber Rifles' mess, the 'arms factory' at Darra near the Khyber Pass where they make guns out of scrap metal. There you can buy a pair of 'Purdeys', indistinguishable from the real thing, complete with proof mark. You can also, if you care to risk having your hand blown off, buy a single shot .25 fetchingly disguised as a fountain pen. I had visited this area before when Commandant of JWE and on that occasion my team and I had lunch in the old Khyber Rifles' mess and had been feasted by the local Pathans, an experience to be treasured rather than repeated. Their leader, a terrifying-looking man, demanded to know apparently in all seriousness when the British were going to come back and help them sweep those bloody Indians into the sea. He looked as though he could have made a good start at it single-handed. By comparison General Tikka Khan, the so-called 'Butcher of Bangladesh', whom we got to know quite well, looked an absolute pussy cat.

128

In Turkey itself, apart from official visits, I made it my business to see as much of the country as possible. By contrast to our attachés, who were confined to a 50-kilometre radius of Ankara other than by invitation, no restrictions were placed on my travelling, though, had I tried to go to the extreme southeast in the heart of Kurdish country, I believe I would have been intercepted and turned back for my own safety. Apart from the heavy schedule of visits and the monthly PMD's meeting I found the workload extremely light and felt able with a good conscience to delegate a large part of it to Brian Pickford. This left a good deal of time for travelling and exploring. Apart from the BMW I had a 3-litre Rover staff car and a long-wheelbase Land Rover, essential for the more adventurous off-piste journeys. We did many thousands of miles in the latter and saw a great deal of the more interesting and most beautiful parts of Turkey.

Apart from the wealth and diversity of architecture, the ruins of different periods, most of them pre-dating Christianity, we saw many strange sights: peasants ploughing with oxen and wooden plough as in Biblical times; nomadic herdsmen with their goatskin tents and heavily veiled women; Whirling Dervishes; Anatolian sheepdogs with spiked metal collars to protect them against wolves, bigger and fiercer than any European dog. On one occasion when Brian Pickford and I were out duck shooting a shepherd with a warped sense of humour set two of these animals on us, only whistling the recall signal at the last moment and bringing the dogs to a skidding halt within a few yards of us.

Two sights in particular had a lasting and profound effect: the stone heads of the Comagenes and the underground city near Nevsçehir. Some 250 miles southeast of Ankara, Nemruth Dagi rises to 8,205ft. I had difficulty in coaxing the Land Rover to the summit as the engine kept cutting out but it was worth the effort. On the very top stands a 100ft mound of small stones reputed to be the burial place of Antiochus I (69–34BC). This mound is surrounded by stone statues about 30ft tall which due to weather, lightning and earthquake have lost their heads over the centuries, though these have been set upright and grouped together, each standing some 10ft high. Adiyaman, at the foot of the mountain, is remote enough but at the summit that remoteness is accentuated to the point of eeriness.

In central Anatolia near the strange churches of Göreme hollowed out of the soft stone are two underground cities. We visited the one just south of Nevsçehir at Kaymakli. This is 250ft deep, with eight floors each designed to hold 200 people. A central airshaft gives perfect ventilation and by some ingenious method smoke from the cooking fires was kept below ground so that the hideaway would not be betrayed. There is a narrow entrance on the spot but the main access is by a cave some miles away and connected by tunnel through which the sheep and goats were driven. A similar tunnel, again of considerable length, joins Kaymakli to another underground city. It is not known who the people were who planned and carried out these amazing feats of engineering, but there can be little doubt that their ingenuity was sharpened by terror and the folk memory of untold horrors.

We made two official visits to London during my time in Turkey and each followed the same pattern. It was gratifying that the UK visit should be regarded as the highlight of the PMD's year but there was no doubt that the perception was well merited. Just as we excel at ceremonial so do we excel at putting out the red carpet. It was fascinating to be an official guest in one's own country and to admire and enjoy the smoothness of the arrangements. We were accommodated in the Carlton Tower and each PMD had a chauffeur-driven Daimler at his disposal. We lunched with the Chiefs of Staff at the Royal Hospital, Chelsea, dined at the Savoy and went to the ballet.

The visits outside London were on a similar plane and the wives' programme, although allowing generous time for shopping, was full of interest. One incident that seemed amusing at the time, but which in the light of subsequent events could with hindsight be seen in a sinister light, was Akbar Khan's visit to Birmingham. His tour of the city by Daimler by all accounts was something close to a royal progress, with Pakistanis turning out in their thousands to cheer him. Although Bhutto was still in power it is not difficult to imagine that word of this incident would have got back to General Zia and would not have been well received.

In October 1973 the PMDs visited America for the second time that year, this time without our wives. We were guests primarily of the US Army and visited Fort Myer, Fort Hood, Fort

Worth, Fort Bragg and the Bell Helicopter company at Dallas — where I was allowed to fly the Cobra, a superb little aircraft.

Sometime prior to this visit I must have been informed of my next posting because instead of flying back to Ankara with the others I flew to London on the 18th and was flat hunting on the 22nd. Again on changeover of CAS my projected posting had been changed and I was to be Vice-Chief of Defence Staff rather than Vice-Chief of Air Staff as forecast and expected. Spotswood was about to hand over to Andrew Humphrey who probably felt that he would not be comfortable with a contemporary and an old friend serving him in a subordinate position. Whether or not that was so it probably made good sense as there was no one else with anything approaching my experience and knowledge of the other two services. I had flown in support of the army during the War and the Malayan Emergency, in support of the Navy during the Korean War and had been Commandant of JWE. Added to that, I knew Mike Carver, now Chief of Defence Staff, well and was on friendly terms with him. So, though I would dearly have loved to be VCAS, I felt only slight regret and dubbed myself the Air Force's sacrificial lamb on the altar of the Field Marshal. I did not in the event come to regret being offered up in this fashion.

I spent a week in London during which time I got a rundown on the job from the then VCDS, Lieutenant-General Sir John Gibbon, another old friend, and attended CAS' Annual Conference. On the 26th I flew to Akrotiri with John Aiken, C-in-C Cyprus, and thence on to Ankara. The last two months in Ankara were busy, particularly with Christmas and a flood of farewell parties, but Sylvia and I eventually flew to Copenhagen on 6 January, a date which conveniently coincided with the January sales, for a few days' leave on our way home.

Of the many farewell calls I had to make, one in particular was unusual at the time and was to become extremely important in the future. General Sancar, the Chief of the Turkish General Staff, had always been very friendly and indeed had shown me especial favour. I had been slightly puzzled as to why the most powerful man in Turkey should behave in that way and on this final call I discovered the reason. He told me on this last time that we were to meet that I was the exact twin of his younger brother who had been killed in a flying accident. I thought this was an exaggeration until some years later Mike Beavis found a postcard in a Cyprus shop of a man on water-skis in a black and yellow wet suit. Except that I have never worn such a suit, I would have sworn that I was the man on the skis. It is an extremely odd and uncomfortable experience to look at what appears to be yourself in every particular and to know that you are in fact looking at a stranger. I have no doubt that that stranger was Semih Sancar's dead brother.

Right:
The doppelgänger.

15. Fifth Interval: January 1974–January 1976
Vice-Chief of Defence Staff

The responsibilities of VCDS in 1974 were wide-ranging on paper but somewhat less so in practice. The Deputy Chief of Defence Staff (Intelligence), the Deputy Chief of Defence Staff (Operational Requirements) and the Assistant Chief of Defence Staff (Signals) were all answerable to VCDS but they were all experts in their own field in which no sensible VCDS would seek to interfere so, in practice, they just kept the Vice-Chief informed of what was of importance at any particular time. That left the Assistant Chief of Defence Staff (Policy), the Assistant Chief of Defence Staff (Operations) and the Head of COSSEC, the Chiefs of Staff Secretariat.

I had known Field Marshal Carver since he was a major-general and had seen him in action as Chairman of the Commanders-in-Chief Committee (Far East). I knew him to be extremely decisive and expected him to give me a clear brief as to what he wanted of me and I was not disappointed in that. I was, however, disappointed when he told me that ACDS (Pol) was to report direct to him as there was no point in filtering his proposals through me. I had thought that my wide experience of dealing with Policy and Planning matters might have been put to good use but Mike didn't really need advice or even a sounding board, so I had to content myself with being briefed by ACDS (Pol) after the line had been determined.

CDS saw no point in us duplicating anything, with which I agreed, and we succeeded in keeping our functions separate and never visiting the same units at anything approaching the same time. By and large I stayed at home while he did the bulk of the visiting. There could be flexibility on that but on one point, when he was laying out his requirements, he was crystal clear. He saw my most important role as that of crisis manager. He said that when there was a crisis he would stand back and give me a free hand and, in the event, when Turkey invaded Cyprus in 1974, he was as good as his word.

Apart from that major incident, life was relatively tranquil although, looking back at my engagement diaries for those two years, inordinately busy. Mike was very often away and I found myself representing him at interminable National Day cocktail parties in addition to looking after visitors at my own level. Very often I was lunching out either as host or guest, and a great deal of business was done in that way without the formality of staffs and minute taking. A good deal of inter-service work naturally fell to me as Chairman of the Vice-Chiefs as did ultimate responsibility for Joint Warfare matters. I was a fairly frequent visitor to Old Sarum, perhaps two or three times a year, and found it somewhat strange to be entertained in what had so recently been my own house.

When matters of inter-service dispute or disagreement arose, as they not infrequently did, it fell to me in the first place to try and bring about a resolution which those concerned could live with. To this task one could only bring the instruments of advocacy, persuasion and appeals to reason as at that time the Centre, as it was known, had no power to make and enforce a decision. The Chiefs of Staff were still strong and although the days when jointly they could have brought down a government had long passed, they still, individually, had retained the right *in extremis* of direct access to the Prime Minister. Successive Secretaries of State for Defence had sought to break their power, which by and large had resulted over the years in the Defence Budget being split three ways almost regardless of perceived strategic priorities. Thus when the RAF had responsibility for the nuclear deterrent in the shape of the V-Force other important elements of air power, notably tactical support for the army in the field, were largely neglected as the V-Force took the major share of the budget. Similarly the Navy later suffered, and is still suffering, from having to bear the cost of the nuclear ballistic missile submarines. I have always felt that this is inequitable and that the strategic force, from whichever service, should be separately funded, perhaps by an increase in the Foreign Office vote, as the deterrent is a symbol of national status and resolve rather than a usable weapon.

John Nott was the Secretary of State who came closest to achieving his objective before falling at the hurdle of the Falklands War. With the defence of Western Europe as priority, he had logically decided to favour the Army and the Air Force in budgetary terms at the expense of the Navy. Had his decisions been put into effect and had the Argentines invaded a year later we could well have been powerless to intervene. Thus can logic, usually a reliable guide, be faulted by a wild card.

The Secretary of State who had the ruthlessness and determination to break the residual power of the Chiefs of Staff was Michael Heseltine. His achievement in reducing the power of the individual services and increasing the authority of the Centre, as represented by the Chief of Defence Staff and the Permanent Under Secretary, was probably inevitable, some might even say overdue, but like so many would-be reforms has perhaps gone too far in tipping the balance the other way. Now the Chief of Air Staff, in place of one 3-star and four 2-star officers (and in still earlier days two 3-star and six 2-star) on his immediate staff, has one solitary 2-star and is in what must be the uncomfortable position of being reliant on the Centre for some of the information he needs to do his job.

In 1974, however, power still resided in the single services and VCDS had influence rather than executive authority. I was also, as I very soon discovered, an object of near suspicion in the higher reaches of my own service as the effort to be non-partisan that the post demanded could so easily come to be seen as a form of treachery. Michael Carver was no stranger to this feeling, but it was new to me and I found it uncomfortable. He was away visiting a great deal in 1974 and, although in his absence one of the Chiefs of Staff was acting CDS, a lot of the minor chores fell to me with the result that it was November before I made an overseas visit of more than a day.

I was then away for a working week visiting Malta and Gibraltar and taking Sylvia with me. Although I had refuelled in Malta on a number of occasions I had not spent a night there since 1943 and the contrast with the bustle and crowding of those days was most marked. Our relations with the civilian authorities, and in particular Prime Minister Mintoff, were cool but

The Vice-Chiefs at Ashford: front row, the author (third left), Treacher (fourth left), Wade (third right) and Fraser (second right); Willison DCDS (1) is to the far right. *Crown Copyright*

we still had facilities in the island and had a Rear-Admiral in command. We stayed with the Lorams, surrounded by the echoes of past glory. His office in particular was immensely nostalgic. Formerly the office of successive Commanders-in-Chief, Mediterranean Fleet, it looked out onto Grand Harbour and was hung with a wondrous collection of photographs, mostly taken during the annual exercises when Home Fleet and Mediterranean Fleet combined. In the earlier photographs Grand Harbour was almost entirely filled with line upon line of battleships with the remaining space being taken up by heavy cruisers. Light cruisers, destroyers and frigates were pushed out to Sliema. Even in postwar photographs Grand Harbour was an imposing sight with several aircraft carriers, with the helicopter carrier *Bulwark* and with the assault ships *Fearless* and *Intrepid* taking the place of battleships, and with still quite a significant array of cruisers, destroyers, frigates and submarines.

In Gibraltar we stayed with the Grandys at the Convent, the charming and historic residence of the Governor and Commander-in-Chief. I visited the remnants of our military presence, notably the naval hospital and dockyard, and formed the impression that Gibraltar was not a good place to be at that time, sealed off as it was from the Spanish mainland. Socially, we met close relations of one of my cousins by marriage. His family had come to Gibraltar hundreds of years ago as Genoese merchants and had prospered exceedingly, being big property owners and, as hardware merchants, were still busily engaged in selling beds to the Bedouins.

This visit to Malta and Gibraltar was almost in lieu of leave which I had cancelled in July because of the Cyprus affair. Leave or not, I certainly needed a break after that crisis, personal as well as international. The details of that emergency are chronicled in Michael Carver's autobiography *Out of Step*. As a record of fact they are accurate, except in the details of one incident, but they give no inkling of the series of small dramas that were almost daily enacted behind the scenes. Neither does he refer, for understandable political reasons, to the equivocal attitude of the Foreign Office — now too supine, now too bellicose — nor to my direct link with Sancar which, officially, he could not recognise or approve. The British system of crisis management in 1974, and I doubt if it will have changed since, is efficient and has an element of the gallows about it. On the recognition of an emergency the three Chiefs of Staff stand back and make their forces available to the Centre. At the Centre, the Chief of Defence Staff stands back and allows his Vice-Chief to run things, only being summoned in aid in a political deadlock. If anything goes wrong it is not difficult to point out the condemned. In spite of being sure of Mike's support, should I need it, I felt extremely isolated.

My personal involvement began early on the afternoon of 16 July 1974. John Aiken, C-in-C Cyprus and an old friend, rang me on Skynet, a secure radio telephone link, to say that he had helicoptered Archbishop Makarios out of Paphos and would not be responsible for his safety if, in accordance with the Foreign Secretary's instructions, he remained on the Akrotiri Base. He said he had an Argosy standing by with engines running and sought authority to send him off for Malta immediately. Michael Carver's memory is at fault in what happened next. He writes in his book, 'I therefore gave him authority without further reference to Ministers.' This was not the case as Michael was not on hand at that particular time and it was I who agreed Aiken's request, having ascertained that the Argosy could be turned round to return to Cyprus at any time within four hours after take-off.

Either Michael's memory is again faulty when he records that, 'reluctant agreement was given by officials to Makarios taking off en route to Malta', or perhaps more probably he was quoting from the official Foreign Office version of events. Either way, no such agreement was given prior to take-off, as I well know from receiving an abusive telephone call from Foreign Secretary Jim Callaghan's PPS. I could tell from whispered asides that Callaghan was in the room and this no doubt spurred the PPS on. At all events he accused me in an exceedingly rude, hectoring and arrogant tone of having deliberately disobeyed the Foreign Secretary's orders. When I gave no indication of contrition he had the impertinence to enquire whether I knew to whom I was talking. I reminded him with such composure as I could muster that he was talking to the Vice-Chief of the Defence Staff, that I had authorised Makarios' departure for Malta because the Commander-in-Chief refused to be responsible for his safety and that, if the Foreign Secretary was prepared to take that responsibility upon himself, the Argosy could be turned around at any time within the next four hours. Needless to say, no such instruction was given.

What had caused the threat to Makarios had been a coup in Nicosia by ex-supporters of Grivas in the Greek Cypriot National Guard largely officered by Greek Army officers. These extremists proclaimed Nicos Sampson to be the head of the Greek Cypriot government and this in turn and predictably brought strong Turkish reaction, with Turkey calling on Britain to intervene and to allow the Turks to bring reinforcements into Cyprus through the Sovereign Base Areas. This request could not possibly be agreed as all our dependants, living in largely Greek communities, would have been at the mercy of an inflamed populace. The denial of that request made Turkish intervention of some nature a near certainty and John Aiken withdrew the families, under escort, from Famagusta, Limassol, Larnaca and Nicosia into the Base Areas of Episkopi and Dhekelia, a difficult and successful operation involving the uprooting and rehousing of some 10,000 individuals.

On 19 July it was clear that a Turkish invasion was imminent and the Foreign Office in the person of Callaghan went into bellicose mode, wishing to threaten the Turks with direct action and to make dispositions which would seem to give substance to this threat. This came to a head in the evening when Mike Carver was at Glyndebourne, subject to my recall *in extremis*. I rehearsed all the arguments against finding ourselves, perhaps inadvertently, in action against the Turks and was supported by Bill Rodgers, the Minister of State, who was nothing but helpful throughout the whole period.

However, when we went to see Roy Mason, the Secretary of State, and asked him to intervene, we got nowhere. Mason clearly recognised that Callaghan was likely to be the next Prime Minister and, that apart, felt that the decisive arguments should be political rather than military. So I had no alternative but to ask CDS to leave Glyndebourne and try to persuade Roy Mason that, although the wider issue was political the immediate risk of disaster was military and, as such, his responsibility. As it turned out, it was a wasted journey and an unnecessary recall as, by the time Mike Carver arrived, wiser counsels had prevailed at the Foreign Office and Callaghan had agreed to a more moderate line.

The Turks duly invaded at dawn the following day in the Kyrenia area, having first bombed the airfield at Nicosia and the Greek area of Famagusta. A foothold obtained, they rapidly established a corridor from Kyrenia to Nicosia. The Greeks had flown reinforcements into Nicosia the previous night and it looked like becoming a battle zone, to the discomfiture of the United Nations force stationed there and to the High Commissioner who, cut off as he was, had no control over events.

The Turkish landing and seizure of the road to Nicosia had left nearly 2,000 non-Cypriots isolated in the general area of Kyrenia. In the main these were British, either tourists or Britons with holiday homes or some who had settled permanently either in Kyrenia or on the beautiful coast both to the east and to the west. It was decided to evacuate those who wished to leave, which was nearly everyone, using HMS *Hermes* and two destroyers. The Foreign Secretary agreed the plan on the evening of the 22nd but muddied the waters by making changes of detail, and by appointing Roy Hattersley as minister with responsibility for the refugees. This was a pointless gesture, meaningful only as a totem of political authority. Hattersley, all puff and self-importance, was just another Foreign Office spoke in the wheel and contributed nothing.

Our ambassador in Ankara, Horace Phillips, whom I knew well from my previous posting had repeatedly failed to get access to Bülent Eçevit, the Turkish Prime Minister, and had repeatedly advised caution. This advice during the night of the 22nd/23rd took the form of a series of Flash Signals, advising that the operation be postponed, which John Aiken stoutly and properly ignored. I was able by the sheer good fortune of knowing Sancar to succeed where Phillips had failed, and to communicate direct not with the Prime Minister but with the man in control in Turkey, the Chief of the Turkish General Staff. To do this I had established a link through our senior military man in Brussels who simply handed the text on to his Turkish counterpart who had a direct link to Sancar. Through this link which I had used previously to avoid misunderstanding, I originated a message warning Sancar not to interfere in the forthcoming rescue operation and urging him to instruct his pilots not to attack either our fighter cover or the ships themselves. This latter urging had particular relevance as they had already sunk one destroyer which they had mistakenly identified as Greek and which was in fact one of their own. In the event, the evacuation went without a hitch.

A ceasefire was signed on 30 July and the families returned to their homes outside the Sovereign Base Areas. Some 10 days later Callaghan summoned both sides to Geneva in an effort to reach some agreement. My representative there was ACDS (Ops) Air Vice-Marshal Mellersh, known as 'Young Togs' to distinguish him from his father Togs who had been my Commandant at Staff College and AOC Malaya when I commanded 209.

On 12 August the Turks delivered an ultimatum that unless a large slice of northern Cyprus, roughly what they now hold, was agreed by midnight as a Turkish Cypriot zone they would walk out of the conference and take military action to secure their ends. This animated the Foreign Secretary to propose that we take action to deter the Turks and protect the UN Force at Nicosia. He produced proposals which Togs Mellersh sent back to me for MOD approval. To my mind and to those of my staff his plan was dangerous in that it provided for reinforcements large enough to make the Turks feel threatened but not sufficiently large to inflict a quick defeat on their forces on the island should fighting break out through miscalculation by either side. Quite apart from the horrendous political consequences of even limited hostilities with a NATO and CENTO ally, we were not soundly based militarily in that we would be reliant on a single airfield at Akrotiri and our families, once more living outside the SBAs, would be very much at risk.

The plan therefore had all the hallmarks of an empty threat; at best it would alienate the Turks and at worst it could lead to a minor catastrophe. My staff drafted a signal setting out these views which started with the words, 'As seen from here the plan seems to combine the maximum of provocation with the minimum of deterrence.' I approved the signal and sent it 'Personal for AVM Mellersh For His Eyes Only from VCDS', leaving it up to him to convey tactfully to Callaghan that the Ministry of Defence had considerable reservations about his proposals. Unfortunately the Foreign Secretary had laid down that he was personally to receive a copy of any incoming signal from MOD, regardless of classification, so he received the full impact of my unflattering views without the tactful filter that had been intended. Eventually Callaghan reluctantly accepted that we should not intervene and in due course the stalemate, which continues to this day, was the result.

Throughout the Cyprus crisis I had caused a log to be kept of Foreign Office actions, advice, interference and general unhelpfulness. This document formed an indictment of one Ministry by another and partly because I was smarting from having had my role as crisis manager made more difficult than it need have been, and partly because I thought an analysis of what had happened might serve to prevent illegitimate Foreign Office interference in any future operation, I urged CDS to make an issue of it. He had not suffered at first hand as had my operations staff and was able to take a more lofty and probably wiser view that, like it or not, we had to work with them and that it would do no good to stir things up. Whether the Foreign Office was a help or a hindrance in the Falklands War, in the Gulf War and in former Yugoslavia I do not know, but they were certainly excess baggage in the Cyprus emergency. The High Commissioner in Nicosia, cut off as he was, could be of no help to the C-in-C; our ambassador in Ankara consistently advised against any action and officialdom in Whitehall was not always helpful.

Compared to 1974, 1975 was idyllic. I was able to fly the Jaguar, the Harrier and the Nimrod and got out and about a good deal more than I had in the previous year. There were interesting visits to Intelligence establishments, to the SAS, to Royal Marine Commandos, and to a mock-up of a Northern Ireland inner city area, compete with snipers, used to train troops before assignment to the province.

Two visits that stand out in my memory were to an oil rig off Aberdeen and to the nuclear submarine base at Faslane. I helicoptered out to the oil rig in perfect weather and this no doubt helped to form my view that the workers were on to a soft touch. Huge wages and every comfort and facility that management could contrive were theirs in exchange for loss of liberty. Had I visited in winter when storm force winds and mountainous seas were battering the rig I might well have taken a different view. The visit to Faslane was fascinating but all too short. I flew up to Glasgow on a Monday morning, spent the day on the base and, on the Tuesday, embarked in an SSKN or nuclear hunter-killer submarine. My previous experience of being submerged had been a night and a day in 1949 in the immensely cramped quarters of a World War II diesel-electric-powered submarine. By comparison, the SSKN was like a cruise liner, a large and formidable craft indeed. A memorable day finished in impressive style. At 17.00 I was winched off the submarine by Sea King helicopter and flown to Prestwick there to be transferred to an HS125 of Metropolitan Comm Squadron. Shortly before 18.15, not much over an hour after leaving the submarine, I was at Northolt.

Two more visits were to the Royal Artillery ranges in the Outer Hebrides and to the Army Air Corps Centre at Middle Wallop. The first involved flying to Benbecula by HS125, then a new and impressive executive jet, and driving to South Uist for a night stop. What I remember most about the visit apart from the wild scenery was the unimpressive performance of Blowpipe, the infantry's shoulder-fired low-level anti-aircraft missile. I did not have time to see the facilities at Fair Isle so we made a diversion to overfly the island, little more than a huge precipitous grass-covered rock with thousands upon thousands of sea birds, on our flight back to Northolt. The visit to Middle Wallop was fun as I flew to and from Battersea by Gazelle and was allowed to fly one of their little Sioux helicopters, a delight to fly except that as in all earlier helicopters there was no throttle linkage with the collective and one was back to watching the rpm like a hawk.

I had known for a long time that I was due to take over from Bob Hodges at Allied Forces Central Europe (AFCENT) early in 1976 and in October I went through some preliminaries, calling on the NATO Supreme Allied Commander Europe (SACEUR), then General Goodpaster, on the Commanders-in-Chief in Germany and on D/CINCENT, a slightly more protracted visit in which Sylvia got her first sight of Vroenhof which was to be our home for over three years. I was happy to be going there for my last appointment rather than finishing up on the Air Force Board with yet another tour in Whitehall. The appointment was in a direct line from some very colourful and distinguished officers going back to, amongst others, Harry Broadhurst and Basil Embry, both of whom, without really knowing me, had had such a profound effect on my career. After them had come Teddy Hudleston, Gus Walker, Fred Rosier and Bob Hodges. It was an elephants' graveyard, a last appointment, but at least you left your bones in good company.

Although I knew I was going to AFCENT and that Andrew Humphrey had nominated Neil Cameron to succeed him as CAS, elements of the aircraft industry did not, and Sylvia and I were assiduously courted and entertained throughout 1975 in the belief that I would be Andrew's successor. This was occasioned largely, I suspect, by my having been tipped by Chapman Pincher, the ace reporter of his day in service and intelligence matters. Pincher had highly placed sources of information and had a legendary reputation for accuracy. The result of his getting it wrong on this occasion was quietly agreeable and slightly amusing as I knew why we were being singled out and that my hosts were blissfully unaware that they were on the wrong horse. I told the chief executive of one company, who was an old friend, that I would not be succeeding Andrew and expected him to pass the word around but nothing changed. Either he did not believe me or he kept the information to himself.

Throughout November 1975 the situation in Belize, formerly British Honduras, had been tense and on the 20th I set out to visit the colony with my MA, Lieutenant-Colonel Charles Ramsay. Charles, the son of Admiral Sir Bertram Ramsay who commanded the combined fleets on D-Day, was a most efficient and charming officer who eventually retired as a major-general.

Although it would have been possible to make the journey in comfort by civil air I elected to travel steerage, as it were, and we left Lyneham by Hercules at 14.00. For some reason I cannot now remember we were routed via Prestwick and arrived in Belize, with one refuelling, at 06.30 the following morning. We had two very full days in the colony, enough to get a feel for the place and for the problems of the garrison, but I would have liked longer. I found it very reminiscent of Malaya but less attractive. On the second day we did an extensive tour by Puma which took us to the Guatemalan border in the extreme south. Turning for home in the late afternoon, it was soon apparent that we were going to have a weather problem as visibility was deteriorating and cloud was building up. The captain of the aircraft determined to make for a pass in the Maya Range at about 4,500ft. This turned out to be an error of judgement and we would have fared better to have stayed at sea level and groped our way back along the coast. I was flying the aircraft and as we climbed up to the pass I could see it closing off ahead of us just as I had seen the same happen in the Cameron Highlands. By the time that it was clear that we could not make the pass the cloud had built up behind us and we found ourselves over solid cloud with tops at 4,000ft and rising. The only thing to do was to head east and let down over the sea where we knew the ceiling to be not more than 300ft in very poor visibility.

It says much for the captain's nerve, and perhaps for my ability to appear calm when close to panic, that he left me at the controls, though instantly ready to take over. Eventually we broke cloud just over the water and headed west in very poor visibility which continued all the way back to Belize. We just hugged the road sometimes making good progress and sometimes having to slow to near walking pace when the cloud and mist came right down on top of the palms. Within a few hours of landing, tired and relieved, Charles and I were off to Nassau to spend the Saturday night and Sunday with some friends of his before flying direct to Lyneham, arriving there just before midday on the Monday.

That same week, as part of a visit by the Swiss CDS, Sylvia and I were guests at Portsmouth and dined aboard HMS *Victory*. That and Trafalgar Night at Greenwich, remain in my memory as two occasions which sharply linked the present with the past. The settings, like the ceremony of Trooping the Colour, were powerful reminders of past glory and of our heritage which was still a presence even in the dull cockpit of the Whitehall of that time.

Although routine continued during December everything had an air of approaching finality. I found myself doing everything for the last time. On the 16th I attended my last meeting of the Chiefs of Staff and on the 23rd after the usual round of Christmas drinks parties I started a long break, not coming back until 5 January for a final round of farewells. I was lunched by my Assistant Chiefs on the 8th, having been lunched by my Vice-Chief colleagues earlier, and gave my own drinks party that night in the Defence Council suite. On the 9th I said goodbye to Mike Carver and had an hour with Henry Leach, who was taking over from me. There was no handover as such as no funds were involved, and no need for any helpful words from me as I knew that Henry would do things his way. After drinks with the staff we had lunch together at Simpsons and that was that; I was no longer the Vice-Chief of Defence Staff.

16. NATO - Second Tour: February 1976–May 1979 Deputy Commander-in-Chief Allied Forces Central Europe

The structure of NATO which I now found in place was somewhat different from that which I had known in the early sixties. For some years postwar there had been two NATO headquarters in Central Region, LANDCENT and AIRCENT. When De Gaulle withdrew France from NATO and expelled the headquarters from Fontainebleau, Supreme Headquarters Allied Powers in Europe (SHAPE) moved to Brussels and LANDCENT and AIRCENT combined to form Allied Forces Central Europe (AFCENT) and moved to southern Holland. In the newly formed AFCENT Headquarters, the commander-in-chief's post fell to the German Army and the deputy commander-in-chief's (D/CINCENT) to the Royal Air Force. It was a less than satisfactory arrangement as the lines of command became somewhat blurred and open to interpretation, when the virtually all-American staff Headquarters Allied Air Forces Central Europe was also established under a 4-star commander. In peacetime command was retained nationally and there was no problem with Commander-in-Chief British Army of the Rhine being responsible for I British Corps with its four armoured divisions and Commander-in-Chief Royal Air Force Germany being responsible for all RAF units. In war or for exercises these two commanders assumed their NATO posts of Commander Northern Army Group and Commander Second Allied Tactical Air Force, the first being responsible to AFCENT and the second to AAFCE. A similar situation prevailed with Central Army Group and 4 ATAF. This made AFCENT's control over air matters in exercises or war extremely nebulous and made it clear that in practice my role as D/CINCENT was just that, Deputy C-in-C with responsibility across the board but nothing was laid down in black and white.

This did not worry me as AFCENT was not there to fight the battle; NORTHAG and CENTAG and the two ATAFs under AAFCE direction were there to do that. AFCENT's responsibility, in my view, having issued suitable directives, was to keep a close watch on developments, to direct reinforcement as required from one army group to the other, to recommend to Supreme Headquarters the use of nuclear weapons if and when that became necessary, and in conjunction with SHAPE to look to the logistic support and reinforcement of its fighting formations. A *sine qua non* of all of this was detailed and up-to-date information and intelligence. Both CINCENTs that I served under demanded information down to brigade level. As an airman I felt that this was overdoing it; there are an awful lot of brigades in two army groups totalling nine corps.

This anomalous position of AFCENT confused even some who should have known better, including Andrew Humphrey, then Chief of Air Staff. He was unfairly critical of my predecessor, Bob Hodges, for not taking control of the air situation during exercises and told me that he wanted me to go down to AAFCE and take a grip of things. Once in post and having found my bearings, I realised that Bob had been quite right. Not only was it no part of the Deputy Commander's responsibility, but it was totally unrealistic to expect to take over, in a NATO hat, the entire staff of the Commander-in-Chief United States Air Forces in Europe together with its highly sensitive intelligence cell which was 'US Eyes Only'. Andrew did not press me, so either he realised that he had been wrong or resigned himself to my failure to carry out his instructions.

I approached my appointment with mixed feelings. Whilst delighted to have reached the 4-star rank that went with this job and enthused with all the challenges that would be ahead in this new environment, I was aware that I was about to become what the Army call a SOONI,

Splinters Smallwood (centre right) visits AFCENT. *Crown Copyright*

a senior officer of no importance, the additional acronym TOOS, to one's own service, hopefully being understood. Each service has at least one: Deputy SACEUR normally for the Army, Deputy SACLANT for the Navy and Deputy CINCENT for the Air Force. I had been accustomed to having an input to certain policy matters at four different levels, as a wing commander joint planner, as a group captain single service planner, as an air commodore briefer to CAS and finally as an air vice-marshal as ACAS (Pol). Since becoming an air marshal I had missed the opportunity to contribute; at CENTO I was totally out of contact and, as VCDS, I had been kept at arm's length as though under suspicion of carrying a contagious disease. And now once more and for the last few years of my service I was fated in ambassadorial style 'to lie abroad for my country'.

It was really only a very minor reservation as overwhelmingly I was looking forward to the new job but it set a train of thought going. It had been Chris Foxley-Norris, probably the best brain and certainly the wittiest officer of his generation, who had first remarked on it to me. His last appointment had been the tri-service post of Comptroller of Personnel and Logistics in which he was instrumental in bringing about index-linked pensions, a huge benefit to all three services, but he had never been able to do anything specifically for the RAF. I remember him saying something like, 'You spend a lot of time as a junior and middle ranking officer being critical of various things and thinking how, if you get sufficiently senior, you will change them all, but in fact you find that your power to change anything is very limited if not nil.' It is limited, of course, primarily by appointment and secondly by time. In practice only Board Members can bring about major change and they are seldom in post for longer than two years, a relatively short period in which to effect anything substantial.

One of the biggest upheavals in my time was brought about by Andrew Humphrey, as Air Member for Personnel, changing the whole nature and *raison d'être* of Cranwell by getting the Board to agree that henceforward a university degree would be a prerequisite for a direct route permanent commission. I disagreed with him strongly and discussed it with him at length as a friend, as I had no official standing in the matter whatsoever. He had been sold the educator's line, fashionable at the time, that a degree was the be-all and end-all for a young man and that no one without one would go to Cranwell as a flight cadet because, if for any reason he left the Royal Air Force, he would be unemployable without a degree. This seemed to me to overlook the fact that past generations of flight cadets had remained wholly dedicated to the Royal Air Force and had been motivated in the first instance by a desire to fly and to fly now, not at the end of a further three years of academic training. I felt that if we changed the function of the Royal Air Force College in the way recommended we would be in danger of ceasing to attract some of our best young men who did not want to go to university but might be chary, or whose parents might be chary for them, of embarking on the short service route to a permanent commission.

I also knew from practical experience that graduate entry could present problems for the individual. I had had a very few such officers on my station and as senior flying officers or junior flight lieutenants they naturally had far fewer hours, especially on type, than their short service contemporaries. This did not matter whilst they were squadron pilots but I foresaw possible problems when they would become flight commanders. I had seen one example of this at first hand. A newly promoted officer was posted in as a squadron leader flight commander to one of my Javelin squadrons. He had relatively few flying hours for his rank and a very limited total on Javelins. The result was sad. He was a good officer, but had been given a near impossible task in the Freemasonry of the Javelin crews. The majority of them had been on night/all-weather fighters for years and had many hundreds of hours on Javelins; their skills had been honed by experience, skills which no newcomer to that particular world could hope to match. I foresaw, or thought I could foresee, that this pattern would become common once all regular officers were graduates and the flight and squadron commanders of the future. I understand that now we have a compromise which satisfies both schools of thought but I remain sad that one of Trenchard's cornerstones has been eroded.

On the occasion of our argument Andrew called me an old reactionary. I think that was fair comment as I am resistant to change and hate to see institutions that have tradition and a good track record on their side being tinkered with in response to the alleged need to 'move with the times'. It is as well that I retired when I did as I would have found many of the changes that have since been forced on the service very hard indeed to come to terms with.

The Board Member with most power to effect change is naturally the Chief of the Air Staff, but not all the ones that I have been able to observe have sought to do so and many, if not all, have found their room for manoeuvre severely restricted by extraneous

AFCENT transport.

Mike Carver arriving at AFCENT. *Crown Copyright*

A touch of colour at AFSOUTH.

considerations, chief among them being foreign policy and finance. Jack Slessor and Dermot Boyle had the build-up of the V-Force and the management of the nuclear deterrent as their primary preoccupation, together with the Malayan Emergency. Tom Pike had a relatively calm passage and came to working arrangements with the Army over the responsibilities of the Army Air Corps. Sam Elworthy had a difficult time with Healey as Secretary of State, with resisting a renewed Navy attempt to take control of Coastal Command and, almost as a sideline, the Confrontation with Indonesia. John Grandy, whilst having a calmer time on the Whitehall front, had all the adjustments following the pull-out from east of Suez to contend with. Only Denis Spotswood and Andrew Humphrey had the opportunity of making changes not dictated by force of circumstances. Both were reformers and both were successful in finding ways of protecting the front line within a shrinking budget.

Having put all yearning to become involved in single-service issues firmly behind me, I set myself to think NATO and to get to know the ropes. AFCENT's area of responsibility ran from the Baltic to the Alps and it was by far the biggest and most important of the three major NATO commands. AFNORTH was in Oslo with responsibility for holding the left flank, consisting of Norway and Denmark. It was a small command not without interest but thought unlikely to be the scene of a major Soviet push. Since the formation of NATO CINCNORTH had traditionally been a British officer, usually an Army general. The incumbent when I took over as D/CINCENT was John Sharp, a charming man who sadly died in post. The Army found difficulty in replacing him and his place was taken by Peter Whiteley who on retirement as Commandant-General Royal Marines was promoted full general in order to fill this gap. Sylvia and I got to know him and Nancy well and were to see a lot of them later when we coincided as Lieutenant-Governors of Guernsey and Jersey respectively.

AFSOUTH had its headquarters in Naples and was always commanded by an American admiral. It was a disparate command of Italians, Greeks and Turks, the two latter somewhat uneasy bedfellows, but had the tremendous asset of the American Sixth Fleet at CINCSOUTH's disposal. CINCSOUTH in my day was Stan Turner, an agreeable officer who had been a friend of Jimmy Carter's at, I think, Annapolis. Almost certainly because of this connection he became Director of the CIA on retirement from the United States Navy.

Above these three regional headquarters was SHAPE, Supreme Headquarters Allied Powers in Europe, commanded always by an American 4-star officer, either Army or Air Force. When I first called on SACEUR as VCDS it was General Goodpaster, USAF, who was succeeded by Al Haig, US Army. I well remember the astonishment of our Chiefs of Staff when the announcement was made of Haig's appointment at the age of 53. He had by their standards very little operational experience, his only active command being that of a brigade in Vietnam when he was a colonel. He was essentially a political soldier and the Chiefs initially were beset by doubts, only Edward Ashmore, The First Sea Lord, making the astute observation that he would not be surprised if Haig turned out to be the best SACEUR we had ever had.

I was to see a lot of Al Haig during the three and a bit years I spent as D/CINCENT and in my view Edward was proved right. A charismatic individual, Haig was dynamic, full of energy and charm and an outstanding ambassador for his country. Adept at dealing with politicians, he was himself effectively a politician in uniform. If war came SHAPE would be concerned primarily with logistics and reinforcements. If the Soviets initiated nuclear warfare Haig had delegated authority to respond, and only if the situation on the ground became so desperate that SHAPE was forced to recommend first use would Haig's judgement and powers of persuasion become of paramount importance. To him would fall the task of convincing the politicians, something he would have been better equipped to do than most generals.

I never served at SHAPE, which in common with all NATO headquarters had a swollen staff, each nation wanting to make sure of the maximum possible representation. The post of Deputy to SACEUR had always been filled by a British officer, starting with Field Marshal Montgomery, and when I arrived the incumbent was General John Mogg whom I had first met when Commandant of JWE. He was followed by Harry Tuzo whom I had also known previously and I found them both to be most likeable colleagues.

The post of D/SACEUR must have been very frustrating at times because the real power under SACEUR lay with the Chief of Staff, always an American, who, whilst responding to D/SACEUR internationally, also worked directly to Haig on a 'US Eyes Only' basis, so that D/SACEUR found himself excluded from discussion of matters which might be deemed to touch on US national interest. As against that, the British held the most powerful 2-star post, that of Assistant Chief of Staff Plans and Policy, solidly from 1972 and we certainly did NATO proud, filling the post successively with very talented officers. From 1972 until 1980 we sent Mike Beetham, Peter Terry, Keith Williamson and Peter Harding. All except Peter Terry became Chief of Air Staff and Marshals of the Royal Air Force and Peter Harding became Chief of Defence Staff. Peter Terry was briefly my successor but one at AFCENT before being switched to D/SACEUR in place of General Bill Scotter who died before he could take up his appointment. Peter subsequently became Governor of Gibraltar.

Although the post of D/SACEUR must have been frustrating it had considerable prestige, so much so that the Germans lobbied for, and finally achieved, the parallel post of a second D/SACEUR. This was a purely political move prompted by national *amour propre* and the general concerned must have found himself seriously underemployed.

The SHAPE showpiece of the year was SHAPEX held over two to three days in the first half of May. It was always a very big affair indeed attended by the Secretary-General of NATO, a number of ambassadors, the national service chiefs, all the NATO hierarchy with commanders and staff officers mostly at 2- and 3-star level but including a few 1-stars in key posts. Al Haig opened and wound up, but the content and stage management of the whole show fell to the D/SACEUR of the day, and they always did it extremely well. It was a high price gathering and a great occasion for meeting old friends. A lot of useful work was done 'in the margins' but the set piece presentations and discussion periods generally yielded little because the more sensitive and interesting subjects were not touched on as the security clearance of some of those attending did not allow of it. It was always a great occasion for Al Haig and he never failed to dazzle his audience. And dazzle is pretty much the *mot juste* as you listened enthralled to this oratory, all delivered in what we knew as Haigspeak, passages so densely obscure that no meaning could be extracted from them whatsoever, although at the time you felt you knew what he meant and wholeheartedly agreed with him. I saw a good deal of Haig as he held fairly frequent meetings with his principal subordinate commanders and, although not one myself, I was privileged to attend. In common with, I think, most people, I both liked and admired Haig whilst having some considerable reservations as to his sincerity. That in itself is not a major criticism as insincerity, at least to some degree, is a necessary part of any SACEUR's make-up, faced as he is with the need to flatter and cajole.

When De Gaulle withdrew from NATO, the headquarters formed to command the Central Region found a welcome in the Netherlands and AFCENT headquarters set up in a disused coalmine at Brunssum in the southern province of Limburg. It was nothing like as bad as it sounds as offices were above ground and Limburg is a nice area in which to live. When the move was decided upon Teddy Hudleston, who was the last COMAIRCENT and about to retire, rendered his last major service to the RAF by being first in the field in seeking a house for his successor. He did well indeed in persuading DOE to buy Vroenhof which was superior to Kastel Puth, the only other house that would have been suitable and which fell instead to the German C-in-C.

Vroenhof was a lovely, old 17th century house that in its earliest times had been a training establishment for novices. My mother, who stayed with us on two occasions, attested to one of the bedrooms and a bathroom being haunted. Although I myself saw nothing I would hesitate to disagree as she had a certain sensibility in that field. Certainly it was a house that could well have been haunted although it had a warm and friendly atmosphere. Largely blind to the nearby main road, which ran from Heerlen near the German border on the east to Maastricht near the Belgian border on the west, it had a lovely garden behind with many wonderful old trees, a walled vegetable and fruit garden, three acres of orchard and seven acres of pasture leading to a small copse, all looking out on the foothills of the Ardennes. The first inhabitant was one-armed Gus Walker who was still remembered with great affection by the locals some six years later. He had been followed by Fred Rosier and Bob Hodges, Fred a charismatic extrovert and Bob immensely solid and wise, so it was a daunting line to try and follow.

Vroenhof. *Crown Copyright*

One of these predecessors, I am not sure which, had persuaded DOE to buy sheep to keep the seven acres of pasture under control and this had resulted in the setting up of a small farm, selling sheep and apples. The profits from this undertaking which was administered by successive ADCs were ploughed back into the farm for the purchase of machinery (the Vroenhof gardener was highly mechanised and ran on vodka like his contemporary at Air House), plants and seed. On top of this the farm made a small profit, even after one or in a good year two sheep had ended up in the Vroenhof deep freeze.

When I took over from Bob we were, I recall, some £400 to the good. Quite apart from that it was great fun in the lambing season and one year Flight Sergeant Viney, my excellent head of house staff, brought up a rejected lamb on the bottle. Very sadly, my successor brought all this to an abrupt end. Inheriting about £400 and some 30-odd sheep, he promptly sold the sheep and demanded grass-cutting machinery from DOE. This they quite understandably refused to provide and I am not sure what happened. John Stacey was a very strange man anyway but we now know that he was terminally ill at the time — he died within a year — and that may have been the explanation.

As I was retired I do not know the details but Stacey was succeeded by Peter Terry, perhaps after a small gap and then, after only some three months, Peter was moved to SHAPE, leaving no doubt another gap before John Gingell took up residence. At all events, at some time during this turbulent period Vroenhof was without a master for long enough for DOE to sell off the land. When Sylvia and I visited Vroenhof in Mike Beavis's time some six or seven years after we had left, they had the small garden and the kitchen garden and did not know that the land behind had originally belonged to the house. The gardener Luckie was still there, needing more vodka than ever to sustain him, and no doubt bemoaning the sad reduction of his fiefdom which John Stacey and DOE had jointly brought about.

But in 1976 Vroenhof stood in all its glory. By today's standards it was luxuriously staffed and a most comfortable place in which to live. The first faint signs of a cutting back were just visible if you looked hard enough. Bob's Pembroke and its crew had been personal to him,

Sylvia with Franz Josef Schultze. *Crown Copyright*

whereas I was just guaranteed a Pembroke whenever I needed one and the crew might vary. Similarly I lost my Dutch ADC soon after arrival as the Dutch Air Force was being forced to economise and his was clearly a non-essential post. Neither of these minuscule economies had any practical effect and in the office I was similarly well served, having a colonel as chief of personal staff, a squadron leader later wing commander personal staff officer, a flight lieutenant ADC, a very efficient warrant officer shorthand typist and my driver, Flight Sergeant soon to become Warrant Officer John Baker, who had moved with me from London and was to stay with me for nearly five and a half years.

The post, as I knew it would be, was frantically busy in terms of visiting. I did a great deal of it in my own right but also accompanied CINCENT on his major tours of inspection. Both of them, Karl Schnell and then Franz Josef Schultze, visited every corps in turn, paying particular attention to the three German corps, in order both to get a feel for the ground and for the relative fighting efficiency of the troops. In the course of these major tours we would spend several nights away, sometimes in hotels close to the East/West border and in these in particular it was noticeable how greatly respected a German general still was. There was a great deal of heel-clicking and bowing and one felt that deep down not a great deal had changed.

We have tended to think in the West of the Berlin Wall as being the big divider of East and West Germany. Whilst it had huge symbolic importance it was minuscule in relation to the real Iron Curtain. The entire border between East and West Germany, stretching literally from the Baltic to the Alps, was impassable. I have flown most of it by helicopter, some stretches more than once, and throughout its length in those days there were watchtowers and barbed-wire, no doubt minefields the whole way, in most areas a high wall and everywhere either a deep ditch or dragon's teeth to make escape by vehicle impossible. It was a sombre sight as were the myriad of tank tracks criss-crossing the giant exercise area or proving ground that one could see when flying up the corridor to Berlin. This I did on a number of occasions when I was able to borrow C-in-C Germany's Berlin residence. Known as High House, it was in fact a small well-built house in a charming setting overlooking and leading down to one of Berlin's lakes. Ideal for entertaining important guests, it was modestly but permanently staffed and had a large Mercedes with RAF driver on call and as many tickets to the opera as one wanted, the whole provided at no cost as part of German reparations.

It was fascinating visiting so many formations and units to see how clearly national characteristics showed through and, to a lesser degree, how national attitudes were reflected in the troops' appearance and bearing. The most striking example of the latter was the tolerance of long hair by some armies and, in Central Region, specifically by the Dutch, always in the forefront of social change. Here I think they got it wrong. There was no real reason to suppose that their hirsute and sometimes effeminate appearance would affect their fighting qualities, but somehow one wondered. The Belgians were punchy and keen but handicapped by their language divide. The British, holding the key geographical position in Northern Army Group around which Western defence might well pivot, were steady and totally reliable but handicapped as ever by equipment shortages and deficiencies, notably at that time, I seem to remember, the poor performance of the gun in the main battle tank and the unreliability of the engine in the armoured fighting vehicles. That the engine could perform when really required was shown when some 98% of them started on cue for the drive past on the occasion of The Queen's review of the army at Sennelager during her Silver Jubilee. The parade, which went off impeccably and which I was one of the few Royal Air Force officers privileged to attend, was led by Nigel Bagnall, then the Major-General commanding the 4th Division, who had worked for me as COSSEC and was later to become Chief of the General Staff and a field marshal.

Part of the received wisdom of the day — probably about as reliable as its predecessor to the effect that Japanese pilots were useless because of poor eyesight — was that Soviet troops were totally inflexible and lacking in initiative. If and when the set plan failed or tactical communications broke down, leadership and improvisation at junior level would be poor and open to exploitation. This doctrine was taught by the Americans, seemingly unaware that they, too, adhered rigidly to any plan and gave little discretion at lower levels. But they would undoubtedly have given a good account of themselves, superbly equipped as they were and with rising morale. It had been a long haul back for the US army after the humiliation of Vietnam and by 1976 they had just about got there, although drugs were still a problem albeit a very much smaller one.

This left three German corps, numerically the largest land force in Central Region. My two CINCENTs seemed well satisfied with them and I am sure they would have been extremely effective in action. They did not look quite so frightening to me as allies as they had done as enemies but there was still the jackboot, now reassuringly relaunched as a 'democratic' jackboot, to remind one of the legendary power and efficiency of the German Army. I had been brought face to face with this in the form of a monolithic guard of honour and band complete with glockenspiel, when soon after arrival I called on Admiral Zimmerman, then Chief of the German Armed Forces. On 9 May 1945, as Lieutenant Commander Zimmerman, he had negotiated the surrender of the German occupying forces in Guernsey on behalf of his commander. It was a strange connection and one which could have been awkward. In the event we got on well and I was sorry not to have seen more of him. He was an unusual man of some charm and sadly died soon afterwards of a brain tumour.

Formal calls bulked large in early 1976 on arrival and again in early 1979 on relinquishing the appointment. Though mostly within Central Region, it was customary to call in addition on CINCNORTH in Oslo and on CINCSOUTH in Naples. The Naples calls were colourful affairs, including as they did a large guard of honour with a mounted element. Apart from the numerous exercises within the region there was a large scale exercise every other year in Norway which I visited to see the performance of ACE Mobile Force, a spearhead reinforcement unit based within Central Region. It also gave me the opportunity to visit British units, notably Royal Marine Commandos, earmarked for the reinforcement of AFNORTH in emergency. The 1976 exercise was called Atlas Express and involved an interesting series of flights. I flew from Beek, a small airfield just north of Maastricht to Oslo by HS125 and from there, again by the same HS125 to Bardufoss. That afternoon and the next day I watched various units on the exercise and had a 10-minute flight in a Scout of the 1st Royal Anglian Regiment. On the third day I flew to Tromsö by Twin Otter of the Norwegian Air Force, visiting HMS *Hermes* from there by Wessex. On return to Tromsö I was flown back to Wildenrath in a C160, a nice scaled-down twin-engined version of the

Hercules, of the German Air Force in 5 hours 10 minutes. In 1978 by contrast I travelled throughout by civil air starting from Washington, arriving in Oslo via London and returning from Bardufoss to Amsterdam.

I started from Washington because I had been lecturing to the US Army War College in Harrisburg, Pennsylvania, a most delightful part of the United States. Lecturing was a fairly constant commitment, as it had been as VCDS and to a lesser degree as ACAS (Pol). But from Brunssum it was more widely spread geographically from Harrisburg to Rome's NATO Defence College with Oberammergau, the nuclear school, in between. The bulk of the lecture venues were however well-trodden ground — Bracknell, Camberley and Latimer in particular being familiar indeed. As rather special items I was invited to address a particular dinner in the House of Commons when I replied for the Guests to a toast proposed by Norman Tebbit, and to lecture at the RUSI of which I was still at that time a Council Member. That was a specially cosy affair as it fell to Harry Tuzo, as Chairman of Council, to welcome me and to sum up.

I visited Rome twice. On the first occasion I arrived in style in an HS125 and, amongst other things, called on the British Ambassador in the controversial Embassy building, so highly regarded by cognoscenti of architecture. A lover of old buildings, I found it stridently out of place, an unnecessarily loud and weird statement. The second time I had to go to Rome I rather fancy there was no HS125 available and, although I could have gone by civil air, I elected to go by Pembroke, probably the longest journey that that venerable aircraft type has ever made. It took for ever with two refuelling stops, one at an air force base near Dijon and one at Cannes, but it was great fun, rather like the London to Brighton race. I was taking my CPS, Colonel John Nichols and his wife for a well-earned break and we played bridge non-stop both ways until towards the end of the homeward lap, it became so turbulent that we could not keep the cards on the table. That as a bridge marathon had only been exceeded by a series of games between Washington and Ankara in the USAF version of a Boeing 707. On that occasion we again flew non-stop, and the game was continuous. All five PMDs were bridge players and Sylvia made a sixth so that each individual got a break part of the time.

Almost all my lectures dealt with the strengths and weaknesses and readiness for war of Central Region forces. One had very much in mind the old Biblical quotation, 'If the trumpet shall give an uncertain sound who shall have prepared himself for the battle?' and needed to strike a positive and optimistic note, whilst at the same time being realistic about at least some of our deficiencies. Our major weakness was the lack of tactical nuclear weapons on the ground and the deterrent effect which their deployment would have yielded. This was not due to the lack of suitable hardware so much as to the lack of political will, principally on the part of President Carter. The prevailing political view was that nothing must be done to provoke or upset the Russians and the result was a dangerous tactical nuclear imbalance which it was left to President Reagan's administration to remedy.

In the late seventies the British government was in severe trouble with Healey at the Treasury, Callaghan at the helm, and the Winter of Discontent just around the corner. Perhaps unsurprisingly we had few visits from senior political figures. Callaghan visited before I had arrived and unfortunately betrayed the depth of his ignorance by asking CINCENT how many Turkish divisions he had under command. Defence Secretary Fred Mulley did no better, though less publicly, by expressing surprise at how mountainous Holland was when landing by helicopter at our war headquarters in Germany. All in all, senior British officers were somewhat doubtful of our political leaders understanding of the role they would have to play and the decisions they would need to take in an emergency. Certainly, in my experience, no Cabinet members took part directly in the war games that were run annually but deputed their decisions to officials. One was left with the cynical feeling that perhaps our best hope nationally was that they would do the same in war.

At the end of May 1977 I was guest of honour at Cranwell and in my 'Reply for the Guests' had to speak *inter alia* to the outgoing course. I wrote down what I wanted to say and still have the script. It said,

'Your generation will soon have charge of the Air Force and you will have to complete and consolidate the change now underway from a world-wide to an essentially European-oriented force, and you will at the same time need to think and plan for the generation which

Schultze, Schnell and Haig. *Crown Copyright*

Vera Lynn.

will succeed yours in its turn. Some things which are wrong now — not through anyone's fault but through force of circumstances — will I hope have been put right in the meantime, and I refer particularly to two matters in the personnel field which are in a way inter-related.

'The first of these is the drift away from station life. In the past, in my view, a great deal of the RAF's spirit and strength has come from a sense of difference — of elitism if you will — engendered in part by our living in cantonments, not only overseas but here at home as well. Now, as we all know, almost the opposite is happening — young officers and airmen are buying houses as soon as (or in some cases before) they can afford to and, to make this possible, more and more young wives are working. The main reason for this is of course obvious — the ever increasing quartering charges and the knowledge that your terminal grant is no longer sufficient to buy you a house. I believe it to be vital that this should be put right and that the drift away from station life should be halted. I am not arguing for a return to the 1930s and I am not against a somewhat greater involvement with the rest of the community than has been customary in the past — what I am against, and what would be the ruination of the Air Force, would be to allow the situation to develop to the point where our young men come to be regarded — or even worse to regard themselves — as virtual civilians who just happened to put on uniform to come to work.

'To put this right we must somehow regain a measure of control over our own pay and conditions of service — not only to halt the drift from stations but also because, without the attraction of overseas service and with a closer comparison being drawn with civilians than previously, pay is going to be much more important in the future than it has been in the past. The crux of both these problems is of course the Armed Forces Pay Review Body. The plain fact of the matter, I believe, is that officers and men alike have lost confidence in the AFPRB with its system of Irishmen's rises and its blatant abandonment of comparability, which was supposed to be the cornerstone of the "Military Salary". I believe, therefore, that as soon as a new government is formed the Chiefs of Staff should insist — and collectively they can insist in such a matter — that the composition of the AFPRB should be changed to ensure that there are people on it who are likely at least to understand and perhaps be responsive to what the Principal Personnel Officers tell them.'

The latter part of this low-key tirade was directed of course at Callaghan's government and with Teddy Donaldson, the air correspondent of the *Daily Telegraph*, in the audience, it was duly featured next day under the headline 'RAF spirit eroded by poor pay'. The article started: 'service Chiefs have warned the government that officers and men alike have lost confidence in the Armed Forces Pay Review Body with its unfair system of "Irishmen's pay rises".' I like to think that what I said that night may have had some small effect on the Opposition — there were questions in the House and certainly there was a massive rise in pay as soon as the Conservatives took over. On the first part of what I had to say, I believe, sadly, that something approaching my worst fears is in danger of being realised.

The fact that Vroenhof was such a charming, spacious and well-staffed house meant that on the big occasions the bulk of the entertaining fell to us. Chief amongst these was Central Fortress, AFCENT's equivalent of SHAPEX, and of course the Change of Command ceremony which is made a lot of in NATO. Karl Schnell retired prematurely to be the right-hand man of the Minister of Defence in Bonn and handed over to Franz Josef Schultze on 7 January 1977. On that occasion we had about fifty to lunch and my visitors' book makes interesting reading. The Germans were there in force, but the best turnout of all was from the UK with CDS, CAS and CGS in the form of Andrew Humphrey, Neil Cameron and Roly Gibbs.

Very soon after that Andrew's health deteriorated suddenly and he tragically died only some six months after becoming CDS. This very sad and unexpected event threw things into confusion. The selection of a Chief of Air Staff is not so secret and ritualised an affair as the election of a new Pope and it is usually clear to insiders where the mantle will fall. It was clear that Andrew had been marked out from his exceptionally early promotion from group captain on. It was almost as clear from the pattern of his appointments that for some years Nigel Maynard had been expected to succeed Andrew and I happened to know that he had most unwisely been told so. Most unwisely because whatever the intentions of a former

RAF spirit 'eroded by poor pay'

By Our Air Correspondent

SERVICE chiefs have warned the Government that officers and men alike have lost confidence in the Armed Forces Pay Review Body with .its unfair system of "Irishmen's pay rises."

They have spoken of the review body's blatant abandonment of comparability, which was supposed to be the cornerstone of military salary.

The recent derisory pay rise was eaten up by increases in other charges which meant no more money to the Services.

The anger and frustration of the RAF is on no less a scale then the policemen and there is added resentment that their case has received little publicity because it has no union or association representation.

They feel that the review body is no longer reflecting in its reports the conditions existing in the Service and that it is unresponsive to the advice of the Services' principal personnel officers whose duty is to speak up and advise.

Serious drift

The result, senior officers say, is a serious drift away from station service life which they maintain was the main reason for the RAF's great spirit and strength that won it the major air battles over the last half-century.

Now young officers and airmen are buying homes as soon as, and in some cases before, they can afford them and their wives are going out to work.

Previously wives have been able to devote considerable time to improve the welfare of families living on a station as well as charitable work in the neighbourhood.

The reason they are buying houses is because of the enormous increase charged for renting married quarters. Some 65 per cent. or about 5,000 of these now stand empty.

Servicemen's knowledge that terminal grants are no longer sufficient to buy houses fills them with apprehension.

Service chiefs have warned it is vital that the situation be put right and the damaging drift away from station life halted.

The ruination of the RAF could follow if the situation developed to a point where young men came to be regarded — or even worse, to regard themselves—as civilians who just happened to put uniform on to go to work.

Measure of control

The Services insist they must regain some measure of control over their own pay and conditions not only to halt the drift away, but also because, without the attractions of overseas service and with a closer comparison being drawn with civilians than previously, pay is going to be much more important in the future.

The Service chiefs want the review board to be changed to ensure people on it should at least understand, and perhaps be responsive to what the Services' principal personnel officers advise.

I am told that many officers who have bought permanent homes and then been posted elsewhere travel hundreds of miles home from their new stations every weekend, further reducing their contribution to service life.

Some of this can be put down to the Rent Act which makes it difficult for officers to get their own houses back after a lease, and the difficulties of getting compensation when tenants do not take care of the property.

They say they cannot afford to allow their homes to stand empty and no officer can afford to run two homes.

Above: Daily Telegraph, 31 May 1977.

hierarchy may have been the final choice of his successor, subject to political approval, lies with the outgoing Chief of Air Staff. Andrew's choice fell not on Nigel but on Neil Cameron. Neil had a fine brain and was an excellent speaker but had been out of favour for some years because he had been handpicked by Healey, on the strength of one of his articles, to form part of a small team at 1-star level reporting to Healey direct. Not unnaturally, the unfortunate incumbents immediately became highly suspect in the eyes of their respective chiefs and the damage to Neil could have been terminal and probably would have been but for Andrew who restored him to favour.

Soon after Neil became CAS Nigel Maynard elected to retire early. Andrew's untimely death then produced a dilemma and a minor crisis. Until by making John Fieldhouse CDS in the early eighties Margaret Thatcher upset the system that appointment had gone to each of the services in turn, and with Andrew dying in office the RAF had something like two years of its expected occupancy of that post still to go. Very understandably Neil did not want to give up being CAS after only six months, so an agreement was reached whereby Edward Ashmore became caretaker CDS to allow Neil to complete a year as head of his service before becoming CDS in turn.

It was clear that, had this turmoil not arisen, Mike Beetham, then about to finish his time in Germany, was planned to be the next CAS after two years or so as AOC-in-C Strike Command. If that plan was to be adhered to an interim CAS would need to be appointed. Mike and I, isolated from Whitehall and ignorant of the arguments going on, discussed the matter at some length and concluded that the sensible solution was to appoint an interim CAS because, if Mike was to become CAS earlier than planned, he would not only miss out on Strike but would either finish the appointment at an unprecedentedly young age or would have to remain in post for an equally unprecedented number of years. Mike and I were also agreed that, if there was to be an interim CAS, it was almost certain to be me. As time wore on, and neither of us heard from Neil, it was obvious that there was a problem. Then, after what seemed like a long time but was probably only a few days, Neil sent for Mike and told him that he was to be his successor. Not long afterwards I was in London and saw Neil, whom I had known since he was a group captain. He obviously knew that I had been expecting, or at least hoping, to succeed him and his manner bordered on the apologetic. It would clearly have been improper for him to have told me exactly what had happened but the one sentence he permitted himself was enough. His precise words were, 'The trouble is that some of us are more politically acceptable than others.' From this it was clear that Jim Callaghan was not only a bluff and genial individual but also had a long and unforgiving memory!

Andrew's death and Nigel's early retirement had left us very thin at the top and soon after taking over as CAS Mike asked me if I would stay on an extra year at AFCENT. This I was only too delighted to do, as I found it difficult to imagine no longer being part of the RAF and suspected I would not be good retirement material. Our house in the Cotswolds had been ideal as a weekend retreat and holiday home but the nearer the reality loomed the more I began to wonder. It was in an idyllic situation but 40 miles from my golf club and 50 miles from our nearest friends. It was in an extremely horsey part of the country and as we had five loose boxes and no horses we were doomed to be outsiders, unaccepted and unacceptable.

One of the bonuses of that extra year was that I just caught a second NATO Air Chiefs Tour of the USAF before retiring. The NATO Air Chiefs Tour took place every other year and had as its object the sale of aircraft to the NATO air forces. Although we all knew this, the sales pitch was extremely muted and the whole tour, which lasted a week, was notable for its hospitality and for the efforts our hosts made to 'show us the US of A'. The itineraries varied somewhat between the 1977 and 1979 tours but both had two things in common. On each occasion we started off in Washington by being entertained by the Air Force Chiefs on the first evening, which was a Saturday, and by playing golf at Burning Tree on the following day. I am not sure whether Burning Tree has survived as the last bastion of male chauvinism in a matriarchal society, but it was going strong 20 years ago and only some weird equal rights legislation could have brought it down. It was, and I hope still is, a club for the very rich. You could not apply for membership but only became a member by invitation. There was no annual subscription but the costs for the year were divided between the members and were

The hardships of Texas.

The Air Chiefs on tour.

Goodbye to Al Haig.

running at that time at about $10,000 a head. It had no 'Ladies Section' and women were not admitted to the clubhouse. They were, however, allowed into the pro shop in Christmas week if they wished to buy presents for their husbands, some might think the final symbol of would-be male dominance!

The second equally memorable but considerably less enjoyable event which each tour had in common was a night in Las Vegas following a day at nearby Nellis Air Force Base. There must be, indeed clearly are, hundreds of thousands of people who adore Las Vegas, just as there are an equal or greater number who think highly of Disneyland, but I am not amongst them. On both occasions we stayed at Caesar's Palace and having lost my parsimonious limit of £10 equivalent at black jack I went to bed early, an action possibly unique in Las Vegas history.

On the 1979 visit we also stayed at the Beverly Hills Hilton and played golf at the Bel Air Country Club. I was told in suitably reverential tones that I was to be partnered by Howard Keel, intelligence which was somewhat robbed of its intended effect by the fact that I had not the slightest idea who Howard Keel was, not being an aficionado of American musicals. He turned out to be a very nice chap, as did Bruce Forsyth who was also present and must have wondered what had happened to Hollywood that it was suddenly full of air marshals.

My final memory of the 1979 tour was of Omaha, Nebraska, the Headquarters of Strategic Air Command which is no doubt now listed as armageddon.co.usa, and was not of the cataclysmic potential of that headquarters but of the antiquated appearance of the so-called Hot Line. It was difficult to realise that in certain circumstances the fate of the world could have depended on such a mundane piece of equipment.

During the latter part of 1978 I learned of the possibility of a further job in the offing, one which ironically would not have been open to me had I become Chief of the Air Staff. But there was to be an anxious waiting period until, about a month before starting retirement leave in May 1979, it was confirmed that, on the recommendation of the Secretary of State for Home Affairs, The Queen had been graciously pleased to appoint me the next Lieutenant-Governor of Guernsey and its Dependencies starting early in 1980. The Royal Warrant, with Her Majesty's signature at its head, was given at the Court of Saint James in the

The Queen's Colour Squadron guard before the author's swearing-in as Lieutenant-Governor of Guernsey.
Guernsey Press

Sylvia and Sir John and Lady Loveridge immediately after being sworn in. *Guernsey Press*

29th year of Her Reign and signed at Her Majesty's command by the Home Secretary, Willie Whitelaw. Unfortunately Willie, in typical laid-back fashion, signed this impressive document with a ballpoint pen and all trace of his signature has now vanished!

This represented a break with tradition in that I would be the first Guernseyman appointed to that office in peacetime for more than 600 years. I say in peacetime because in 1940, the lieutenant-governor having left the island, the then bailiff, Sir Victor Carey, was appointed in his place and held the office under German occupation for the remainder of the war. But quite apart from that, and much more importantly to me, it robbed retirement from the Royal Air Force of much of its sting. I would have a strong link with the service and would wear uniform on occasion for a further five years and could perhaps persuade myself that I had not retired after all. This illusion was strengthened by being flown in on an aircraft of the Queen's Flight and by being met by a guard of honour found by Queen's Colour Squadron commanded by Nick Acous, a former ADC of mine at AFCENT, on the occasion of my swearing-in. Thus began a new phase of my life which has no place in this book.

Author as Lieutenant-Governor.

Index